Praise for Hunting Season

"An account that is as unflinching as it is important. Both an incisive reconstruction of a heartbreaking murder and an unsparing diagnosis of a national malady . . . with *Hunting Season* Ojito has done truth an invaluable service. Extraordinary."

—JUNOT DÍAZ, author of *The Brief Wondrous Life of Oscar Wao*

"Mirta Ojito tells a powerful story, connecting us with the real-life people who are all too often left out of the immigration debate. In doing so, Ojito plumbs the depths of what it means to be an American, a nation of immigrants, whose narrative and identity are deeply tied to this journey of arrival and assimilation—and sometimes rejection. This book should be required reading in any community grappling with the issues of immigration, which often remain abstract and divisive. Ojito helps us understand ourselves as a nation, whose motto, *E pluribus unum*, 'Out of many, one,' celebrates our unity in our diversity, as she does in this book. A powerful story, masterfully written, imbued with a deep, compassionate, and healing intelligence."

—JULIA ALVAREZ, author of *A Wedding in Haiti*

"An Ecuadorean immigrant's ethnically motivated murder is at the heart of Mirta Ojito's compelling and complex narrative; but beyond laying down the tragic machinations of prejudice, she gives us an up-lifting tale about the universality—and wonder—of ordinary folk—in this case, Latinos—pursuing the American dream. All this is told with the authority of a much-respected journalist, whose own experience as an immigrant lends this book the depth, insights, and poignancy that only someone of her experience can convincingly—and right-fully—convey."

—OSCAR HIJUELOS, Pulitzer Prize–winning author of
The Mambo Kings Play Songs of Love

HUNTING SEASON

Immigration and Murder
in an All-American Town

MIRTA OJITO

Beacon Press · Boston

BEACON PRESS
Boston, Massachusetts
www.beacon.org

Beacon Press books
are published under the auspices of
the Unitarian Universalist Association of Congregations.

17 16 15 14   8 7 6 5 4 3 2 1

This book is printed on acid-free paper that meets the uncoated paper
ANSI/NISO specifications for permanence as revised in 1992.

Composition by Wilsted & Taylor Publishing Services.

LIBRARY OF CONGRESS CATALOGING-IN-PUBLICATION DATA
Ojito, Mirta A.
  Hunting season : immigration and murder in an all-American town /
Mirta Ojito.
    pages cm
  Includes bibliographical references.
  ISBN 978-0-8070-6122-0 (paperback) — ISBN 978-0-8070-0182-0
(ebook)
1. Murder—New York (State)—Patchogue—Case studies. 2. Latin
Americans—New York (State) —Patchogue—Case studies. 3. Racism—
New York (State) —Patchogue—Case studies. 4. Immigrants—New
York (State)—Patchogue—Case studies. 5. Patchogue (N.Y.)—Ethnic
relations—Case studies. 6. Patchogue (N.Y.) —Emigration and
immigration—Social aspects—Case studies. I. Title.
  HV6534.P38O35 2013
  364.152'30974725—dc23   2013023313

For my children:
Juan Arturo, Lucas, and Marcelo,
Americans in the truest sense of the word.

And for my father,
Orestes Ojito,
who made it all possible.

Hate, as a single word might lead us to believe, is not a single emotion or behavior, but instead stands for a variety of complex psychological phenomena that can be expressed in many different ways by different people. Why some people express "hate" in the form of criminal behavior is something that we do not yet fully understand.

NATHAN HALL, *HATE CRIME*

CONTENTS

Author's Note · xi

PROLOGUE · 1

CHAPTER 1
A Bloody Knife · 15

CHAPTER 2
Painted Birds in the Air · 27

CHAPTER 3
Welcome to Patchogue · 43

CHAPTER 4
Not in My Backyard · 58

CHAPTER 5
Beaner Jumping · 79

CHAPTER 6
Unwanted · 105

CHAPTER 7
A Murder in the Suburbs · 118

CHAPTER 8
A Torn Community · 139

CHAPTER 9
A Little Piece of Heaven · 167

CHAPTER 10
Trial and Punishment · 188

EPILOGUE · 206

Acknowledgments · 227
Notes · 230
Bibliography · 250

AUTHOR'S NOTE

To re-create events that transpired fifty, twenty, or five years ago is always an act of faith that depends mostly—but not only—on the kindness of those who witnessed the events and on their willingness to share. The other way to re-create events is following a paper trail, and I've made liberal use of that option, mining court records, transcripts, and news accounts.

I'm lucky and grateful that many people in Patchogue, New York, and Gualaceo, Ecuador, shared their stories with me. I asked them to remember in great detail events that happened years before we met. Since it is difficult to recall precise details of conversations held so long ago, I've opted not to use quotation marks unless I'm quoting from a published or aired source, such as a newspaper story or a TV clip, using transcripts of interviews, confessions, or court proceedings, or referring to notes I took when the words were uttered.

Only nine people know what happened on the night of November 8, 2008. One who knew—Marcelo Lucero—is dead; his friend, Angel Loja, spoke to me. But the seven young men who are still in prison for attacking Lucero and Loja and killing Lucero refused to, as did all their parents but two—Bob Conroy, the father of Jeffrey Conroy, and Denise Overton, the mother of Christopher Overton. Their cooperation allowed me to convey a more nuanced portrayal of their children.

From prison, Jeffrey Conroy wrote me a letter, which for more than a year I kept on my bulletin board, next to the picture of a serious-looking Lucero as a fourth-grade student in Ecuador, his body partly blocking a map of North America. In his letter, dated July 16, 2011, Conroy wrote that he believed I would "write a fair book" and that my work would be "balanced and respectful." For more than three years I've labored to live up to that expectation and to honor the stories of those in Patchogue and Gualaceo who opened their lives to my curiosity and scrutiny.

PROLOGUE

On November 8, 2008, having had a few beers and an early dinner, Marcelo Lucero, an undocumented Ecuadorian immigrant,
took a late-night stroll with his childhood friend Angel Loja near
the train tracks in Patchogue, a seaside village of twelve thousand people in Suffolk County, New York, a county that only
three years earlier had been touted by *Forbes* magazine as one of
the safest and wealthiest in the United States.[1] It is also one of the
most segregated counties.[2]

Before the mild moonlit night was over, Lucero was stabbed
and killed by a gaggle of teenagers from neighboring towns, who
had gone out hunting for "beaners," the slur that, as some of them
later told police, they used for Latinos. Earlier that night, they had
harassed and beaten another Hispanic man—a naturalized US
citizen from Colombia named Héctor Sierra. The teenagers also
confessed to attacking Hispanics at least once a week.

Lucero was not the first immigrant killed by an enraged mob
in the United States, and he most certainly will not be the last. At
least two other immigrants were killed in the Northeast in 2008,

but Lucero's case is especially poignant because he was killed by a high school star athlete in an all-American town where people of mostly Italian and Irish descent proudly display US flags on the Fourth of July and every year attend a Christmas parade on Main Street. If it happened here, it can happen anywhere.

Patchogue, in central Long Island, is only about sixty miles from Manhattan—far enough to escape the city's noise, dirt, and angst, but close enough to feel splashes of its excitement, pluck, and glamour. Lucero, who probably didn't know about the *Forbes* ranking of the village as an idyllic place to live and raise children, had come from Ecuador to Patchogue in 1993 on the heels of others from his hometown who for thirty years now have been slowly and quietly making their way to this pocket of lush land named by the Indians who once inhabited it.

In Ecuador, too, Lucero had lived in a small village called Gualaceo. The town has lost so many of its people to Patchogue that those who remain call it Little Patchogue, a way to honor the dollars flowing there from Long Island. Month by month, remittances from New York have helped Gualaceños prosper despite a profound and long-lasting national economic crisis that forced the government to toss its national currency and adopt the US dollar more than a decade ago.

The day before he was killed, Lucero, thirty-seven, had been talking about going home. Over the years he had sent his family about $100,000—money earned working low-paying jobs—to buy land and build a three-story house he planned to share with his mother, his sister, and his nephew. He was eager to join them. The sister, Rosario, had asked him to be a father figure for her son. It's time to go, Lucero told his younger brother, Joselo, who also lived in Patchogue.[3]

"He was tired," Joselo recalled. "He had done enough."

Lucero was planning to leave before Christmas, an early present for their ailing mother. I'll take you to the airport, Joselo promised. He never got the chance.

• • •

I read about the murder of Marcelo Lucero when it was first re-ported in the news, but I learned some of the more intimate details through a Columbia University graduate student, Angel Canales, who had immediately jumped on the story and was working on a documentary about it for his master's thesis. The story resonated with me for several reasons, not the least of them being my own condition as an immigrant. Though I never felt the burden of being in the country "illegally," I have carried a different kind of stigma.

I came from Cuba in 1980, at sixteen, aboard a boat named *Mañana*, as part of a boatlift that brought more than one hundred twenty-five thousand Cuban refugees from the port of Mariel to the shores of South Florida in the span of five months. Several thousand of those refugees had committed crimes in Cuba and kept at it in their new country. Quickly, quicker than I could learn English or even understand what was happening around me, all of us were tainted by the unspeakable actions of a few. We became saddled with the label "Marielitos," which carried a negative connotation, and with the narrative of *Scarface*, the un-fortunate but popular film by Brian De Palma in which Al Pacino played a "Marielito" drug lord. It was a difficult stigma to shake. In 2005, when a book I wrote about the boatlift was published, people still felt the need to point to my story as a rarity—a suc-cessful "Marielita" who had done well and had even made it to the *New York Times*.

In fact, the opposite was true. My story was not unique. Most Mariel refugees were honest, decent, hard-working people. The exceptions had given us all a bad name. Those experiences taught me what it's like to live under the shadow of an unpopular label, and while "illegal" is not as detrimental as "criminal," it is close, and it has endured far longer than the "Marielito" curse.

The murder of Marcelo Lucero also resonated with me for a professional reason. It brought back memories of a story I had written for the *New York Times* on September 30, 1996, about a Hudson Valley village called Haverstraw, where, according to

3

the 1990 census, 51 percent of the residents were Hispanic, although everyone knew the ratio was closer to 70 percent. Just thirty miles north of Manhattan, Haverstraw had been a magnet for Puerto Ricans since the 1940s. In more recent years, Dominicans had followed. The mayor, Francis "Bud" Wassmer, told me he no longer recognized the village where he had been born and raised. The public library carried an extensive selection of bilingual books, a local store that once sold men's suits was selling work boots, the strains of *merengue* spilled from the pink windows of riverfront Victorian mansions, and the old candy store had closed down while eighteen bodegas had opened.

My story included the following paragraphs:

> The suburbs, long the refuge of fleeing city dwellers, are quietly becoming a magnet to newly arrived immigrants, who, lured by relatives and the promise of a better life, are bypassing the city and driving to the proverbial American dream straight from the nation's biggest international airports.
>
> The trend, entrenched everywhere there is a significant immigrant population, is transforming the character of many suburbs, sociologists and demographers say. It is making suburbia more heterogeneous and interesting. But, like never before, it is also pressing onto unprepared suburban towns the travails and turmoil of the cities.
>
> New immigrants, unlike immigrants who have lived in the country for a while, have special needs. They are likely not to speak English. They need jobs, help in finding affordable homes, guidance to enroll their children in schools, and information on how to establish credit and even open a checking account. They may also need public assistance to make ends meet until they find jobs. And they need it all in their own language.

Cities, where immigrants traditionally settled, have the services and the expertise to help new immigrants make a smoother transition to life in America. Places like the village of Haverstraw are not always fully equipped to deal with the needs of new immigrants.

"We have social problems just like urban communities," Mr. [Ronaldo] Figueroa said, "but we don't have the resources to address them in the same way, so they tend to accelerate at a greater pace than we can keep up with."[4]

Throughout the piece, I quoted the work of Richard D. Alba and John R. Logan, both sociology professors at the State University of New York at Albany, who had been researching how members of minority groups get along in suburbs of New York City, Chicago, Miami, San Francisco, and Los Angeles.

"The question is how are they going to meet the needs of these new immigrants in a suburban environment?" Professor Logan told me. "This is very new for suburbia and it poses a challenge to public institutions."

Twelve years later, when I heard about Lucero, I thought of Professors Logan and Alba, and I remembered the words of Mayor Wassmer, who told me that one of the problems he had with Hispanics in Haverstraw was that they produced a lot of garbage. Perplexed, I asked what he was referring to. He replied, "I mean, rice and beans are heavy, you know." The other problem, as he saw it, was that Hispanics tended to walk in the streets and congregate at night by the tenuous light of the village's old lampposts.

In fact, Lucero had been taking a stroll when he was attacked by seven teenagers and killed. Was it unusual in the village of Patchogue for people to walk late at night in its deserted streets? Was anyone there threatened by two Latino men out for a stroll?

Was this the challenge that Logan had talked about, the turmoil that Figueroa had envisioned? The "problems" that the mayor had been able to discuss only by referring to garbage?

The Haverstraw story had always felt unfinished. As many reporters do, I had swooped in to collect information, filed a story, and moved on to the next assignment. I had never followed up. Patchogue, I thought, was my chance to connect the dots, to explore what could have happened—but, to my knowledge, never did—in Haverstraw.

That Lucero had been killed in a town so close to New York City and by youngsters who are only two or three generations removed from their own immigrant roots came as a shock even to those who for years have known that there was trouble brewing under the tranquil surface of suburbia.

"It's like we heard the bells but we didn't know if Mass was beginning or ending," said Paul Pontieri Jr., the village's mayor, who keeps in his office a photo of his Italian grandfather paving the roads of Patchogue. "I heard but I didn't listen. I wish I had."[5]

But the killing did not surprise experts who track hate crimes and who knew that attacks against Hispanic immigrants had increased 40 percent between 2003 and 2007.[6] According to the FBI, in 2008, crimes against Hispanics represented 64 percent of all ethnically motivated attacks.[7]

In the two years that followed Lucero's death, hate crime reports in Suffolk County increased 30 percent, a ratio closely aligned with national trends.[8] It is unclear whether more attacks have taken place or if more victims, emboldened by the Lucero case, have come forward with their own tales of abuse.

Lucero's murder, as well as the growing number of attacks against other immigrants, illustrates the angst that grips the country regarding immigration, raising delicate and serious questions that most people would prefer to ignore. What makes us Americans? What binds us together as a nation? How do we protect what we know, what we own? How can young men still in high school feel so protective of their turf and so angry toward new-comers that they can commit the ultimate act of violence, taking a life that, to them, was worthless because it was foreign?

Global movement—how to stimulate it and how to harness it—is the topic of this century. Few issues in the world today are as cru-cial and defining as how to deal with the seemingly endless flow of immigrants making their way to wealthier countries. Even the war against terrorism, which since 9/11 has become especially prominent, has been framed as an immigration challenge: who comes in, who stays out.

The relentless flow of immigrants impacts the languages we speak (consider the ongoing debate over bilingual education and the quiet acceptance in major cities, such as Miami and New York, of the predominance of Spanish), the foods we eat, the people we hire, the bosses we work for, and even the music we dance to. On a larger scale, immigrants affect foreign policy, the debate over homeland security, local and national politics, budget allocations, the job market, schools, and police work. No institution can ig-nore the role immigrants now play in shaping the daily life of most industrialized countries of the world.

In the United States immigration is at the heart of the nation's narrative and sense of identity. Yet we continue to be conflicted by it: armed vigilantes patrol the Rio Grande while undocumented workers find jobs every day watching over our children or deliver-ing food to our door. In 2011 members of Congress considered debating if the US-born children of undocumented immigrants ought to be rightful citizens of the country, while in Arizona La-tino studies were declared illegal.

While the federal government spends millions of dollars build-ing an ineffective wall at the US-Mexico border, the 11.1 million undocumented immigrants living in the United States wonder if the wall is being built to keep them out or in. In fact, 40 percent of undocumented immigrants, or more than four million people, did not climb a fence or dig a tunnel to get to the United States. They arrived at the nation's airports as tourists, students, or authorized workers, and simply stayed once their visas expired.[9]

The immigration debate affects not only Hispanic immigrants, who comprise the largest number of foreign-born people in the United States, but all immigrants. The Center for Immigration Studies, a Washington, DC, think tank, reported in August 2012 that the number of immigrants (both documented and undocumented) in the country hit a new record of forty million in 2010, a 28 percent increase over the total in 2000.[10]

In a 2007 report researchers at the center generated population projections and examined the impact of different levels of immigration on the size and aging of American society. They found that if immigration continues at current levels, the nation's population will increase to 468 million in 2060, a 56 percent increase from the current population. Immigrants and their descendants will account for 105 million, 63 percent of that increase.[11] By 2060, one of every three people in the United States will be a Hispanic.[12] Another study, released in 2011 by the Brookings Institution, revealed that "America's population of white children, a majority now, will be in the minority during this decade." Already minorities make up 46.5 percent of the population under eighteen.[13]

As a nation we remain stumped over immigration. Are we still a nation of immigrants? Or are we welcoming only to those who follow the rules and, even more, look and act like us? In Suffolk County, the answers are complex.

The county likes people who have legal documents, who speak English, who don't play volleyball in their backyards late into the night while drinking beer with buddies, who don't produce a lot of garbage, who pay taxes, who know when and where to put the garbage outside and keep the lid on it, who support—or at least don't interfere—with school sports programs, who don't urinate behind 7-Elevens, who don't look for jobs on the sidewalks, and who keep bushes trimmed and fences painted, preferably white.

"As I often say to immigrants," said John F. "Jack" Eddington, the grandson of Irish immigrants and a former Suffolk County legislator, who lives in Medford but kept his legislative office in Patchogue, "When you move to a new town, the moment you walk in your new house—in fact, before you walk in—stand on the front steps and take a look around. The way people maintain their homes, their lawns, their cars: that's what you must do."[14]

Paul Pontieri, the mayor of Patchogue, said almost the same words to me in two separate interviews. Others in Patchogue have given similar answers to questions of assimilation. It is clear that in this town—if not the entire country—the notion of what it means to be an American is tightly woven with the idea of home ownership: how to get it, how to keep it, and how to protect it from strangers. And nowhere is home a more sacred, almost sanctified, concept than in suburbia, the very place where, for decades, the middle class has sought refuge from urban blight, despair, poverty, and the kind of social ills that cities confront and suburbia—mythically, at least—narrowly escapes.

In the last decades, though, immigrants have been following jobs to rural and suburban areas. In 2010, census data showed that "immigrant populations rose more than 60 percent in places where immigrants made up fewer than 5 percent of the population in 2000," while in big cities "the foreign-born population was flat over that period." The data also showed that the country's biggest population gains were in suburbia. "But, in a departure from past decades when whites led the rise, now it is because of minorities. More than a third of all 13.3 million new suburbanites were Hispanic."[15]

A study released in September 2012 by Brown University confirmed that trend, and found that "of the roughly 15,000 places in the country—defined as cities, towns, suburbs or rural areas that govern their own fiscal affairs—some 82.6% were majority white in 2010, down from 93.4% in 1980. Places where whites made up at least 90% of the population fell even more sharply, to 36% in 2010 from 65.8% in 1980."[16]

And so the process of acculturation that an immigrant used to experience in the anonymity of the city—from learning the essential first English words to understanding how close to stand when speaking to an American—now occurs in the wide-open spaces of suburbia and under the scrutiny of neighbors who worry about property values, taxes, and the height of a blade of grass on the lawn, just like Alba and Logan envisioned so many years ago.

Suffolk County, where the population's growth in the last two decades has been fueled by immigration, fits squarely in this demographic trend. Some towns have gone from being practically all white to having a 17 percent Latino population.[17] In 2008 the Latino population in Patchogue and Medford, mostly from Ecuador, had reached 24 percent.[18]

In Patchogue, learning how to mow one's lawn the proper way is a serious, defining matter—a milepost on the road to assimilation. Francisco Hernández, who was born in New York City and moved to Patchogue from Queens, remembers how a neighbor had to teach him what products to use to keep his lawn pristine. "Spanish people [Hispanics or people who speak Spanish] do learn," he told a documentary filmmaker in 2009. "Look at Raúl, my neighbor. His lawn was like crap. He's got one of the best lawns now in the neighborhood. He won't let one car park on his lawn."[19]

Such are the issues that can turn neighbor against neighbor in Suffolk County, particularly if the one who won't use the right fertilizer speaks a language other than English.

While six of the zip codes in Suffolk County are among the hundred wealthiest in the United States, Patchogue and Medford are predominantly middle-class towns with strip malls and pizzerias. These are towns where teachers, police officers, and deli owners live, not where Wall Street tycoons vacation or where pint-size Park Avenue trust-fund children learn to ride their first horses. Thus, working-class families that live in places like Patchogue and Medford are likely to view immigrant newcomers not as hired help but as competitors for the jobs they too covet.[20]

Immigrant advocates say that the attitudes young people develop against Hispanics are fueled by the rhetoric they absorb in the hallways and classrooms of their schools, in the news media, or in conversations at home.[21] In fact, research has shown that to be the case. Research has also shown that much of the immigrant-bashing rhetoric is caused by fear.

"I think the difference in the situation now," Eddington, the former legislator and Medford resident, told me, "is that you have people . . . moving into Patchogue that can't speak English, didn't grow up in the community, and I think what happens in that situation is that people become afraid because there are cultural differences."[22]

It would be easy and convenient to have a villain in this book. Take Jeffrey Conroy, for example, the teenager convicted of killing Lucero. He was seventeen, restless and unruly in school, and he once asked a friend to tattoo his body with symbols of white power: a swastika and a lightning bolt. But many in Suffolk County see Jeffrey as a victim as well—a jock who, though friendly to the Latinos in his circle of friends, absorbed the hateful rhetoric of those around him in positions of authority.

No one had more authority in Suffolk County when Jeffrey was growing up than Steve Levy, a man with such striking anti-immigration views that a report released after Lucero's death by the Southern Poverty Law Center, of Montgomery, Alabama, called him "The Enabler," blaming him for fueling the attack on Lucero and others before him. He was fond of calling critics "communists" and "anarchists," and he cofounded Mayors and Executives for Immigration Reform, a national group that advocates for local ordinances against undocumented immigrants. On one occasion he said that immigrant women were crossing the border to have "anchor babies," a term used by those who claim the country is under siege by invading Mexicans.[23]

While it is true that Levy was the most vocal and most visible of the Long Island politicians who continuously stoked the flames against immigrants, he wasn't the only one. More important, shrewd politician that he was, Levy would not have used immigrant bashing as one of the pillars of his campaigns and speeches if he hadn't recognized that his words would be well received by the majority of the registered voters in the county.

Lucero's death has left a mark on Patchogue, and placed the village in the eye of the political storm that immigration has become. On the night of November 8, 2008, a Saturday, everyone went to sleep in a town that was almost totally anonymous and awoke the next morning to find satellite trucks in their front yards. Pontieri found out about the attack as he sipped coffee and read the Sunday paper in his backyard. Diana Berthold, a local artist, heard the story on TV. In desperation, and out of habit, she began to quilt. Jean Kaleda, a local librarian, was coming back from a short vacation when a friend told her about it; her stomach lurched at the news.

Film and television crews descended on the town. A half-hour documentary was promptly filmed and released, PBS taped a show, and a local theater group staged a well-received play about the murder. In addition, college students wrote essays about Lucero and hate crimes to win scholarship money. Later a separate scholarship fund was established by the Lucero family to help seniors from the local high school—the same school where the attackers had been students—pay for college. (At the end of 2012, four students had received scholarships ranging from $250 to $500.) A group of about twenty women worked for more than a year on a three-part quilt that has been used in a local anti-hate campaign. Soccer tournaments that include Latino teams have become yearly events spearheaded by Eddington, the former legislator, and a group of Ecuadorians, under the banner of the Lucero Foundation, has met regularly to discuss issues that affect their community. (At a meeting in November 2011, the discussion wavered between two issues: whether to give toys or candy to children at a Christmas gathering, and how to react to a man who disrupted a town parade because Latinos had been included.)

But beyond the headlines, sound bites, and community meetings, and after the satellite trucks left, what remains is daily life in this seemingly sleepy and charming village. It is here, in the mundane details of personal stories and relationships, where my book dwells. This two-way process of assimilation and adaptation—a drama unfolding every day, in every small and not-so-small town across the United States—is how stereotypes are shaped and cemented, opinions are molded, and political decisions are made. When the process works well, as it usually does, America is at its best: welcoming and gracious, showering newcomers with handouts and opportunities like no other country on earth. When it doesn't, as has been increasingly the case, America is at its worst: parochial, protective, and dismissive of the other. (Arizona and Alabama, with their punitive anti-immigration laws, are relevant examples.)

In Patchogue, Marcelo Lucero thought he had found a home, albeit a temporary one, but to the town he was always a stranger, a foreigner, an invisible other. Pontieri is still upset when he recalls that a few days after Lucero's death a local Hispanic man approached him to talk about his fears. Pontieri asked him where he lived. Over there, the man said, pointing to a small, white, wood-framed home two doors from the house where Pontieri grew up, the house he visits every day to check on his mother. "How is it that I never saw him?" Pontieri asked me rhetorically. "He's been living here for years and I never saw him before, and I know everybody in this town." Four years later, wanting to meet that man, I asked Pontieri what his name was. He had forgotten—or never learned it.[24]

Of course, Pontieri does not know everybody in his village. He didn't know Lucero either, just like most people in Patchogue. Only in death did they learn his name. Only in death were they forced to see him.

CHAPTER I

A BLOODY KNIFE

From his perch on the witness stand, Angel Loja knew he was doing well—composed, in control, hands folded on his lap. Just as he had been instructed, he was giving straight answers, looking at the lawyer as he spoke, occasionally glancing at the prosecutor or the judge for reassurance, trying to enunciate every word carefully and truthfully, to the best of his recollection. But then the lawyer for the defense mentioned the knife, and Loja, thirty-seven, almost lost his composure.

"Did you ever see a knife?" asked William Keahon, the lawyer representing Jeffrey Conroy, the young man who, at seventeen, had confessed to stabbing and killing Loja's friend, Marcelo Lucero.

"Never."

"Did you ever see anyone stab Marcelo?"

"No, because in the second attack . . ."

"I'm not asking—please stop."

"Sorry. I'm sorry about that."

"That's fine," the lawyer said, and he went on to the next question.[1]

But it was not fine. A simple no couldn't convey Loja's feelings, the nights he had stayed awake thinking "what-if," the hours he had mulled over his actions on the day of the attack. It wasn't fair that the lawyer wanted a simple yes or no. Neither of those answers could accurately describe his fears or his regrets.

The truth was that Loja had turned his back momentarily on his friend and their attackers to run for safety to a nearby alley. He had called out to Lucero to follow him, but Lucero had stood his ground and fought. The truth was that he had not seen the knife. He wished he had.

"And when you got to the police precinct did you talk to a detective or a police officer right away or did you have to wait?" the lawyer continued.

"I had to wait."

"Do you know about how long?"

"Two, three hours. Three hours."

"And during that time, that two or three hours that you were waiting to speak to a police officer, did you learn about what had happened to your friend, Marcelo Lucero?"

"No."

"Okay. So, when did you learn that?"

"I didn't find out until the detectives approached me. They introduced themselves. They said they were detectives. The first thing I asked was, 'How's my friend?'"

"And what did they say?"

"They said, 'I'm sorry. Your friend passed away. He's dead.'"

At this point in the trial, Loja could no longer hold back the tears. He wanted to go back in time to Lucero's one-room apartment, shut the door, and stay inside with his friend, watching TV. He wished he had never gone out that day at all. If he hadn't, if he had said no instead of yes when Lucero called the afternoon of November 8, 2008, if he hadn't been so accommodating to his older, wiser friend, perhaps Lucero would still be alive.

He had briefly considered turning down Lucero's invitation that day, but in his friend's voice he had detected something akin to desperation or loneliness. Later Loja would wonder: Did Lucero know that he was going to die that day? Did he somehow intuit that he had hours to live and that's why he didn't want to be alone? Lucero may not have needed a savior that day, for Loja knew he couldn't have saved his friend. What Lucero had needed, he had concluded after the attack, was someone to bear witness.

And so here he was, more than sixteen months after that day, bearing witness.

"And how did you know Marcelo Lucero?" the prosecutor, Megan O'Donnell, asked, unleashing a flood of memories.

Loja cleared his throat before answering.

"I have known Marcelo Lucero since I was five years old."

There was little they didn't know about each other. They were born sixteen months apart, and their mothers were friends and neighbors in Gualaceo, a dusty speck of a town in a valley near Cuenca, a mid-size city in Ecuador known for its colonial buildings, narrow streets, and a river that divides it in two. Their town, though, has little in common with Cuenca, which for Gualaceños is more like a point of reference, a way to anchor them to the better-known geography of a place. Gualaceo, with only one main street, one cemetery, and one bus station, does not have the colonial charm or tourist-fueled relative wealth of Cuenca. There are no fancy hotels or restaurants in Gualaceo, and not one that serves, say, an omelet for breakfast. A tourist would be hard-pressed to find a place to eat after 7:00 p.m., but there are dozens of stores that sell leather shoes in a dizzying array of colors and styles, at least two food markets, two churches, and two local weekly newspapers. What beauty Gualaceo has it owes to nature. Cleaved by the Santa Bárbara River—once believed by the Spanish conquistadors to be brimming with gold—and surrounded by majestic mountains, some locals call it *pedacito de cielo*—little piece of heaven.

For Lucero and Loja, Gualaceo proved to be too small a piece of heaven. They wanted more.

Loja came from a large family, one that had known unimaginable pain and addiction but also redemption, prosperity, and perhaps even a miracle.

He was the second-oldest boy of a family of nine, but knew only six of his siblings. By the time he was born, his parents, who had once been too poor for medicine or doctors, had lost three daughters, ages three, five, and six, to mysterious ailments that no amount of home remedies could cure. At that time, Loja's mother was supporting the family, while her husband buried his helplessness and sadness in alcohol. The couple and their surviving children lived with Loja's father's parents in a modest house in the countryside; the arrangement upset Loja's mother, who thought each family ought to have its own house.

She moved out with the children and, with sticks and stones, built a hut with her own hands. Jolted by her move, Loja's father sobered up, pulled his family from the makeshift shed, and became a devout follower of the Virgin Mary. During the day he worked in construction. At night he prayed the Rosary with friends and neighbors. The family prospered and moved to the center of town. The father did so well that he eventually began selling construction materials, a much less demanding and better-paying job. The Lojas, though never rich, managed to reach a lower-middle-class status. Loja, unlike Lucero, never went to bed hungry.

When he was nine, Loja had a vision that changed his life. He was playing with his brother Pablo, then seven, outside their grandfather's stone house. An uncle had died and the family had just returned from the funeral. The adults were inside, tending to their elderly and setting out the food. Eventually stars became visible in the twilight. The brothers looked up, marveling at the beauty of the sky, at the sudden way the sun had disappeared behind the regal mountains of the Azuay province in the highlands of the country, where some peaks reach fifteen thousand feet above sea level.

It was quiet but for the faint sounds of sobs coming from inside the house and dogs barking in the distance. Suddenly, it seemed to the boys, the brightest star exploded and its light traveled down to where they were playing, illuminating a spot a few steps from them. It shimmered and flowed, like the river in summer afternoons. Loja wanted to touch it but held back. Open-mouthed and paralyzed by fear and excitement, the boys saw an image of Jesus Christ take shape in the light. The figure, which appeared to be floating and looking directly at them, wore a white tunic; the arms were extended, and the pale hands were pierced and bleeding, just like in the countless images of Christ they had seen in church. Pablo took off running to get his parents, but Loja stayed put. After a few seconds, the image went up with the light, leaving behind a thick curtain of fog and a boy who, from then on, felt special, protected by a divine force.

Later, after he had become a star athlete, Loja had no doubt that God had been illuminating a path for him. Later still, after he had survived a desert passage and made it to New York in a nineteen-day journey, he felt indebted to God. With God on his side and his well-honed athlete's instincts, he felt invincible, an indispensable feeling for a dark-skinned Latino to have in Suffolk County at the dawn of the twenty-first century.

Every Latino in Suffolk County knew that gangs of youngsters roamed the streets looking for immigrants to harass or beat. Some people were even afraid to go to the library at night for the free English classes because they knew that, upon leaving, thugs could be waiting for them. Loja and Lucero had heard the stories, but they thought the attacks happened mostly in Farmingville, a nearby community where tensions between Latinos and non-Latino residents had made news for almost a decade.

They had heard about the two Mexican day laborers who in 2000 were lured with promises of work to an abandoned building in Shirley, about fifteen minutes from Farmingville, by two white men who beat them savagely. More recently there had been reports of beatings and confrontations in other towns in Suffolk County, and they knew that Patchogue was not immune.

From his kitchen window overlooking a parking lot, Loja once saw a Latino man being attacked by a group of white teenagers. The youngsters pushed the man down, made him kneel and brace himself as if for a rough landing in an airplane, and then ran their bicycles over his back. The teenagers took off on their bikes and the man got up, dusted himself off, rubbed his face with his hands, and left the parking lot before Loja had time to react. Loja, if not Lucero, knew that Patchogue too could be a dangerous place.

The improbable road that had taken Loja from the streets of Gualaceo to a courtroom in Suffolk County, New York, started in 1990, when, at eighteen, he decided that he could no longer be a burden to his parents. It wasn't an original thought. At that time just about every able teenage male was leaving Gualaceo for the United States, especially New York, and even more specifically

Patchogue, where Gualaceños had begun to settle years earlier. In Gualaceo going north was a rite of passage for young men.

In August 1994, Loja thought his time had come, but first he had to visit the mountaintop shrine of El Señor de los Milagros de Andacocha. Before setting out in the long and difficult journey north, virtually every emigrant goes to that shrine to pray for guidance and help, ascending a steep hill of 2,780 meters, or almost two miles in altitude. Some drive or ride horses but many more walk, and a few get on their knees and crawl for at least part of the way. Loja drove for about an hour in punishing, uneven, and twisting country roads before he got to the salmon-colored building with the wooden door that remains open almost around the clock, always ready to receive migrants in need of hope.

The veneration of El Señor de Andacocha began in 1957 when a drunken farmhand found a tiny image of Jesus Christ, about an inch long, in a cross in the ground. He picked it up and kept it for a few years until, the locals believe, he had a dream in which God told him to give a Mass on His behalf.[2]

That dream eventually led to the building of a small chapel, and then, in 1974, the current one, where Loja found himself in August 1994 kneeling on the cold tiled floor below the imposing altar, asking for a miracle: to arrive safely in the United States and prosper. From where he knelt he could hardly see the image of Jesus found by the farmhand. It is nestled inside a glass case at the center of an enormous metal cross that is surrounded by dozens of vases with flowers. Behind the cross and to its sides, large stained-glass windows allowed the first scant rays of the sun as Loja quietly prayed.

He knew that El Señor would listen to his prayers, not only because Loja was deeply religious but also because when he looked around he saw the smiling pictures of young men and women, people like him, who survived their journeys and had sent pictures from the United States. Under his breath, Loja recited the Prayer of the Peregrine:

> Lord, Jesus of Andacocha, accompany me every day, from dawn to evening. Give me strength and courage for my journey. Guide me in the path of goodness and virtue. Fill my mind and my spirit with love and patience to forgive and forget. Give me intelligence to face all the adversities of life and to face pain with a smile. Give me faith to walk in high spirits and with hope in my heart. Señor de Andacocha, do not allow failures to make me weak. Protect my family always. In my plans and work, bless me. In my studies, give me wisdom and perseverance. If I fall, pick me up. If I'm sad, give me hope. If I'm lost, find me a way out. If I'm ill, give me health. If I'm alone and old, you be my company. If I migrate, guide me to the goal. If I'm happy, bless my happiness, Señor de Andacocha: bless me now and always. Amen.[3]

The next day, August 15, Loja left home early in the morning, after receiving multiple blessings from his parents. Along with a friend, he boarded a flight to a coastal city in Guatemala, where a coyote—a smuggler—guided them to a small room in a whorehouse. Loja had never been separated from his family and had never visited a brothel. He was uncomfortable but not afraid. If so many had followed this very route before him and lived to tell the story, it couldn't be all that bad, he reasoned.

For two full days they hid in the room with several others and took turns sleeping on cement beds with no mattresses. They were fed chicken, tortillas, and beans once a day. The heat was unbearable and so was the lack of information. No one seemed to know what would happen next. They had to trust handlers they didn't know but to whom they had each given about $6,000.

On the third day they were taken from the room to a port and ordered to board a boat to Veracruz, Mexico. Two dozen men and women crowded every surface of the vessel. For more than twenty hours they sailed silently over the treacherous waters of the Gulf of Mexico. Some, unable to control themselves, urinated where they sat or stood. Loja, who was hunched over for most of the voyage, could barely walk when they docked in Veracruz. His back was throbbing painfully.

At the time, Loja's journey by sea was unusual, but it quickly became common. Statistics show that between January 1982 and March 1999, the US Coast Guard caught only two Ecuadorians in the high seas. In March 1999, however, the Coast Guard intercepted a fishing vessel carrying 1,452 Ecuadorians, and in the following months other boats were also intercepted. From October 1999 to September 2000, the service found 1,244 Ecuadorians at sea, more than any other nationality.[4]

Once in Mexico, Loja's group stayed hidden for three days in a hotel. Eventually the group was split in two. About a dozen people, including Loja, were driven in a minivan for about six hours until they reached Matamoros, a border town across from Brownsville, Texas. For three days they walked in the desert, crossing the border, each carrying two gallons of water and some food. The food ran out almost immediately. The water did too.

Loja was blinded by thirst. For the first time he thought that God had abandoned him and that he was going to die. Just as he was adjusting to the idea of not feeling God's presence in his life, he found a pool of putrid water, brushed aside trash and dirt, and cupped his hands to drink. It tasted like poison, he thought, but it allowed him to go on.

He dreamed of catching one of the buzzards that circled over the group as if knowing that a meal would soon be available. He wanted to tear one apart and eat it raw with his hands, without breaking his stride. He knew he couldn't lag behind, not even for food. Instead he started to pull chunks of cacti from the plants he encountered on his way. His hands bled from their thorns and his mouth puckered with the bitter taste of the flesh.

At some point he came upon a woman who had fallen in a pit and was moaning for help as men and women passed her, ignoring her pleas, afraid to be separated from the group. Loja stopped and pulled her out effortlessly.

What's your name? she asked.

Angel, he said.

Then you are my guardian angel, she told him.

Loja liked the sound of that and began to feel responsible for the others in the group. His youth, energy, and athleticism gave him an edge over others who could barely walk. When an elderly, heavyset woman fell, Loja picked her up and carried her on his wide back until the woman started to complain that he reeked of cigarettes. He extricated himself and set her down. The woman then began yelling insults, but Loja didn't say a word. He just kept walking and made a mental note of how fluid everything was, including gratitude. A man could go from hero to pestilence in a matter of hours.

Loja had turned twenty-two a few days before leaving Gualaceo. He had learned more about the world in two weeks than he had during two decades at home.

Sometime during the night, a van picked up the migrants and delivered them to a ranch in Houston, where for $40 each they purchased cheap new clothing from the coyotes, took showers, and ate ham-and-cheese sandwiches. Soon Loja boarded a bus to New York, and in three days, on September 2, 1994, he found himself in Times Square, with nothing but the clothes he was wearing.

In Gualaceo Loja had memorized the phone number of relatives, and during his journey he would often review it in his mind to make sure he wouldn't forget it, but when he tried dialing the number from a phone booth in New York, a recording indicated he had dialed a number that was not in service. Though he didn't understand the actual message, he knew he had reached a dead end. Another young man from the group offered to take Loja to his brother's place in Manhattan. Loja accepted and joined eight other men in a one-room apartment in the basement of a building on Thirty-fourth Street and Third Avenue; he found a place to sleep on the floor.

The city did not intimidate Loja, who was used to traveling all over Ecuador for basketball tournaments, and he had also visited big cities with his father. The one thing that gave him pause was the subway system with its loud noise, dirty cars, and untold number of people riding next to each other with vacant eyes. Like millions of immigrants before him, he set out to conquer the city. First, he needed a job.

He found one in two days, after someone told him a local Chinese restaurant was always looking for dishwashers. Loja went to the restaurant and as soon as he walked in, he was immediately ushered to a back room and shown an enormous column of greasy pots, taller than him, at five foot nine, and tottering perilously. Undaunted, he started, but he could never make a dent in the pile. The faster he washed, the faster the restaurant's owner piled more pots on top.

Hurry up, you lazy bum. Quickly, quickly. Where do you think you are? Work, work, work! the man urged him on.

Loja didn't understand English, much less Mandarin-accented English, but he understood the tone and asked another dishwasher to translate for him. At the end of the day, he took off his apron and walked out, without pay, never to return. Hard work didn't scare him; the abusive language did. At home no one ever had treated him like this. He felt small and unwanted, but he figured that one Chinese restaurant couldn't possibly thwart his idea of America or his plans to save enough money to help his family and to eventually go back home.

He found a job at a Sbarro restaurant across from Madison Square Garden, making salads, and was soon promoted to cook. The job was good and steady, and it helped Loja to pay the $6,000 he had borrowed to make his way to New York. In two years, paying $300 every month, he canceled the debt, with interest. In 1996 he moved to Woodside, Queens, to live with a sister who had just crossed the border. Life in Queens, surrounded by so many other immigrants, many from his own town, was more tolerable than his lonely life in Manhattan had been.

After six years at Sbarro, where he was making about $240 a week at a rate of $7.25 an hour, a friend mentioned that jobs on Long Island paid better. A man could make $400 a week working construction or picking up leaves from manicured lawns, the friend said. Loja didn't think about it twice. He threw a few items of clothing in a bag and took the train, leaving his job and the city behind.

It was late summer in 2000, and he was headed for Patchogue, where, his friend had assured him, a lot of Gualaceños had found jobs, clean and ample homes, and a measure of peace and contentment. A former shoemaker, the friend said, had paved the way.

CHAPTER 2

PAINTED BIRDS IN THE AIR

From his window seat in an Aerolíneas Argentinas flight, Julio Espinoza could see the city, sprawling and twinkling underneath him, just like he had seen it countless times in the movies back home. Only now New York seemed more imposing, larger, and forbidden, even dangerous. He focused not on the lights but on the darkness.

What don't I see? he thought, and immediately covered his eyes because he had begun to cry again. The Argentine couple seated next to him ignored him, as they had for the entire five-and-a-half-hour trip. Almost three thousand miles away, at home in Ecuador, his wife, Ana, and three daughters, the oldest just seven, remained. He was traveling with a visa that allowed him to enter the country and return whenever he wanted. Because he was a businessman, the US government did not fear that he would want to stay. Besides, he didn't look like someone who would need to stay.

He was tall and good-looking with fair skin and a broad, open face that seemed trusting and therefore trustworthy. He had an easy smile and friendly eyes that narrowed to slits when he smiled; his straight dark brown hair was trimmed in the back and worn a little long in the front, lending him a boyish look. He wore his one good suit—dark, with a blue tie and an impeccably white long-sleeved shirt. Surely he was coming for a short visit, perhaps to make a business deal or to find new buyers for his seemingly thriving shoemaking business in Bullcay, a hamlet just outside Gualaceo, a place so small that even some Ecuadorians have trouble locating it on a map.

Espinoza hadn't lied to the immigration officers who checked his passport before he left the country earlier that day, August 15, 1981. He was indeed a businessman. What he didn't tell them was that he was penniless and that he had borrowed the $1,200 in his pants pocket. He was coming to the United States not to visit the Empire State Building and have drinks at the Plaza with business associates, but to do what he had to do—wash dishes, sweep floors, mow lawns—to pay off a $30,000 debt that had placed him in an increasingly common but uncomfortable situation for many Ecuadorians of his class: the sudden need to migrate north to support a family.

The debt weighed heavily on Espinoza, who was twenty-five. The oldest boy of a single mother who would eventually have six children, Espinoza had worked since he was six, when one sizzling hot day he realized that thirsty and sweaty young men playing volleyball in the park would buy anything fresh and cool brought to them. The only thing he could think of buying was fruit, so he bought oranges at the market, and then sold them at the endless games in his neighborhood. On a good day, he could make 5 sucres, enough to buy himself a pair of pants, maybe even a pair of shoes. (The sucre was the official currency in Ecuador until January 2000 when the country switched to the US dollar.)

Espinoza had an unhappy childhood. He didn't know who his father was until, at eighteen, a man approached him and introduced himself as his father. By then, Espinoza was engaged to be married and had no use for a repentant father. His maternal grandparents had raised him and that had been enough for him. He loved his grandfather's gentle character and the quiet, dignified way he provided for his daughter's growing family without criticizing her choice of partners. As a child, Espinoza was not as forgiving. With every pregnancy, he would look at his mother's swelling belly and ask why. Why do you keep having children when we don't have enough for all? Instead of responding, she would whack him on the head.

Pained and in tears, he would run away to relatives or a friend's house. In a day or two, he was brought back, and his mother would hit him again. The cycle of shame and abuse was broken when the last baby was born—a fair-skinned girl with round, deep blue eyes. Without saying a word to anyone, he left the house and boarded a bus to Guayaquil, where he knew a friend of the family lived. The family embraced him and put him to work as an apprentice in a shoe factory. He was thirteen.

He returned home two years later carrying a twenty-five-pound sack of rice because, even when he was angry, Espinoza understood that family came first and, like his grandfather, saw himself as a provider. Twenty-five pounds of white rice, he was sure, would last for a long time even for a family of nine. His mother was so relieved to see him that this time she did not beat him. Besides, he was now fifteen and a working man. His childhood was long over.

At a local dance a few months later he met his neighbor Ana, whom he had previously ignored because she was a year younger. In his absence, Ana had blossomed. They fell in love and Espinoza thought his fate was sealed. He would marry Ana, work as a shoemaker, eventually open his own factory, and build a home for the family he hoped to have one day. Three and a half years later, in August 1973, Espinoza and Ana married in a Roman Catholic ceremony. The reception lasted until four the next morning.

The year the Espinozas wed, Ecuador had been ruled for

a year by a military junta that remained in power until 1979. Though less fierce than other military governments in South America—notably Argentina and Chile—Ecuador's junta failed to deliver the economic progress and stability it had promised the people. Ecuadorians were used to ineffective and volatile governments since gaining their independence from Spain in 1822, but for people like Espinoza whose livelihood depended on their work and on the vagaries of the US dollar that determined the value of the ever-fluctuating sucre, one government mirrored the other.

Yet in 1979 there was cause to rejoice as the country found its economic footing with a worldwide demand for oil—one of the natural resources Ecuador is blessed with—and democracy returned with the election of a young, popular president, Jaime Roldós Aguilera, who stood up to the United States and quickly gained a regional reputation as a champion of human rights. As if the country were cursed with chronic instability, Roldós died in a plane crash less than two years into his term. Upon Roldós's death, his vice president and constitutional successor, Osvaldo Hurtado, became president and immediately faced an economic crisis precipitated by the sudden end of the petroleum boom.[1]

Espinoza and his wife, who in the six years of their marriage had established a shoemaking factory at home, began to feel the impact of the crisis when the shop owners who used to pay for their shoes with cash started delaying payment. Every time Espinoza traveled to Quito or Guayaquil with a shipment of shoes, he returned with a check that he was told he couldn't cash for two or three months. If he didn't like the arrangement, the shop owners would tell him, he could take his shoes elsewhere; there would always be another shoemaker willing to take their worthless checks. So Espinoza turned to loan sharks, *chulqueros* in the local argot, to keep his business afloat.

By the time Espinoza realized he was losing his business, he was in debt for three hundred thousand sucres, about $30,000, and he was dangerously close to losing his home because he had offered it as collateral for the high-interest loans. It wasn't easy for Espinoza to find another job; all he knew was how to make shoes. In Ecuador, though relatively poor by US standards, he was considered a middle-class man, and middle-class men, by culture and tradition, didn't lose their businesses to start anew washing dishes or working in a factory. There was only one solution and it came to him suddenly one day as he was returning from Guayaquil with yet another worthless check he would have to turn over to the *chulqueros*.

I'm going to the United States, he told Ana as soon as he walked in their small, modest home by the side of the main road. There, he explained, he could reinvent himself, doing whatever was necessary to support his family and get out of debt. In the United States, practically all immigrants were expected to start at the bottom. Espinoza had no fear of starting at the bottom, as long as it was not at home.

How would you manage to go? Ana asked, surprised at his sudden declaration. We have no money, no bank account, she insisted.

True enough. But Espinoza had a plan. He had a cousin who had enough money to have a healthy bank account. Back then, bank statements were rudimentary and didn't include the client's name. Espinoza asked his cousin for his latest bank statement, and, armed with that, and wearing his black suit with the same tie and shirt he would later use to leave his country, he took a regional bus to Guayaquil, the largest and most populous city in Ecuador and the site of the US consulate. From the bus station, he went straight to the consulate and waited in line, along with about one hundred other people who, like him, were seeking travel visas.

His chances were not great. In 1981, the US government granted just 690 "temporary visitor for business" visas to Ecuadorians, fewer by far than the number of visas extended to Bolivians, Brazilians, Chileans, Colombians, Peruvians, and Venezuelans.[2]

When his time came, Espinoza was sweating under his black suit. Embarrassed at the moisture he could feel under his arms, he kept the jacket on and—with a smile that exuded a confidence he didn't feel—walked into the main office. A pretty blonde American secretary greeted him with a smile. Espinoza flirted a little, not so much because he desperately wanted a visa but because it was his nature to be flirtatious.

The secretary helped him fill out the application, which he had left incomplete; he had been afraid to make a mistake. Then the hard part came. Why are you traveling to the United States? she asked.

Espinoza had prepared for such questions.

I'm going to Miami. I want to buy new machines for my shoe business, he said, showing her his graduation certificate from a shoemaker's school in Gualaceo.

That and the bank account must have impressed the secretary, who whispered, Come back at three.

What for? asked Espinoza, who was sure he needed to see the consul before his visa could be granted.

To pick up your papers, she said enigmatically and called the next person in line.

Espinoza didn't ask any more questions. It was mid-morning and he had the equivalent of one dollar in his pocket, not enough for breakfast or lunch, not even a soda. He stopped at a café and asked for a glass of water. Then he took a long walk around the port city, which was warm and humid, with the temperature hovering around eighty, typical for a summer day. To kill time, he walked toward *el malecón*, the promenade along the Guayas River, which flows into the Pacific Ocean. He entertained himself by looking at the dark waters and thinking about what he would do once he arrived in the United States. Not once did he contemplate not getting the visa.

By two thirty that afternoon, Espinoza was back at the consulate.

You are early, the secretary teased him, before handing him his passport back.

Now what? he asked.

Now you get your ticket. Your visa has been approved, she said.

Espinoza had to work hard to contain his elation. After all, a businessman like him should be used to getting his way, including a travel visa to the United States. He shook her hand, said thank you, walked out of the consulate, and went straight to the bus station for the five-hour trip home. On the bus, he tried to get his thoughts organized and make plans for the future, but he didn't get very far because his only plan was to find a job the moment he arrived in New York.

When he got home, his wife was waiting for him. At the sight of her expectant face, the tears that he had been holding back for hours could no longer be contained.

So you are going to leave me alone with the girls after all, she said, but there was no bitterness in her comment for she too understood that this was the only choice they had left.

When Espinoza uncovered his eyes, the plane was about to land at John F. Kennedy Airport in Queens, and all that he could see ahead of him was the seemingly endless runway. It was almost midnight, and the pilot made a perfect landing. Because he was a man in need of good luck and reassurance, he took the soft landing as a good sign and immediately felt lighter, ready to face the future, optimistic even.

At the baggage carousel, he grabbed his large suitcase, which contained only two pairs of pants, three shirts, and two pairs of shoes. His wife's cousin, David, met him at the airport and took him to the home he shared with his wife and five-year-old son in Jersey City, New Jersey. By then it was the early hours of Sunday, August 16, 1981, and Espinoza felt he had been born anew.

He didn't know how to speak English. He didn't know anybody except a smattering of friends and relatives who had come only months or a few years before him and could guide him a little. He rested for two days, and on Tuesday, accompanied by David, he set out to find a job in Manhattan. They had been told that the factories near the Avenue of the Americas, south of Thirty-fourth Street, were hiring.

As they drove through the Lincoln Tunnel, Espinoza found it endless and futuristic. In the cities he had traveled to in his country, Quito and Guayaquil, there were no underground tunnels connecting the mainland to an island. When they emerged, another surprise awaited: smoke was rising from the streets in midtown Manhattan. Espinoza didn't say anything, but wondered who could possibly be cooking underground? It took him a while to learn that the smoke billowing from the innards of the city was steam from a heating system.

Espinoza found a job in the first place he asked for one: a shoe factory on Twenty-first Street and Avenue of the Americas, where he would sew ballet slippers eight hours a day for $200 a week. Given that his workday started at eight in the morning and ended at four, Espinoza thought he could add a second shift to his schedule, and he found another job two blocks away, on Twenty-third Street, doing the same work. He toiled eight hours there, from 4:30 p.m. to 12:30 a.m., for $185 a week. Then he headed to the Port Authority and took a bus to Jersey City, where he would collapse into bed at one thirty and rise five hours later to head back to work. At the end of the week, Espinoza could barely focus his eyes. Whenever he looked up from his labor, he would see dots—like small black insects—fluttering around on the edges of his vision. He would have to close his eyes for a moment before he could refocus on the shoe at hand. He feared he would go blind.

He kept at it because it pleased him enormously to chip away at his debt and send money home to take care of his family, and because he felt comfortable in his new job, surrounded by recent arrivals, just like him, but from the Dominican Republic. He could speak Spanish with his coworkers during their lunch breaks and express longing for his family, which they understood. There were about fifty thousand Ecuadorians in New York then, so few that they were hardly noticeable in the city.[3] The majority of Hispanics were from Puerto Rico, who are born US citizens and therefore not considered immigrants.

Three months into his punishing routine, Espinoza was called into the manager's office at his second job and told his hours and his pay would be reduced. The season was over, and the demand for their shoes had plummeted. Espinoza began looking for another job.

A relative of David, his wife's cousin, told him that in Bay Shore, Long Island, a fine restaurant called Captain Bill's was looking for workers. Espinoza went to the waterfront restaurant the following Sunday and got a job washing enormous pots encrusted with tomato sauce. The pots were so big he had to rinse them on the floor with a hose. The pay was about the same as in the city, but food was included. To Espinoza, that seemed like a raise. He quit his jobs and moved to Bay Shore with another friend, who had rented a two-bedroom apartment. After a year washing dishes and pots, he was promoted to making salads. At first Espinoza struggled with the language. Someone would ask for an onion and he would hand him a tomato, but in time words such as "chicken," "salad," "cheese," and "dressing" became part of his vocabulary.

Two years later, in 1984, a friend mentioned that he had

found a job at a restaurant called South Shore, in the Long Island town of Patchogue. Espinoza had never heard of it but was ready for a new job, especially one that came with a $40-per-week raise. Where he lived was less important than how much he made.

When Espinoza arrived in Patchogue, he and his friend Galo Vázquez discovered they were the first Ecuadorians to move to the village, where a little over eleven thousand people lived then in an area of 2.2 square miles. Espinoza liked Patchogue. It seemed peaceful, pretty, and safe, a good place to raise the family he desperately wanted to get back. He rented an apartment in a twelve-unit building at 5 Lake Street, just off Main Street, and, because he was always fixing things, the owner made him superintendent.

Inflation in Ecuador had made it possible for him to pay his debt to the *chulquero* faster than he would have otherwise, but he was still supporting his family while spending about $300 a month in phone calls, at $1.50 a minute. From the moment Espinoza arrived, he had developed a system that allowed him to speak with his wife and children at least once a month. Since his wife didn't have a telephone at home and no one in Bullcay or nearby Gualaceo had one they could use, the family traveled to a relative's house in Cuenca, about seventeen miles away, to use the phone. In letters that Espinoza wrote frequently, he would alert them to the day and time of his call. For the family, that was a sacred appointment.

From early in the morning, Ana would remind the girls that today they would get to talk with their father. They would wash and dress and leave the house hours before the appointed time: better to be careful and early than risk an accident or traffic jam that would jeopardize their window of opportunity for the call. They would board the bus or catch a ride and arrive at least an hour early. On the phone Espinoza would tell his family about his life, his work, and how much he loved them and missed them, and the girls would mostly listen and cry.

In his letters and during the calls, Espinoza told them also about how jobs were plentiful and well paid. He would mention that schools were free and that all children were expected to graduate and go on to college, and how in the town where he lived there were playgrounds and safe beaches nearby and clean streets with orderly traffic. Ana would relay the stories to their friends and relatives and they would spread the word.

Before Christmas of 1984, Ana arrived in New York from Ecuador with a visitor's visa, leaving the girls behind for a year and four months. In February 1986, Espinoza returned home to get his daughters, now twelve, ten, and eight. By then Espinoza had become a legal US resident—he benefited from a 1986 amnesty that legalized about three million undocumented immigrants. With his family finally together, Espinoza felt he was working for their future and not merely for survival. For the first time in his life he was able to save money, and he began feeling more ambitious about his job prospects. Though he was still making salads, Espinoza was also observing the chef. His attentiveness would serve him well. Four years later, a job as an assistant chef opened up in the kitchen of a local country club. Espinoza took it and brought his wife along. They would stay for fourteen years.

While the Espinozas were busily working at the country club, Gualaceños started arriving in Patchogue, following the lead of those, like Espinoza, who had encouraged them to come. It didn't take much to convince them. Ecuador, always a tumultuous country plagued by natural disasters, difficult to govern, and even more difficult to keep afloat economically, was hemorrhaging its most entrepreneurial citizens—mostly men—to the American dream at an unprecedented rate.

The Azuay province of Ecuador, where Gualaceo is located, had had a business relationship with New York since the first half of the twentieth century because of the incorrectly named Panama hat, that handwoven, blindingly white straw hat popularized in the movies of the time. But when demand for the hat decreased in the 1950s and 1960s, the Ecuadorian economy suffered, particularly for two groups: the businessmen who exported the hats and the peasants who made them. Both groups, taking advantage of the established business patterns and relationships they had formed over the years, began to slowly migrate to the city they were somewhat familiar with: New York.[4]

That first wave of migrants was nothing compared with what was to come. In the 1980s and 1990s a migration fever seized the country. Crippled by a mounting debt crisis, Ecuador began to export people instead of hats. Unable to find jobs at home or elsewhere in their own country, thousands of Ecuadorians left for New York in whatever way it was possible: either legally, with a visa, or illegally, by crossing the border surreptitiously or buying fake visas. Everyone seemed to be migrating north or knew someone who had already left on the perilous and costly journey.

In a 1990 survey conducted by the University of Cuenca, 45.5 percent of the respondents reported having at least one family member living in the United States. By 1991 the New York Department of City Planning estimated that there were approximately one hundred thousand Ecuadorian migrants in the New York City area (this figure did not account for undocumented immigrants, which would likely have doubled that number).[5] The Azuayan branch of the Central Bank estimated that remittances from migrants abroad amounted to $120 million in 1991, equivalent to sixteen years of straw-hat exports.[6]

Espinoza himself helped at least twenty Gualaceños find jobs. On one day alone he placed seven men in a flower shop. At times it seemed as if every Gualaceño who came to Long Island went to see him first. As a building superintendent, he either had a space to rent or knew who had it and was willing to rent to newly arrived immigrants, often men who shared a room.

In this way, Espinoza quickly became what those who study migration patterns have called a "pioneer migrant"—immigrants

who have a "decisive influence on later migrants," who are guided
not by job ads or recruiting agents but "by spontaneous individual and family decisions, usually based on the presence in certain
places of kin and friends who can provide shelter and assistance,"
as Alejandro Portes and Rubén G. Rumbaut note in their classic
Immigrant America: A Portrait.[7] After a group settles in a certain
place, an enclave is established and others from the same town
or nationality follow. "Migration is a network-driven process,
and the operation of kin and friendship ties is nowhere more
effective than in guiding new arrivals toward preexisting ethnic
communities," Portes and Rumbaut wrote.[8] Once this process is
well established, the authors conclude, "migration becomes self-
perpetuating through the operation of ethnic networks." In theory, they explain, "this process may continue indefinitely."

In 1993, twelve years after his arrival in New York, Espinoza,
who by then had had two other children with Ana, a son and a
fourth daughter, realized that practically everybody he knew from
Gualaceo had at least one family member in Patchogue, which
gave him an idea for a business. Most immigrants he knew, himself included, had to travel to Queens whenever they wanted to
send a package or wire money to relatives at home. Wouldn't it
be great if they could do it right here in Patchogue? Espinoza described this idea to his wife, who was hesitant about leaving their
stable jobs but knew enough not to stand between her husband
and his unwavering optimism.

With their savings and a loan of $5,000 from a relative, Espi-
noza rented a seven-hundred-square-foot space on Patchogue's
Main Street and called it Envios Espinoza. Failure was not an option, but, just in case, the ever-careful Espinoza team kept working at the restaurant on the weekends. By the time they opened a
second store, a few blocks away and also on Main Street, Espinoza
decided to stop working for others and focus on his own thriving
business. Eight years after he opened the first store, Espinoza
opened a third store in 2001. Every day he shuttled from one

counter to another, where he sold products—such as *manichos* (chocolates) and *galletas* (crackers)—that Gualaceños yearned for. He offered immigration advice, rented Spanish-language movies, wired money home, and sold phone cards. Gualaceños would stop by after work or on their lunch break and greet him as they would back home, respectfully and in Spanish. *Buenos días, Don Julio,* they would say, and Espinoza felt right at home.

Yet Espinoza was aware that Patchogue was not home. It was where he lived and where he had settled and where he hoped to stay, but he was not naive enough to assume that just because he liked Patchogue, Patchogue liked him back. Though he had a thriving business, he knew that his business depended entirely on the Ecuadorian population. No one who was not Hispanic had ever ventured into his shop out of curiosity or need. It was as if there was an invisible line separating the Ecuadorian immigrants from the rest of Patchogue.

His children admitted that they experienced the same line running through the hallways of their local high school: those who spoke only English stayed on one side, while those who spoke only Spanish stayed on the other. Then there were the rumors Espinoza had heard of young people harassing and attacking immigrants late at night, particularly if they had had too much to drink, stealing their money and sometimes their bicycles, and calling them ugly names.

Espinoza knew there was a name for that, racism, but he himself had not felt it. He was content in his small world, tending to his customers, paying the rent on his shops on time, and rushing home at night to share a meal with his family. In 2002, Espinoza and his wife bought their first home in the United States, a three-bedroom house on a busy road, built far enough from the street that it was possible for them to ignore the world outside, even the traffic.

One of the Espinozas' most loyal customers was a young man

who had arrived in New York in 1993 and had moved to Patch-ogue soon after, just like Espinoza a decade earlier, looking for a better-paying, more stable job. His name was Marcelo Lucero and he was the son of a small, walnut-skinned woman who had a reputation for being the best cook in Gualaceo. On market days, people would line up to buy Doña Rosario's home-cooked meals.

Almost every day after work at a dry cleaner's, Lucero would stop at Envios Espinoza and buy a $2 phone card so that he could call home and talk with his mother for about twenty-five minutes. Espinoza was fond of Lucero. He admired especially how often Lucero wanted to speak to his loved ones, but also understood what Lucero was feeling: he was homesick and alone, though sur-rounded by people he knew from childhood, people who were his neighbors in Gualaceo and who had become his neighbors in Patchogue as well.

Between 1999 and 2000, four hundred thousand Ecuador-ians joined their one million compatriots already in the United States.[9] Almost two-thirds of them were living in the greater New York area.[10] According to the 2000 US census, there were 2,842 Hispanics in Patchogue then, more than an 84 percent increase from the previous census in 1990.[11] Most of the Hispanics were from Ecuador; the majority of them were from Gualaceo and its surroundings. Yet for a while Ecuadorians in Patchogue remained under the radar—not because they weren't visible but because most people didn't want to see them.

At first, immigrants were working menial jobs in the stately homes near the waters of the Great South Bay, in nurseries, and on construction sites. That was the case for years and the towns-folk had accepted and even welcomed the cheap labor of immi-grants, as long as at the end of the day they left and went home— wherever that was. What was different with the Ecuadorians in Patchogue—and a little unsettling for those who noticed—was that at the end of the day they stayed, living in the small apartments behind Main Street and in the subdivided grand houses of absentee landlords who long ago had moved to Florida. Patchogue had become their home, not just the place where they worked.

Suddenly, it seemed, there was a proliferation of signs in Spanish asking for dishwashers, ads for restaurants serving "Spanish" food, and even a bilingual teller at the bank on Main Street. Darkhaired delivery boys predominated, and men gathered on main roads looking for daily construction work.

Ecuadorians had become a visible but quiet presence in the streets of the village, scurrying off Main Street whenever a police car approached or a large crowd gathered. Few wanted to engage with them, but some people tried to bridge that divide. One who tried, perhaps more persistently than anyone else, was a local librarian, a Long Island native with an ear for languages and a stubborn and particular love for Spanish.

CHAPTER 3

WELCOME TO PATCHOGUE

In 1997 Jean Kaleda became a reference librarian in the Patchogue-Medford Library. At thirty-eight she had finally found her dream job in a library that served a vast and diverse population in Suffolk County. Practically from childhood, Kaleda had trained precisely for this career.

Kaleda was born and raised in Hicksville, a hamlet within the town of Oyster Bay, Nassau County, which became a bustling New York City suburb during the construction boom years after World War II. Her father, who was from Brooklyn, had two jobs: providing customer service for the then-thriving Eastern Airlines and cleaning offices at night. Her mother, who had been a flight attendant, stayed home after her first child was born. The couple had five children in seven years. Jean, their second-born, was the oldest of three girls.

Growing up in a boisterous house and sharing a room with her sisters, Kaleda found her refuge in literature. She would spend hours in bed reading, mostly British mysteries. Her first job, when she was twelve, was delivering newspapers. Kaleda would peek at the headlines before throwing the bundles on her neighbors' manicured front lawns. Though her paternal grandparents had been born in Lithuania and her mother's father in Sicily, only English was spoken at home. Her ancestors, Kaleda understood, had wanted to assimilate quickly, put their unhappy memories behind them, and restart their lives in a new country.

At home Kaleda's parents stressed a sense of fairness, respect, and hard work. The "golden rule" was a teaching tool. Even as a child, the simple idea of treating others as she would like to be treated herself resonated with her. In ninth grade, the curriculum of the Catholic school she attended dictated that students take a foreign language, and she chose Spanish. Kaleda then studied English at Towson University in Maryland, and in the fall of 1979, her junior year of college, she decided on a whim to go to Spain. It was there, in the narrow streets and smoky bars of downtown Madrid, where Kaleda fell in love not only with the language but also with the bohemian culture of a country that felt electric and giddy with possibilities. General Francisco Franco, the strongman who had ruled Spain for thirty-six years, had died four years earlier, and Spain had transitioned to a democracy with a new constitution.

Kaleda's political sense heightened in Madrid, where she followed the Spanish media coverage regarding the fifty-two Americans taken hostage in Iran that year, and she was surprised and saddened to see that some Spaniards found joy in the suffering of Americans. She thought she understood the reasons for it. She remembered as a child reading the daily news coverage of the Vietnam War, with the photos of dead children and soldiers in caskets. If that's the way the war had played in America's living rooms, she could only imagine what the world had seen and how that had influenced how other countries viewed Americans.

Upon graduation, with a major in Spanish and a minor in English, Kaleda stayed in Maryland, first working as a secretary in an accounting firm, and then for three years as a translator from Spanish to English for the Defense Department. When her father became ill with emphysema, Kaleda moved back home and switched careers, enrolling in St. John's University, in Queens, for a master's degree in library science.

Her first job after graduation was as a librarian in an investment bank in New York City, where she had done an internship during graduate school. She worked there for three years, though the job never fulfilled her. She wanted to be a librarian to share knowledge, not to be a facilitator of data for a big corporation. Taking a pay cut, Kaleda, at thirty-one, returned to Long Island to work as a librarian in Riverhead, near where she had grown up.

From 1990 to 1997 she was relatively content with her job as a reference librarian, but barely used her Spanish. Then, in 1997, the offer came to work at the Patchogue-Medford Library, where, she was assured, her Spanish would be put to good use. So it was with eagerness and a great sense of mission that she accepted the position, seeing herself as a link between the library and the growing Hispanic population on the south shore of Long Island. She envisioned all she could do with her language skills and her curiosity for a people who she knew were underserved and often misunderstood, as many newcomers are.

Kaleda was surprised and disappointed to find that the library's patrons were not as diverse as the population she could see right outside the library's front windows. Where is everybody? she wondered. And who are they? Where are they from?

She would strain her ears walking up and down Main Street trying to identify the soft Spanish accent she had come to know and love in Spain, or the more musical but truncated Spanish of the Caribbean that she was used to hearing from the Dominicans and Puerto Ricans in New York City. What she heard in the streets of Patchogue resembled neither of those accents. This was a more formal, clipped way of speaking that seemed to skip over the vowels and end each word with an expectant tilt, as if the other person was supposed to finish the thought.

Kaleda couldn't place it, and didn't know who could. She didn't know anybody in Patchogue outside the library or at least not anybody who shared her interest in Hispanics and her love of Spanish in particular. But she was determined to attract Hispanic patrons to the library.

There was plenty of history to draw from. Chartered by the state of New York in 1900, the Patchogue-Medford Library is the main library for Suffolk County, serving a population of more than fifty thousand people.[1] During the 1970s and 1980s, Puerto Ricans made up the vast majority of Spanish speakers in the community. A librarian named Barbara Hoffman decided to reach out to that community by focusing on the youth. With her support, a local band of teenage musicians, mostly Hispanic and African Americans, was hired for a library dance. Local teens who thought of themselves as graffiti artists were enlisted to redirect their talents to paint a mural for the library, and the library provided video equipment and a videographer to film events in the Hispanic community. To develop a young adult collection in Spanish, English-speaking librarians asked local teenagers to accompany them to the Borders Bookstore to select books they thought other teenagers would like.[2]

The program was a victim of its own success: as the community became more bilingual and more integrated into the fabric of Patchogue, there was no longer such a need for a Spanish program. Eventually the library's outreach to Spanish speakers came to a near-standstill. While the library blinked, the Spanish-speaking community was reinventing itself, but this time with the Ecuadorians.[3]

In early 2002 the library revised its long-range plan, and Spanish-language outreach was designated a priority. Soon after, the library established a Spanish Outreach Committee, which was chaired by Kaleda. A Literacy and Languages Center with materials to learn English and other languages was established, printed materials were translated into Spanish, and the bilingual and Spanish collections were greatly expanded. Bilingual suggestion boxes were placed everywhere in the library.[4]

The only problem for Kaleda was that there seemed to be no clear path to reach out to the community. The library was like a perfectly laid-out buffet with all the trimmings and no takers. Unlike other groups that tend to unite to lobby for recognition, jobs, or political power, the Ecuadorians in Patchogue seemed to be leaderless. Everyone went about his or her business individually, a behavior typical of recent arrivals. Ecuadorians were not yet seeking a presence in the town's life; they were trying to survive.

Then, in the early fall of 2002, Kaleda found an item on the front page of the local paper, the *Long Island Advance*, that caught her eye: "Planting Roots on Long Island, Surging Hispanic Population Hopes to Break Barriers in America."[5]

Finally, Kaleda thought as she read, somebody else has noticed the obvious:

> Martha Vázquez is a long way from home, but she has lots of company.
>
> A native of Gualaceo, Ecuador, Vázquez says there are more than 16,000 people from her South American homeland who have migrated to Long Island during the past 30 years. The Patchogue Village resident, who moved here 15 years ago and officially became a US citizen on Aug. 15, 1998, also says that at least 4,000 Ecuadorians now live in the greater Patchogue areas.
>
> The most interesting statistic, according to the 32-year-old wife and mother of one, is that all of them came from the same small village in Ecuador.
>
> [...]
>
> On a local level, the Hispanic population in Patchogue village, for example, has increased by 84.1 percent between 1990 and 2000, according to recent census figures. Approximately 2,842 individuals of Latino descent now live within

the borders of the 2.2-square-mile village. The cultural meta-morphosis is most apparent on South Ocean Avenue, where Spanish bodegas and meat markets now dominate the commercial corridor.

[. . .]

In addition to seeking employment opportunities, the majority of Ecuadorians living on Long Island either are or hope to become full-fledged tax-paying American citizens, according to Vázquez, spokeswoman for the newly incorporated Ecuadorians United in Long Island. The Patchogue-based group now boasts almost 60 members, but only two speak good English, highlighting one of the barriers that the growing local Hispanic population must contend with.

Kaleda had found her answers. In a few paragraphs she had noted a need she knew she could fulfill—English lessons—and learned the name of a person who seemed poised to help, Martha Vázquez. She picked up the phone and called Vázquez. The article had identified her as working for a local bank.

Vázquez was receptive, immediately grasping Kaleda's intentions, and invited her to the next meeting. The group—no more than ten that night—met in a space above a Chinese restaurant on Main Street. Kaleda went and mostly listened. Group members were discussing one of their first projects: a community garden on South Ocean Avenue. Kaleda understood that if she wanted to attract Ecuadorians to the library she needed to reach many more than ten. She needed to do it in Spanish and through a publication they trusted. Someone at the meeting mentioned that the most trusted publication among Hispanics in Patchogue was not on Long Island, but in Ecuador, more than three thousand miles away: a weekly newspaper called *Semanario El Pueblo*, which was edited and published in Gualaceo on Sundays, and arrived in Patchogue by Thursdays.

The next day Kaleda composed an e-mail in Spanish to the publisher, Fernando León, telling him that the doors of the library were open to the Ecuadorian community and that library employees were eager to work with them. She also asked him for advice on how best to reach the community. She was hoping for an e-mail response, or even simple confirmation that her e-mail had been received, but heard nothing. A few days later, the first three Gualaceños walked into the library looking for Kaleda.

How did you find me? she asked, startled but pleased.

They pointed to a copy of *El Pueblo* they carried with them. The publisher had used Kaleda's e-mail as a letter to the editor. The ice was broken.

The outreach program was set into high gear. *Bienvenido al Pueblo* welcome packets, modeled on the library's English-language "Welcome to the Community" packets, were created and distributed to all patrons applying for library cards. Spanish-language and bilingual workshops were offered on topics that ranged from immigration and health awareness to fair housing, and bilingual story times were started.[6]

For much of the translation work the library relied on Kaleda, who had learned Spanish as an adult, a part-time clerk who was not in a public service area, and a part-time custodian. No one else in the library spoke Spanish. Kaleda knew she needed to find a full-time employee who was truly bilingual. She found what she was looking for right under the library's roof, but it took time and a dash of luck to make it happen.

One day Kaleda was speaking with a man who had attended one of the bilingual workshops and who stressed that what he and other Latinos in the area needed was a primer on how Patchogue worked. For instance, how to pay a parking ticket, understanding the difference between the local constables and the Suffolk County police, or how to apply to use the soccer field for a game. Kaleda listened and set out to organize the first bilingual village/

library meeting. She spoke to the mayor, Paul Pontieri, who was interested. The meeting was set for November 3, 2004, and it was billed as "*Viviendo en la Villa de Patchogue*"—Living in the Village of Patchogue.

A supervisor for the Patchogue-Medford Adult Literary Consortium agreed to bring some of their English-language learners to the meeting. The consortium held citizenship classes at the library as well, and, by coincidence, one was scheduled the same day as the meeting, so those students too were expected to attend. The woman who taught the citizenship classes was Gilda Ramos, a part-time employee of the school district, who had been born and raised in Peru but who had lived on Long Island for six years.

Flyers all over the village advertised the meeting, and though the text was riddled with mistakes and spelling errors it was understandable. Mayor Pontieri was expected to explain everything from where to park legally to how to apply for low-income housing.

When Pontieri arrived shortly before 7:00 p.m., dozens of people were waiting for him. In the end, about one hundred crammed into a small room in the library basement. The mayor began to speak, but it was clear from the beginning that the community volunteer who was helping to interpret his words to Spanish was unable to translate. From her seat in the front, Ramos started whispering the correct translation to the beleaguered interpreter, who finally gave up, turned to Ramos, and asked, Do you want to do this? Because I can't.

Ramos leaped at the chance, went to the front of the room, and flawlessly translated the mayor's words.

From the side of the room, near the door, Kaleda liked what she saw and realized she had found just the person she was looking for. In 2005 Ramos began working in the library part-time as a clerk. Two years later, Kaleda was able to hire her in a new full-time civil service category called "Spanish speaking library assistant," and Ramos became an indispensable member of the library, teaching computer classes in Spanish, English as a second language, Spanish conversation, and, of course, her citizenship classes.

Gilda Ramos was, like Kaleda, the right person at the right time in the right job. Trained as an interpreter in English and German in her native Peru, and endowed with a passion for public service and a terrific work ethic, Ramos was eager to help the newly arrived immigrants.

She had started to learn English as a toddler in a Catholic preschool. Her love of the language and facility with it was such that, at night, before she said her prayers in Spanish, she recited the Lord's Prayer and Hail Mary in English. When she was twelve, Ramos, one of two daughters of a single mother who worked as an assistant nurse and studied psychology, started earning money for the family tutoring older kids in English. By sixteen, she was translating for missionaries while going to school and continuing her training in English. The language school was far from her house, and it took her hours to navigate the city. At that time, the terrorist Maoist group Shining Path was keeping Lima alert and in fear with constant bombings. But nothing could deter Ramos in her drive to succeed.

At twenty-two, secure in her knowledge of English, Ramos turned her attention to German, and moved to Stuttgart, Germany, to work as an au pair. Her plan was to stay for a year and then return home and find a job in a pharmaceutical lab or a German brewery, but she fell in love with an American soldier. When she returned home, the soldier followed her. On his third visit, the two married and he whisked her off to an apartment in Center Moriches, on Long Island. The couple had two children, but the marriage quickly soured.

In 2000, just two years after she arrived in the country, Ramos started working for the Patchogue-Medford School District as a teacher of English for newcomers. Then her supervisor asked her to begin teaching citizenship classes at the Patchogue-Medford Library, and that's how she found herself translating the mayor's words in the village/library meeting in November 2004.

Both Kaleda and Ramos started 2008 with great hopes. Kaleda was finally seeing the fruit of years of effort in trying to attract diverse patrons. Ramos, who still sees herself as the voice of the voiceless, translated all kinds of materials—from flyers to calendars—and the library truly became a hub for newly arrived English learners.

But things began to change in the fall. Ramos and Kaleda noticed that the Spanish-language materials—dictionaries, films, and compact discs—were not being checked out as often as they had been just a few months earlier. The classes were packed, but when there were no classes, few Hispanics went to the library, especially at night.

In late October, as Halloween approached, Ramos asked her students what was happening, and what she heard made her shiver with fear. The library had become such a magnet for immigrants that, at night, when they left classes walking or riding their bicycles, gangs of young men would follow them to harass and beat them or steal their money and bicycles. One had suffered a cut on his scalp from an attack, and a woman had been chased by a group of young men, who threw soda cans at her. The attacks were taking place all over Patchogue, not just near the library. That's why some of them were staying away, they said. They were afraid to be targeted, but risked attending the classes because they were so hungry to learn.

Ramos was horrified and immediately found Kaleda.

"You won't believe this," she said, a little out of breath and resting against the doorframe in Kaleda's office. "I want you to hear this with your own ears."

With Kaleda in the room, she asked her students to repeat their stories. Kaleda, who was aware that racism was rampant on Long Island and had heard stories of harassment and violence against immigrants elsewhere, immediately grasped the urgency of the matter. She was shocked that she hadn't known what was happening at night in the streets of Patchogue, and she felt vulnerable, exposed, and, above all, scared.

The year had not been kind to immigrants. Though 2008 was an election year, the candidates, US senators Barack Obama and John McCain, rarely talked about immigration. The issue was not raised at all during their three debates.[7] One of the few times McCain discussed immigration he was campaigning in Mexico City and yet stressing the need to secure the border. Few heard him because his talk in a helicopter hangar "was interrupted by the deafening sound of a heavy rainstorm that made his remarks unintelligible," the *New York Times* reported.[8]

As it has happened with certain periodicity in the United States, immigration had become the nation's most heartwrenching, divisive, and vexing issue at the turn of the century. Even before George W. Bush assumed the presidency in 2001, he had announced his intention to mend the country's broken-down immigration system. Specifically, he had called for legislation to legalize the twelve million immigrants who were then believed to live in the country illegally. The bill he championed died in Congress in June 2007, with only twelve of forty-nine Senate Republicans supporting him on a key procedural vote.[9]

In fact, any possibility of immigration reform died long before that vote, perishing in the rubble of the World Trade Center on 9/11. After the terrorist attacks perpetrated by foreigners who had entered the country with visas, the nation closed in on itself. Fluid borders turned rigid and the national conversation swiftly changed: it was no longer about helping immigrants assimilate and become Americans. Rather, it was about keeping aliens out. Caught in the rhetoric were the millions of immigrants, many of them Hispanics from Mexico, who were already in the country and—in their eyes, at least—part of the United States, though with no documents to prove it. Funding was diverted to enforcement, deportation, and homeland security. Indeed, the former Immigration and Naturalization Service became the Department of Homeland Security.[10]

In the spring of 2006, millions of immigrants took to the streets in cities all over the country, demanding immigration reform. But the effort backfired. It didn't help that the most visible flags in all demonstrations were not red, white, and blue, but red, white, and green Mexican flags. Instead of raising consciousness of their plight, the protesters managed to raise consciousness of their numbers. In television interviews, they came across as angry and ungrateful. Americans wanted to hear them asking for permission to stay, not demanding a change of the laws they had already flaunted by crossing the border illegally or overstaying visas. Middle America became even more afraid of a so-called Hispanic invasion.

Every day, it seemed, newspapers carried stories that detailed the mood of the country, and it was clear that the country was torn. On the one hand, businesses and liberals advocated for less restrictive immigration policies and a kind, generous approach to legalizing the millions who were in the country illegally. On the other hand, conservatives and anti-immigration activists decried the lax security at the border and angrily demanded that the federal government establish a coherent way to control illegal immigration.

In a 2008 editorial titled "The Great Immigration Panic," the *New York Times* described the situation as a war:

> Someday, the country will recognize the true cost of its war on illegal immigration. We don't mean dollars, though those are being squandered by the billions. The true cost is to the na-

tional identity: the sense of who we are and what we value. It will hit us once the enforcement fever breaks, when we look at what has been done and no longer recognize the country that did it. . . . The restrictionist message is brutally simple—that illegal immigrants deserve no rights, mercy or hope. It refuses to recognize that illegality is not an identity; it is a status that can be mended by making reparations and resuming a lawful life. Unless the nation contains its enforcement compulsion, illegal immigrants will remain forever Them and never Us, subject to whatever abusive regimes the powers of the moment may devise.[11]

With more than 175 bills relating to immigrant employment introduced by states in 2008, it was obvious that the war was being waged at the local level.[12] Two years earlier, municipalities and towns had started to propose—and sometimes pass—resolutions and laws aimed at curbing illegal immigration. Towns from Long Island to Palm Beach, Florida, and beyond tried to dictate what documents employers had to check when hiring workers to fix a roof or cut the grass, where day laborers could stand while looking for jobs on street corners, and even whether they could wave their arms at incoming trucks looking for workers. In the summer of 2006, the city council of Hazleton, Pennsylvania, passed the Illegal Immigration Relief Act to target employers and landlords who hired or rented their homes to undocumented immigrants. The act also declared English the city's official language. Courts prevented most elements of the ordinance from going into effect, but it brought national attention and much angst to a divided Hazleton.

"What I'm doing here is protecting the legal taxpayer of any race," the then-fifty-year-old mayor of Hazleton, Louis J. Barletta, the grandson of immigrants, told the *Washington Post*. "And I will get rid of the illegal people. It's this simple: *They must leave.*"[13]

From June 2008 until Election Day that year, the war against immigration played out on the front pages of local and national newspapers. Everyone knew about the factory raids: 595 workers, said to be in the country illegally, were detained in Laurel, Mississippi;[14] 300 were arrested at a kosher meat plant in Postville, Iowa;[15] and 160 were arrested at a used-clothing and rag-exporting plant in Houston.[16] Everyone heard about the detention centers and the growing number of deportations and about the 670-mile high-security fence along the US-Mexico border that was to be built by the end of the year.[17] Often the words "illegality," "terror," "detention," "crime," "prison," and "drugs" were linked directly or indirectly to immigrants.

In Suffolk County, the tone of the debate regarding immigration had become openly hostile. On September 17, 2008, *Newsday* reported that nearly two dozen immigration advocates had asked the Suffolk County legislature to "tone down what they say is the legislature's hostility toward immigrants, especially Hispanics." Some were particularly frustrated with legislator Brian Beedenbender, a Democrat from Centereach, who introduced a bill requiring "those with occupational licenses to verify that their workers are in the country legally," *Newsday* reported. The legislature passed the bill, but the state supreme court voided it. The county appealed. The battle was raging here as well.[18]

So Ramos and Kaleda were not inclined to take any comments about threats and violence lightly. If this was indeed a war, who was protecting the immigrants? Did you call the police? Have you told somebody? Ramos and Kaleda asked their students, who said they had, at first, but when the police ignored their calls, claiming that because the attackers were underage there was little they could do, they hadn't bothered calling again. Although it wasn't articulated, it was understood that undocumented immigrants were afraid to bring attention to themselves by pressing charges.

Best to pick yourself up from the street, stay quiet, and buy another used bicycle.

Kaleda rushed to her office and composed an e-mail message to Mayor Pontieri. We have to talk, she told him. The next morning, for good measure, she called Pontieri's number in Village Hall.

This, she felt sure, was a phone call he would want to take himself.

CHAPTER 4

NOT IN MY BACKYARD

Paul Pontieri picked up the phone knowing Jean Kaleda was on the line. His secretary had transferred the call and said it sounded urgent.[1]

She must be really concerned, thought Pontieri, who knew Kaleda to be a calm and caring woman: a librarian, not an agitator. He understood her urgency, though. He too was concerned after reading her e-mail. No one should be afraid of using the library, he thought. No one should fear walking the streets at night because an accent or a skin color made one the target of hatred.

It wasn't as if Pontieri hadn't heard about violence against Latinos before, but not in Patchogue, not in the streets he knew so well. He refused to believe that anti-immigrant hatred had seeped into his home turf.

Pontieri, sixty-one, was born and raised in Patchogue, a town he had always known as an immigrant enclave. His grandparents were Italians: from Calabria on his mother's side, from Bari on his father's side. In a drawer of his desk he kept a copy of *From*

Steerage to Suburb: Long Island Italians, a book that chronicled the arrival and settlement of Italians in Patchogue and other towns of Long Island. One of the men shown on the faded cover was his maternal grandfather, Frank Romeo. On a shelf in Pontieri's office was another picture of Romeo, shirtsleeves rolled up and a fedora hat on his head, helping build the village's roads.

Pontieri liked pointing to the photo any time someone came to his office to discuss the growing number of Hispanics in town. "We are the same," he would stress. "Small, dark men with thick arms and heavy souls working to build a better life."

In fact, there are numerous similarities between the Italian immigrants who settled in Patchogue in the late nineteenth century and the Ecuadorians who started arriving after Julio Espinoza moved to the village in 1984. Both came to find better work opportunities. Many in both groups settled in Patchogue immediately or soon after arriving in New York City, lured away from the city by the promise of jobs in the open pastures and vast spaces of Long Island. Most Italians in Patchogue came from a specific region, Calabria, which is at the tip of the boot-shaped Italian peninsula, and most Ecuadorians in Patchogue are from one region in Azuay, a south-central province of Ecuador. Both groups worked primarily in construction, and, like Ecuadorians would more than a century later, the pioneering Italians on Long Island encountered discrimination. It wasn't unusual at the turn of the twentieth century to find a sign excluding Italians in advertised properties for sale on Long Island communities.[2] Though there are no such signs rejecting Hispanics now, many say they have felt the sting of racism.

Just as Gualaceños migrated once Espinoza and others sent word about the wonders of Patchogue, Calabrians had moved there at the urging of relatives or friends who had preceded them and who often had found them housing and jobs once—or even before—they arrived in town. That's how Pontieri's maternal grandmother, Rose Mazzotti, happened to find a home there, and that's how Frank Romeo, who knew Rose from Calabria, happened to build a life with her.

In 1896, Rose Mazzotti, born in Terranova di Sibari, was brought to the United States in the first of three transatlantic journeys her family made over ten years before settling permanently in the United States. The Mazzotti family came to Long Island because an uncle of Rose's mother, Louis Lotito, had sent for them. Lotito, the earliest Italian to reside in Patchogue, was a caretaker at a farm that needed more laborers, and Rose and her parents joined him.

In their seminal work *The Polish Peasant in Europe and America*, first published in 1927, William I. Thomas and Florian Znaniecki explain this process of transoceanic migration to America from Europe almost the same way that Rumbaut and Portes would eighty years later. "When many members of a community are settled in America and keep contact with their home, America appears almost as an extension of the community," they observe. "When a member prepares to leave, though he may travel alone, he goes at the invitation of another member and goes to him; from the standpoint of his group, it is not so very different from going to a Polish city to visit a friend and earn there some money."[3]

One of the families to follow Lotito was the Romeo family. Frank Romeo had met and fallen in love with Rose in Italy during one of her trips home. Because she was still so young, her parents regarded Frank's interest as a premature infatuation. In 1902 Frank arrived in New York City with no money, family, or employment, but he quickly found a job as a contractor's helper finishing sidewalks. After learning that Rose had returned to Patchogue with her family, Frank resumed his courtship, riding sixty miles on weekends on his bicycle from New York City to Patchogue and then sixty miles back. He soon moved to Patchogue, however, and started working as a mason and a bricklayer, crafts he had learned in Italy from his father. On

January 16, 1910, when he was twenty-five and she was sixteen, Frank and Rose were married. Frank started a road construction business, Romeo Construction Company, and the couple went on to have seven children.[4] One of them, Marguerite, would one day become the mother of Paul Pontieri, the town's first Italian American mayor.

For thousands of years Patchogue was inhabited by Native Americans who spoke an Algonquian dialect. The name "Patchogue" is derived from "Pochaug," which means a turning place or "where two streams separate." The area was first settled by the Dutch and eventually became part of New England, but it remained undeveloped by European settlers for decades. In the eighteenth century, because of its abundant lakes, rivers, and extensive shoreline, Patchogue became a mill town—producing paper, twine, cloth, wool, carpet, lumber, leather, and iron products—an irresistible draw for many immigrants, including Italians.[5]

By the turn of the twentieth century, Patchogue, incorporated as a village since 1893, had a thriving fishing industry and had made a name for itself as a tourist town that attracted the moneyed class from New York City seeking a respite in the hot summers. A new railroad in 1869 had made it easier for city residents to reach Patchogue. Large hotels were built on or near the shoreline that could accommodate over 1,600 guests. The twenties—the golden age of the silent era of Hollywood movies—brought stars, including Gloria Swanson, to Patchogue's theaters for opening nights. Because of its privileged location and buoyant economy, the town grew as a commercial and shopping hub for central and eastern Long Island. With the advent of the car, however, came greater choices for travel and shopping. The heyday of the grand resorts on Long Island started to fade as the automobile gave city dwellers a wider choice for travel.[6]

The proliferation of the car also made it easier for people to move to suburbia, even towns as far away from the city as Patchogue, which remained a good place to raise a family. In her book *Gangs in Garden City*, Sarah Garland explains how "by the 1940s, 17 percent of the country lived in the outer rings of cities." Some suburbs of New York, where the growth was particularly notable, grew even more than the city.[7]

Those who moved to suburbia—a concept that originated in Great Britain and the United States around 1815—were not like the original residents of Patchogue.[8] They were middle-class families who felt they had paid their dues after years of toiling in the city and were hoping to reach their own version of the American dream in the promised land of suburbia: a backyard with fragrant trees and an immaculate lawn with clipped grass, a barbecue with like-minded neighbors on the weekends, and good schools that children could walk to and where they would be shielded from the grittier dimensions of urban life.[9]

Despite the influx of newcomers, after the postwar baby boom Patchogue suffered another setback: strip malls began to pull shoppers away from the downtown area in the late 1960s, leading to several decades of decline on Main Street.[10] The one theater left became a ruin, as the big department stores moved elsewhere and small shops struggled to survive in a changing economy and rapidly evolving demographics. It was precisely because of that decline that newly arrived immigrants were able to move from the city to Patchogue. They could afford the rents.

Mayor Pontieri's life neatly fits the narrative of the 1950s and the growth and changes of suburbia in the postwar years. Born in 1947, he was the second child—and the only boy—of four children born to Marguerite Romeo and Paul Pontieri, who were high school sweethearts. (Paul was the president of his junior class and Marguerite was the secretary.) Paul, who didn't attend college, worked a variety of jobs. For a while he was a salesman for Sunshine Biscuits, a company that manufactured and sold cookies, crackers, and biscuits. Then he opened and operated a luncheonette next to the movie theater on South Ocean Avenue. Later he drove an oil truck. His wife stayed home, taking care of the children.

The Patchogue that the mayor remembers, seemingly without nostalgia, was a great place to be a kid. From Cedar Avenue, where he grew up, a kid in possession of a bike could go anywhere, from the park to the movies, and from school to the shore. Everything was three to five blocks away—ball fields, theaters, and the bay. More important, they had what he calls "a real neighborhood," one where parents didn't have to make play dates for their children. The children simply stepped outside looking for company, and they would always find another child ready to play.

There were dozens of stores on Main Street, including J. C. Penney and Woolworth, and three movie theaters: Granada, Plaza, and Rialto. Pontieri and a friend would often steal posters of films such as *Moby Dick*, *Davy Crockett*, and *The War of the Worlds* and keep them inside the pages of a large Peter Pan book. (Pontieri still has some of the posters; at least two are framed in his home now.) Riding his bicycle down Main Street, it wasn't difficult for young Pontieri to imagine that Patchogue was all his.

The Pontieris and the Romeos were large families. Growing up, Pontieri had seven aunts and uncles, all within a few blocks. He could have breakfast at home, lunch with an aunt, and dinner with an uncle. Christmas Eves were always huge events that would begin mid-afternoon and end with midnight Mass.

The idyll of Pontieri's childhood was altered when his father died of a heart attack at forty-one while pulling a heavy oil hose down a driveway. Pontieri, who was coming downstairs from the second floor of the house when a police officer and a priest were delivering the terrible news to the family, sat on the steps, deaf and blind to the world. He was fourteen years old. Everything was a blur after that but Pontieri clearly remembers feeling a mantle of responsibility descending over his already broad shoulders: he was now the man of the house. Much would be expected from him.

Soon after the funeral, the mayor of Patchogue called the house offering the family not only his condolence but also jobs as lifeguards in the village pool for Pontieri and his oldest sister. It was a gesture that Pontieri treasured and that one day would put him on the path to the mayoral seat: politics, he thought then, was about taking care of people when they need it the most. His mother too went to work, as a secretary, but Pontieri remained pampered by the family. Aunts and uncles, particularly the uncles, looked after him. Each uncle took on a different role. One would take him fishing, one would lecture him on the importance of being a good man, and yet another would explain to him why he always needed to put family first. All kept him on the straight path.

When time came for college, Pontieri, at two hundred pounds and five foot ten, with a strong back and large hands, won a football scholarship to Hofstra University. But he was not sure what he would do with the rest of his life other than play football and protect and help his family.

Then, in the summer after his freshman year, fate intervened. One morning, on his way to work, he left the house in a rush, wearing only swimming trunks and flip-flops. Less than half a block from his house, he lost control of his motorcycle and crashed against a parked car, breaking his right leg. He stayed in the hospital for fifteen days while doctors pieced his leg together with pins and placed it in a full cast, then a brace that he had to wear for months. Because he now walked with a slight limp and always in pain, football was no longer an option. He transferred to the State University of New York at Buffalo and got serious about school.

In 1971, the former athlete graduated with a bachelor's degree in elementary education, with a specialization in the education of physically disabled children. Three years later he got a master's degree to work with children who have learning and behavioral disorders. Along the way Pontieri met and married Mary Bilan, who was from Ashland, Ohio, but visited Patchogue with a friend one summer and never left. They went on to have three children, while Pontieri developed a career working with emotionally disturbed children.

In 1984, Pontieri left the classroom and bought a courier business. He grew it to just over $5 million in sales annually and 125 employees, but he stayed as low-key as always, seldom leaving Patchogue, a place he found so enchanting that he took few vacations. He couldn't imagine a better place to be in the summer than his own town, with its public pool, bay views, and easy access to the beaches on Fire Island.

He entered politics in 1986, when a neighbor who was chatting with him while he mowed the lawn suggested he run for village trustee. Pontieri, who had never forgotten the way the mayor had helped him after his father's death, didn't have to ponder the idea for long. He won that first election and continued in politics until he lost his seat in 1994.

Two years later he sold the business and returned to education, working as an assistant principal at Bellport High School. In 2001 he reclaimed his trustee seat, and three years later he ran for mayor and won, becoming the first Italian American mayor of Patchogue one hundred years after his grandfather Romeo came to America. In November 2008, when tragedy struck and the village became the focus of national attention, Pontieri had been mayor for exactly four years.

Pontieri does not recall a day when he suddenly noticed that 30 percent of the residents were Latinos. To him Patchogue had always been a magnet for immigrants, and though technically Puerto Ricans are not immigrants, to him Ecuadorians did not look that different from the Puerto Ricans who had once been the only Latinos in the village. In fact, Ecuadorians, he thought, did not look that different from his grandfather Romeo and the men who had helped build his town.

Sure, they had different customs, they spoke a language he

didn't understand, and they ate different foods. But Pontieri saw no reason why they couldn't coexist with the more established residents of the village. He valued their entrepreneurial spirit and was pleased to see that, along with the renovated theater on Main Street, their small businesses were breathing new life into the moribund downtown area. Where there had been boarded-up storefronts or nearly defunct, dusty stores, the new immigrants were opening up restaurants, cafés, travel agencies, boutiques, and video stores. One such businessman, José Bonilla, went to Pontieri's office to ask for permits for a new supermarket that would sell the products Ecuadorian immigrants couldn't get elsewhere.

Fine, Pontieri said, but he issued a warning: along with the Goya cans, keep the Progresso products.

Pontieri wanted to make sure that his mother wouldn't be "intimidated" by products she did not recognize. He wanted her to feel that even if she didn't understand the murmuring of the stock boys or the accent of the young women at the cashier, she wouldn't feel like a stranger in her own town.

In the first decade of the twenty-first century, Pontieri was feeling good about life in his village. He took pride in Patchogue's ordered civility, in its old stately homes and proximity to the sea, in the library, which was large and modern, and in the Italian bistros that coexisted with Greek eateries and Colombian and Peruvian restaurants. If there was turmoil and ill will, he didn't know it. If Hispanics were being harassed, he hadn't noticed. If teenagers were going around attacking men at night because they thought them to be "illegal Mexicans," Pontieri hadn't been told. He wasn't even sure he knew the difference between an Ecuadorian and a Mexican. And he didn't much care for legal status. The way he saw it, his job was to make sure the village worked for all. Immigration, as he likes to put it, was a few notches "above his pay rate." It was a federal issue, not a village concern.

He was aware, though, that elsewhere, in towns that surrounded Patchogue like a string of pearls, trouble had been brewing for a long time.

Farmingville, a blue-collar hamlet of about fifteen thousand residents, is less than five miles north of Patchogue. In the late 1990s,
Mexican laborers from the state of Hidalgo, west of Mexico City,
settled there during a construction boom. Farmingville's geographic location—seventy miles east of Manhattan, in the center
of Suffolk County and just off the Long Island Expressway—
attracted contractors and others looking for cheap labor from all
over the county. Word of the abundant job opportunities spread,
and even more immigrants, not all Mexicans, moved there looking for jobs in construction, roofing, masonry, lawn care, and
landscaping.[11]

The day laborers in Farmingville—short and brown-skinned,
with dingy worker's clothing and the general demeanor of rural
folks, people who want to be noticed by a *patrón* but ignored by everyone else—became an eyesore to those who looked at them and
saw only one side of the story: large groups of desperate men who
spoke no English standing outside two neighborhood 7-Eleven
convenience stores. In spring and summer there could be as many
as eighty men on one corner and forty on another.

Neighbors began to complain. They were also upset because
their sleepy town had found its way to the front page of *Newsday*
after police officers raided two homes and evicted forty day laborers on the charge of overcrowded housing. For people who are
concerned about the value of their property, as most homeowners are, the story was unwelcome, but the raid was necessary. All
of a sudden, concerned and angry residents began showing up
at meetings of the Farmingville Civic Association, a nonpartisan
community organization that dealt with town issues. The meetings often became shouting matches, and in 1998 about forty of

the most vociferous and angry residents of Farmingville formed a group called Sachem Quality of Life, named after Farmingville's school district.

Members of the group—working-class, nativist, and militant —accused undocumented Latino immigrants not only of harassing young women with catcalls and of urinating and defecating in public but also of being inherently prone to rape, armed robbery, and other violent crimes. They approached the media, demanding that public officials at local and federal levels act immediately. Specifically they wanted to get rid of the one hundred or so men in their midst who were standing on street corners daily in search of work. They organized protest rallies right across the streets from where the laborers waited, harassing and yelling epithets not only at the workers but also at the contractors who approached the pickup sites. Eventually the group even demanded that the US military occupy Farmingville so that immigrants could be effectively rounded up and deported.[12]

The arrival of the Mexican laborers in Farmingville—and the backlash against them—coincided with a global rising tide of xenophobia. In 1996, Paul J. Smith, director of the Pacific Forum's project on migrant trafficking, wrote a piece for the *International Herald Tribune*, in which he described how 1995 had been "a critical turning point in an era of growing international migration." It was the year, he said, "in which the backlash against immigrants, once believed to be a xenophobic reaction limited to rich, industrialized countries, went global." He cited examples of countries—in Africa, the Middle East, East and South Asia, and the Americas, as well as western and eastern Europe—where immigrants had become the targets of fierce campaigns to "track, persecute and ultimately drive them away."

The global backlash, Smith noted, "reflects the emergence of international migration as the most serious social and political crisis of the 1990s, one that is certain to worsen as population pressures, unemployment, and economic disparities between countries become even more acute."[13]

If Farmingville were a country, what happened there could have easily bolstered Smith's point. The members of Sachem Quality of Life lobbied hard against a bill authorizing the building of a day-laborer hiring center. County executive Bob Gaffney vetoed the bill, the site was never built, and incidents of harassment against immigrants continued, becoming almost daily occurrences. People threw rocks and bottles at the workers, fired BB guns at them, and broke the windows of houses where they suspected immigrants lived. Television cameras captured most of the action.[14]

With so much press and the potential for more, Farmingville came to the attention of the Federation for American Immigration Reform (FAIR), a nonprofit organization based in Washington, DC, that advocates for immigration control. The federation sent an organizer to step up recruiting efforts, organize street rallies, promote media outreach, and contribute to a propaganda campaign that, among other things, blamed laborers for a nonexistent rise in crimes such as burglary and rape. With the help of the organizer, Sachem gained four hundred members, who began referring to Latino laborers as "invaders" and labeled anyone who helped them as "traitors" to America. Together Sachem Quality of Life and FAIR heavily influenced the way immigrants were perceived in Suffolk County and helped set the tone for public discourse on immigration.[15]

Sachem Quality of Life also contacted American Patrol, a national nativist group associated with anti-immigrant vigilante activities on the US-Mexico border. With the intervention of outsiders and the heated rhetoric of many of its residents, Farmingville quickly became ground zero for the lingering national debate on immigration.[16]

All this tension finally culminated in a particularly vicious incident during the early Sunday morning hours of September 17, 2000. Two young men in a silver station wagon approached one of the 7-Eleven corners and picked up a Mexican laborer for a job. The laborer indicated that he already had work for the day, but he directed the men to his house where two friends, Israel Pérez, nineteen, and Magdaleno Escamilla, twenty-eight, were staying and looking for jobs. The men with the station wagon, Ryan Wagner, eighteen, and Christopher Slavin, twenty-eight, said they needed help repairing a floor and took the workers to an abandoned warehouse in a nearby town.

They were asked to crawl into a basement—presumably the place where the floor needed repair. There Wagner and Slavin attacked the workers with a crowbar and a shovel, and stabbed them with a knife. Pérez and Escamilla fought back, wrestling a shovel from the attackers, who fled the warehouse. In pain and bleeding, the Mexican men stumbled out. They stood on the street, flagging down cars for help until someone stopped and, thinking the men had been in a car accident, called the police.

The police took them to Brookhaven Memorial Hospital, where a reporter from the *New York Times* interviewed them. They told the reporter that from the start they'd had an uneasy feeling about the white men who lured them to the abandoned building with the promise of work. Escamilla was treated and released. Pérez had to have surgery for a severed tendon in his left wrist. The attackers were eventually caught, tried, and convicted. Slavin was sentenced to twenty-five years in prison, while Wagner got fifteen years.[17]

The reporter also interviewed Ray Wysolmierski, a leader of Sachem Quality of Life. Wysolmierski rejected the idea that his group had helped to inflame racial hatred in the community. "This was inevitably going to happen whether we existed or not," he told the reporter. "People wait on the corner for people to hire them. Those who hire them aren't going to win a Nobel Peace Prize. As far as I'm concerned, they are all criminals."[18]

It isn't difficult to imagine how a child might have internalized the events that were happening a few blocks from his home, right outside the local 7-Eleven where his parents stopped to buy Coke, gum, or a lottery ticket. In a child's imagination, the crimes could easily get confused. Who were the criminals and who were the victims here?

On July 5, 2003, sometime during the night, five white teenagers in Farmingville threw a firebomb at the house of a Mexican family.[19] The family escaped but the hatred did not. It stayed in Suffolk County, barely hidden, gathering strength, festering. Five years later all of that hatred would finally culminate in a murder committed by seven teenagers who grew up with the turmoil of Farmingville as background noise.

The rhetoric of groups such as Sachem Quality of Life was not unlike the steady anti-immigration diet the rest of America was receiving, particularly on television programs such as *Lou Dobbs Tonight* on CNN. Dobbs, who boasted of receiving two thousand e-mails a day—not all of them congratulatory—unleashed a campaign against undocumented immigrants, whom he repeatedly and with apparent relish called "illegal aliens," that lasted more than six years.

Reporters on his show filed stories, such as the one that aired November 4, 2006, highlighting the amount of money "illegal aliens" were costing the government: $12 billion in primary and secondary education, $17 billion for the education of so-called anchor babies—the US-born children of undocumented parents —and $1 billion to reimburse hospitals for the care of undocumented immigrants, they claimed. The report ended with a somber Dobbs stating that the issue of "illegal aliens" was "a problem that is certainly not going to go away."

On his program he often claimed to be pro-immigration, but against illegal immigration. He advocated for a fence between the United States and Mexico and called the daily arrival of undocumented immigrants "an invasion." They used "illegal benefits," he claimed, and undercut jobs that should go to the less-educated US citizens. He blamed undocumented immigrants for crowding schools and using taxpayers' money to get free health care and education for their children, services that they could not receive in their own countries.

While immigrants do come to the United States for opportunities that are unavailable in their home countries, Dobbs's tone communicated a sense of urgency and danger: Mexicans were a problem, a nuisance, a pest. Once, he went as far as to link undocumented immigrants to a spike in the number of leprosy cases in the United States. Later a *60 Minutes* piece proved him wrong.[20]

Dobbs wasn't alone in his relentless criticism of undocumented immigrants. From his perch at Fox News, Bill O'Reilly expounded nightly on the evils of illegal immigrants, at least once engaging in a shouting match with a guest, veteran television journalist Geraldo Rivera, over whether or not the immigration status of a drunk driver who killed a young woman in Virginia was relevant. While the men sparred, viewers saw text moving slowly through the frame below their images: "Daughter Killed by Illegal Alien." For Rivera, the issue was about drunk driving. O'Reilly insisted the driver should have never been in the country to begin with. Rivera asked him if he wanted to start a mob scene. "Do you want your viewers to go knocking on people's doors and ask them, 'Are you illegal? I want to take you outside and do something to you.'" He went on, "History has seen what happens when you single out people like that."[21]

On another occasion O'Reilly talked about a man from Houston who had shot and killed two men who were burglarizing his neighbor's house. The discussion centered on the burglars' immigration status instead of on the fact that the man had left the safety of his house to hunt down and kill two immigrants who were not endangering his life. "Talking Point says, 'Enough is enough,'" O'Reilly said, looking squarely into the camera.[22]

In 2006, Patrick J. Buchanan published *State of Emergency: The Third World Invasion and Conquest of America*, which quickly became a *New York Times* best seller. From the prologue on,

Buchanan's book is a frontal attack against immigrants, particularly Hispanics:

> In 1960, there were perhaps 5 million Asians and Hispanics in the United States. Today, there are 57 million. Between 10 percent and 20 percent of all Mexican, Central American, and Caribbean peoples have moved into the United States. One to 2 million enter every year and stay, half of them in defiance of America's laws and disdain for America's borders. No one knows how many illegal aliens are here. The estimates run from 12 to 20 million.
>
> This is not immigration as America knew it, when men and women made a conscious choice to turn their backs on their native lands and cross the ocean to become Americans. This is an invasion, the greatest invasion in history.[23]

The United States, he went on, was being destroyed by Mexican invaders.

Samuel P. Huntington struck a similar note in *Who Are We? The Challenges to America's National Identity*, published in 2004. "In the contemporary world," he wrote, "the greatest threat to the societal security of nations comes from immigration."[24] One solution, he claimed, was to strive for assimilation, but there was a problem. "Assimilation is particularly problematic for Mexicans and other Hispanics," he declared.[25]

The word "invasion" became part of the discourse, and the ominous threat of this very visible "invasion" didn't escape those who had absconded to suburbia behind their proverbial white picket fences. While most of these fences were metaphorical, real white fences had been erected in part to keep strangers away, unless the strangers happened to be mowing the lawn at a really cheap rate.

• • •

Though immigrants were not new to Patchogue and the surrounding towns, few people there have the personal experiences—such as Pontieri's—or the historical memory or the intellectual curiosity to know that. Many residents felt having immigrants so close to them was an aberration, a troublesome issue they thought they had left behind in the city, along with overcrowded public schools and tiny, overpriced apartments. Many in Suffolk County trace their ancestry to immigrants from Ireland and Italy, but their links to the past are weak. Practically no one speaks Italian anymore, and, like Pontieri, they are more likely to have visited Cancún than Calabria.

The disconnect comes, in part, because of the way immigration patterns changed in the United States in the second decade of the twentieth century, when the government restricted the flow of immigrants from countries such as Italy, Germany, and Ireland. The other notable change regarding immigration took place when President Johnson signed the Immigration and Nationality Act of 1965 into law, prioritizing family reunification. By then the pattern of immigration had changed, as Europe had found its footing and eastern Europe was under the control of the Soviet Union, allowing virtually no migration to the United States.

Immigrants from Latin America and Asia stepped into that void. Many of them were coming from the Dominican Republic, Cuba, Ecuador, and other countries of South and Central America. And when they did, they often found their way to suburbia, which had remained mostly white, middle-class enclaves for decades.

The movement of immigrants to suburbia caught many by surprise—sociologists, demographers, and suburban dwellers alike. Previous generations of immigrants had viewed suburbia as the culmination of their American dream and worked hard in overcrowded cities, enduring all kinds of discomfort and penury while saving for their ticket to places such as Patchogue or

Farmingville. But as cities lost manufacturing jobs to a changing economy, the immigrant experience changed as well: the suburbs became the beginning of the journey for many who simply by-passed the city experience and moved straight to suburbia.[26]

In the mid-1990s, the influx of immigrants was noticeable in the suburbs of New York, Chicago, Miami, San Francisco, and Los Angeles. So many were settling there, in fact, that the authorities began to wonder publicly how to meet their needs and who would pay for it. That was precisely the issue in Suffolk County: how to deal with a growing number of newcomers looking for jobs, housing, schools, health care, and language training while maintaining the illusion of suburbia. How do you reconcile the fact that the city's issues have followed you to the front yard across the way, where your kind elderly neighbor used to live and now five men share a split-level home and park their unsightly trucks in the streets where your children play ball? What to do about the new neighbors who don't understand or don't know what days they should get the garbage out and place it curbside? Why do they have to play volleyball so late at night? And why, above all, don't they speak English already?

These are not easy questions, and the answers are even more difficult to fathom because, beginning in the 1990s, the United States began receiving an ever increasing number of undocumented immigrants. In the absence of clear laws from Washington, local governments tried to exert some form of control over immigration. Lawmakers who couldn't alter or make federal policy started to do what they could to protect the interests of their voters and keep undocumented immigrants out of Long Island. In Suffolk County, where homeowners pay some of the highest taxes in the country, that meant legislators were pressed to protect property values. No one would want to buy a house next to one occupied by a dozen foreigners who failed to keep their own lawn under control.

In September 2000, the Suffolk County legislature narrowly

voted down a proposal to file a lawsuit to get the federal government to detain and deport undocumented immigrants. By then the town of Brookhaven had passed a law limiting the number of people who could occupy a rental house.[27]

County legislators and other officials, attuned to their voters and neighbors or perhaps acting out of their own impulses and biases, fueled the arguments by making inappropriate and violent statements. In August 2001, county legislator Michael D'Andre of Smithtown warned during a public hearing on immigration that if his own town should ever experience an influx of Latino day laborers like that of nearby communities, they would be "up in arms; we'll be out with baseball bats."[28]

In 2006, a school board member in the Hamptons distributed an online petition to parents, teachers, and a school principal to try to prevent undocumented immigrants from receiving any "free services." That same year, the same official sent an e-mail with a description of a doll called Brentwood Barbie: "This Spanish-speaking only Barbie comes with a 1984 Toyota with expired temporary plates & 4 baby Barbies in the backseat (no car seats). The optional Ken doll comes with a paint bucket lunch pail & is missing 3 fingers on his left hand. Green cards are not available for Brentwood Barbie or Ken."[29]

In March 2007, county legislator Elie Mystal of Amityville, also on Long Island, said of Latino immigrants waiting for work on street corners, "If I'm living in a neighborhood and people are gathering like that, I would load my gun and start shooting, period. Nobody will say it, but I'm going to say it."[30]

That same year during a public hearing, county legislator Jack Eddington asked two immigration advocates who were speaking from the podium if they were in the country legally. Eddington also issued a warning to all undocumented immigrants. "You better beware," he said. "Suffolk County residents will not be victimized anymore."[31]

The spotlight was on the county's top legislator, Suffolk

County executive Steve Levy, elected in 2003, whose job was to set the agenda for local government throughout the county. Among other things, upon taking office Levy proposed that Suffolk County police officers act as immigration agents and detain undocumented immigrants. He called for routine checks on the immigration status of all foreign-born people detained by the police and defended housing evictions for overcrowding. In one month alone, June 2005, he oversaw raids on eleven houses in Farmingville. He demanded increased federal support against "illegals," and, in a 2006 forum, he said that women who crossed the border pregnant wanted to give birth in the United States so their American-citizen children could become "anchor babies" to help their families legalize their status.[32]

When activists demonstrated against hate crime violence and the selective enforcement of zoning laws which led to the mass eviction of Latino residents from their rented homes, Levy stated, "I will not back down to this one percent lunatic fringe. They evidently do not like me much because I am one of the few officials who are not intimidated by their politically correct histrionics."[33]

Reelection in 2007, with 96 percent of the vote, further emboldened him.[29] In an interview with the *New York Times* that year about his drive to push undocumented immigrants out of Suffolk County, he said, "People who play by the rules work hard to achieve the suburban dream of the white picket fence. If you live in the suburbs, you do not want to live across the street from a house where 60 men live. You do not want trucks riding up and down the block at 5 a.m., picking up workers."[34]

Like many others in the county, Paul Pontieri was concerned about overcrowding in homes with absent landlords. To that end, the village began to issue citations against those who violated ordinances. Pontieri thought the solution was to focus on ordinance violations—particularly excessive noise and overcrowding—and enforce the law, regardless of who lived in a house and who owned it. In six years, from 2004 to 2010, the village evicted people from about fourteen dwellings. At least half were occupied by Latino residents.

Pontieri was also worried about the rhetoric flowing down from Steve Levy's office and others in Albany. As he understood the concept of leadership, leaders led by example and conviction but also with empathy and humility. Near his desk he kept a framed poster of his favorite Robert Kennedy quote: "The task of leadership, the first task of concerned people, is not to condemn or castigate or deplore; it is to search out the reason for disillusionment and alienation, the rationale of protest and dissent—perhaps, indeed, to learn from it."

That was Pontieri's mood the day he received the call from Jean Kaleda—concerned but optimistic. He agreed to go to the library to meet with immigrants, hoping to allay their fears, on Wednesday, November 12. The meeting was set for 7:00 p.m., in conjunction with a regularly scheduled ESL class. Kaleda would organize the meeting and Gilda Ramos would translate. Pontieri wrote it in his calendar and then called the public safety department and ordered that an officer (one of the retired police officers who worked as unarmed constables for the village) be sent to patrol the library at night.

The officer, though unarmed, would deter any further harassment, Pontieri hoped. The meeting would both inform him and show the community he was taking action. Pontieri was pleased with how he had handled the call.

The meeting took place, but not as scheduled. It was not the kind of meeting that either Kaleda or Pontieri had envisioned.

CHAPTER 5

BEANER JUMPING

Christopher "Chris" Overton was at home, eating pizza with his mom and his younger brother Dylan, when the phone rang. José Pacheco was on the line. José was a new friend, a classmate from Patchogue-Medford High School, the school that Chris was finally attending after two years of being homeschooled. At sixteen and in eleventh grade, he was eager for social contact and friends. He had begged his parents to find him a high school that would take him, one where he could play basketball, which, along with girls, was his passion.[1]

Chris was banned from attending his previous school, Bellport High, because two years earlier, at fourteen, he had participated in a home burglary in East Patchogue with older teens. In the break-in, the homeowner had been shot and killed, but Chris, who later told his parents he had had no idea that anyone was armed, was treated as a youth offender and sent home to wait for a probation hearing.

He was still waiting for the hearing when the phone rang just after 7:30 p.m. on November 8, 2008, and José urged him to join him at the home of a mutual friend, Alyssa Sprague. Chris knew Alyssa from his previous high school. Bellport kids rarely mingled with kids from Patchogue and Medford, but sometimes, like this night, they found connections in their various social circles. Patchogue, East Patchogue, Medford, Bellport, and Farmingville are within minutes of each other.

That night was one of those times when a gathering occurs somewhat serendipitously: a mixture of old and new friendships, coincidences, and a dose of luck. In this case, really bad luck. By the end of the night, a man would lie bleeding to death near the train tracks in Patchogue and seven teenagers would be pressing their backs against the wall of a realtor's office—the one that looked like an old fishing supplies store, the one they had walked by hundreds of times and used as a meeting point with friends—as a cop frisked them and searched their pockets, looking for the knife that one of them had just plunged into the man's chest.

Chris was just getting over a bout of bronchitis and wasn't sure he wanted to go out. José mentioned that his friend Jeff Conroy, a wrestler who also played lacrosse and football, was there as well. Chris, who was into basketball, wasn't impressed and hung up, uncommitted. But his mother, Denise Overton, thought it would do him good to meet other jocks. I'll take you, she told him.

After José called a second time that evening, Chris said yes, he would join them at Alyssa's house. His mother drove him, but before they arrived José called a third time. The group had moved on; they were now hanging out outside a Stop & Shop in Medford, where Jeff lived.

Overton didn't relish the idea of her son "hanging out," so she took him to the store and gave him thirty minutes while she ran some errands. José walked over to the car to greet Chris and they left. Twenty minutes later, Overton texted her son. All was well, he replied, but shortly after that, in typical teenage fashion, the group was on the move again. Chris called his mother and said they were going to Jeff's house.

Okay, said Overton. Let me speak with his father when you get there.

Chris did just that. The elder Conroy came to the phone and said the boys were watching TV in the basement. It was all peaceful and normal, he assured her. They do it every weekend, he said.

All right, Overton agreed. I'll pick him up at eleven, she said and hung up, feeling relieved that her son was finally mingling with kids from his new school. Overton stayed home watching television herself, but soon started to nod off. At ten twenty, she called Chris and told him she was on her way, but he begged for more time, explaining that more people had come over and they were having too good of a time to leave.

Overton assumed he was still at Jeff's house, watching TV. Okay, stay, she said. Your father will pick you up on his way home from work at one thirty. Chris's father, Warren Overton, worked security at a nearby club.

By the time the elder Overton called his wife to tell her he couldn't reach their son by phone, it was close to 2:00 a.m. and Chris was far from the Conroy house. In fact, he had left Jeff's house almost as soon as his mother had hung up the phone after promising to come back for him at eleven. His parents wouldn't learn about that until much later, after their son had been arrested and charged with a crime his family was sure he couldn't have committed.[2]

Jeffrey "Jeff" Conroy, seventeen and a senior, had gone to Alyssa's house that night with José to have dinner, but the two left half an hour after they arrived, because Jeff had gotten the feeling that Alyssa's mother didn't like seeing him around her daughter. He and José had walked over to the Stop & Shop, a five-minute walk, to wait for Chris and later for Jeff's father who picked them up. Conroy took them home where they ate peanut-butter-and-jelly sandwiches and hung out for a few minutes. It was getting colder, so Jeff put on his Patchogue-Medford Raiders basketball sweatshirt before heading out the door. The teenagers walked to the Medford train station a few blocks away. This time Chris didn't call his mother to alert her of the changing plans.[3]

Several friends were at the train station when Jeff arrived with José and Chris. They were Jordan Dasch, Nicholas "Nicky" (or "Nick") Hausch, Kevin "Kuvan" Shea, Anthony Hartford, Michelle Cassidy, Nicole Tesoriero, and Felicia Hollman. Jeff knew them all from school. They had beers. Nick was carrying his BB gun.

The Medford train station is a two-level Plexiglas structure painted in neutral colors. Penn Station in Manhattan is only 55.9 miles away, but the Medford station belongs to a world so different from the city that it almost seems located in another country. In Medford there is very little for bored, restless teenagers to do on a Saturday night. They can get together at a friend's house or a mall—or, as it happened this night, the platform of a train station. As Jeff later told his lawyer, the station was "just somewhere to go."

Jeff, José, and Chris climbed a flight of stairs and sat on the platform with the others, where Jeff, after a beer or two, began playing with Felicia. He lifted her up and spun her around, and, when he put her down, cut his left thumb, which bled. No one had a Band-Aid or a tissue, but Michelle gave him a tampon to stanch the blood.

More people arrived: Matt Rivera, Frank Grillo, Jason Eberhardt, and Jason Moran. The playful banter continued and Jeff started wrestling with José. Then Nick and Kuvan fired at a ticket machine with the BB gun. An alarm went off and the group scattered quickly before the cops arrived.

They all crammed into two cars. Jeff, José, and Chris rode in Jordan's SUV, along with Anthony, Kuvan, Nicky, and the three girls. The others left in Jason's car. As they drove aimlessly, a little drunk and in fear, they decided to go to nearby Southaven County Park, where many of them had played as children. Of all the kids in the park that night, Jeff was closest to José and Kuvan.

Kuvan, seventeen, lived in Medford with his father, his father's girlfriend, her daughter, his two brothers, and the girlfriend of one of the brothers. He did not think of himself as racist. "I just like to fight," he would later tell investigators. José, seventeen, who is half black and half Puerto Rican, lived with his mother in Patchogue. By all accounts he was popular and outgoing.

Individually they all seemed like average teenagers. Anthony, seventeen, lived in Medford with his mother, three siblings, an uncle, and a grandfather. Nick too was seventeen and lived in Medford with his parents and five siblings. Jordan, another seventeen-year-old Medford resident, told police during his confession that he did not drink that night because he was driving, and he didn't fight because he had had back surgery the year before and didn't want to injure himself.

Aneesha, a classmate who was particularly close to Kuvan, Anthony, José, and Jeff, described them to a reporter as "sweet," "fun," and "great." She called José a "comedian" because he was always making them laugh. She said she loved them all.

"Like I used to talk to them about, like, my problems and they would tell me, like 'Eesha, don't worry about it.' They would give me good advice, like what to do. Every time I needed someone to talk to, they were always there," she said.[4]

Jeff Conroy shouldn't have been at the park that night. It was his friend Nick Cleary's birthday and he was supposed to spend the night at the Clearys', along with Nick's cousins and brothers and Jeff's best friend, Keith Brunjes. Jeff's father, in fact, thought that his son was headed to the birthday party when he left home. Jeff was going to call him when he arrived, but the call never came and Conroy didn't notice: he had fallen asleep on his couch.

At the park, by the semi-dark basketball courts, the teenagers sat around, killing time and drinking. Then, about half an hour after they arrived, Anthony had an idea. "Let's go fuck up some

Mexicans," he told Jeff and Michelle when the others were about twenty feet away. Michelle wanted no part of that. "No, chill," she counseled Jeff. "Don't go with them. I don't want you getting in trouble."

But some of the boys liked the idea, and about ten minutes later they left. Kuvan, Anthony, Nick, Jordan, José, Chris, and Jeff got in one car. Seven of them. Later they would come to be known as the "Patchogue 7," a name that some of their parents have objected to because it made them sound like a gang. Although they all got in the car voluntarily, it's still unclear how many of them knew exactly what they were going to do or where they were headed. At least two would later say they were in the wrong place at the wrong time. All they had wanted, they insisted, was a ride home.

Later too it would become clear that for some of them attacking Hispanics had become a sport. It has been established that when Nick announced a destination—"Let's go to Patchogue because there's a lot of Spanish people over there"—no one asked to be let out of the car.

On they went. On their way to Patchogue hunting for Hispanics. "Let's go! Let's beat up some beaners!" Nick yelled. Everyone laughed. That's when Chris, his mother says, learned that among his new friends, Mexicans—and, by extension, all Hispanic immigrants—were called "beaners." As in rice and beans, the same food staple that years earlier had so offended the mayor of Haverstraw.

Those who write about hate are in agreement: hate crimes are not usually committed by members of well-known racist organizations. Instead, perpetrators tend to be unremarkable types, including bored teenagers looking to show off in front of their friends. Hate crimes tend to be excessively brutal and random— the perpetrators often attack total strangers—and are usually committed by a group, seldom by a lone attacker.[5]

When Anthony blurted out his entertainment idea for the night, "Let's go fuck up some Mexicans," and the others agreed to go along with it (or at least said nothing), everyone was acting in concert with generally accepted theories on why and how hate crimes take place, and why groups of teenagers—some of whom may not have been known as racists before—are often perpetrators.

"Clearly, there is safety in numbers," write Jack Levin and Jack McDevitt in *Hate Crimes Revisited: America's War on Those Who Are Different.*

> In a group, the hatemongers who instigate an altercation believe that they are less likely to be hurt because they have their friends to protect them. The group also grants a certain degree of anonymity. If everyone participated, then no one person can easily be singled out as bearing primary responsibility for the attack. Because they share the blame, it is diluted or weakened. Finally, the group gives its members a dose of psychological support for their blatant bigotry. Feeding initially on the hatred of one or a few peers, escalation becomes a game in which members of the group incite one another toward ever increasing levels of violence. To do his part and "prove himself," therefore, each offender feels that he must surpass the previous atrocity.[6]

The authors further explain that "many who commit hate crimes are at the margin of their community. They may have dropped out of school either spiritually or physically and see little likelihood of ever making it in terms of the American success ethic."[7]

All the young people in the car that night were in school, but Levin and McDevitt could have been referring to Jeffrey Conroy when they talked about the "spiritual" withdrawal. Between 2006 and 2008, he accumulated twenty-four incidents documented in his school's disciplinary record. He was subject to detentions, in-school suspensions, and multiday out-of-school suspensions for infractions that ranged from being late to insubordination, disorderly conduct, disruptive behavior, using foul language toward teachers, and skipping classes. He had also cursed at a coach and a security officer at a high school football game and later admitted he had been drunk.[8]

It had not always been like this, and it is not how his father saw his oldest son, or how others, including his longtime Latina girlfriend, remember Jeff.

Jeffrey Conroy, the first boy and the second of four children born to Robert "Bob" Conroy and Lori Conroy, had a thoroughly modern—and white American—family tree. His ancestors came from Poland and Ireland on his father's side, and from Italy and Germany on his mother's side.[9]

Jeff also has an older sister, living in California, who is his father's daughter from an early marriage that ended in divorce decades ago, and another, younger sister, who is his mother's biological daughter but not his father's. The Conroys live in a small, modest home in Medford, a solidly middle-class town with none of the charm of Patchogue. Unlike the houses in the village, which can be large, multistoried, and colorful, with flowering lawns and inviting porches—some resemble Victorian bed-and-breakfasts—most houses in Medford are ranch-style, split-level, functional, and uninspiring.

The Conroys' house had been a wedding gift from Lori's mother. When I visited for the first time, the front lawn was in disarray, with dry grass and debris from old toys and cars dotting the driveway. Near the front door was a faded and peeling garden ornament of a sleeping man with a large sombrero, atop a burro, the stereotypical portrayal of a Mexican at rest. Two large dogs roamed freely through the green-carpeted living room, where the walls are canvases for family portraits and the school pictures of every year for every child in the family. Jeff's room was off the small living room, and its every flat surface was covered with shiny trophies. A promising wrestler, he also played football, and his father said he excelled at lacrosse. He dreamed of playing midfield on a lacrosse team for a state university, either Albany or Plattsburgh, the latter in the northern reaches of New York.

"I knew he would be famous one day, but not for this," Bob Conroy told me during my initial conversation with him in December 2010. "I used to think he would go to college on a lacrosse scholarship and become a phys ed teacher, and get married, and settle in a house not far from ours."

Tall and muscular, with a chiseled face and buzz cut, Jeff was popular with the girls. On and off, he had been dating Pamela Suárez since the two had been fourteen years old. Pamela, who was born in Bolivia, is a beauty with two birthmarks on her face, tiny hands and straight, white teeth framed by shapely lips. She says she fell in love with Jeff the moment she saw him in seventh grade. She went home and told her mother, Mom, I think I'm in love. That feeling, Pamela noted in June 2011, seven years after that meeting, never subsided.[10]

By eighth grade, they were seriously dating. Jeff played football; she was a cheerleader. In tenth grade they broke up, but got back together in eleventh grade, though the relationship was rocky that year. "Too many girls in his life," Pamela says sweetly, tears bordering her eyes. "I wanted no part of that." But they remained friends. In many ways, Pamela says, Jeff was a typical suburban teenager. He smoked pot, drank, and hung out with friends at the mall. At her eighteenth birthday party, in her house, he got so drunk that she had to help carry him to a car that would take him home. But he could also be a sweet young man, who dreamed of having three children with her, and who was very close to his family—especially his father and his little sister. He listened to hip-hop, loved rap and Daddy Yankee, and hated country music.

They went to the movies all the time, Pamela said, and he preferred comedies like *Failure to Launch*, a 2006 romantic comedy about a thirtysomething man who would not leave his parents' home. During *The Exorcism of Emily Rose*, a 2005 horror movie she insisted they go to, "he was so scared, he wouldn't let go of my hand," Pamela recalled.

Conroy says Jeff was the family's jokester, the kind who would dump a bucket of cold water on his brother or sisters while they were taking a shower or playfully wrestle his mother to the ground. From an early age, he showed an interest in sports. He was on an elite lacrosse traveling team, which took him to several cities throughout the United States. The summer before Lucero's killing he had made a name for himself as a "faceoff" specialist, which requires both physical strength and psychological skill. (The player has to guess how the opponent will move by the way his hands and wrists are positioned around the lacrosse stick.)

If Jeff's typical week was a blur of school assignments and sports, the weekends were dedicated to helping his father on the fields where he coached neighborhood kids in football, baseball, and lacrosse. About a decade before, Conroy had founded the Pat-Med Booster Club, which raised hundreds of thousands of dollars to enable sports to continue to thrive in the community at a time when voters had failed to pass the school budget and the district was under "austerity" rules, meaning no new sports equipment could be purchased. With the initial funds raised by the club, about $372,000, Conroy also founded the Patchogue-Medford Youth Football and Cheerleading Club to establish Pee Wee football and cheerleading for children aged five to thirteen. Its mission: to "promote, foster and increase camaraderie and socializing among youth."[11]

The athletic fields, two miles from his house, became Conroy's "church"—he shuns organized religion—and Jeff's second home. Jeff helped load the snack stand in the evenings before games and helped maintain the fields in top form. Too old for the Pee Wee leagues, he became a mentor to many children. At sixteen, Jeff helped coach eleven-year-old football players, and he spent one summer improving a boy's lacrosse skills because the boy's mother had asked him for help.

At home, Jeff mowed the lawn, did the laundry, and babysat his siblings when needed. Although sports and school kept him busy, he held some occasional jobs. Once, Pamela recalled, he worked for Wendy's, but he was fired after two or three weeks when he was found eating chicken nuggets in the back.

"He was my back," Conroy said. "The one who literally split the wood."

Conroy, who dropped out of college after just one year, had once wanted to be a cop, but that dream died when he sliced the tip of his right index finger in a deli machine and realized he would never be able to pull a trigger. Later he became a manager at Kmart, but in 1997 he injured his back taking down a heavy box from a store shelf. He has not been able to return to work since, even after six back surgeries, supporting his family with his social security and disability checks. Still, he managed to take the children camping several times a year, and once a year they would splurge with a trip to Lake George, in New York's Adirondack Mountains.

Conroy said his son was a "sweet loving kid, who never tolerated bullies" and had a 10:00 p.m. curfew most weekends. Neighbors say that he was the kind of young man who offered to mow the lawn for them and smacked their children if they cursed in front of their parents.[12] But others who knew him primarily as a student say that Jeff was "obnoxious" and had absorbed his father's displeasure toward his Latino neighbors.[13]

For much of Jeff's childhood the Conroys lived across the street from a house shared by at least six Latino men, though Conroy believes there were as many as two dozen people living in the house at one time. One of them catcalled one of his daughters, who was then thirteen or fourteen; Conroy spoke to the neighbors and the whistling stopped. The episode is etched in his memory as one of the few times—perhaps the only time—he interacted with a Latino immigrant in Medford. Those who knew him then recall that Conroy was obsessed with the house and its residents and feared that his daughters would one day be raped by the men who lived there.[14] He was upset by their loud music and their backyard fires. What they were burning, he doesn't know. Still, he said, if they didn't bother him or his family, he "didn't care" who his neighbors were.

Conroy's focus was his family and coaching. Because he was surrounded by youngsters, he said, he would have heard if packs of teenagers, including his son, were roaming the streets looking for Latinos to attack. He never did. If Jeff had been carrying a knife, he would have known, he said. If his son harbored any ill feelings toward Latinos, he wasn't aware, and he finds it impossible to believe it given that he used to think of Pamela as his future daughter-in-law and of kids named José and Juan as Jeff's good friends.

The day before November 8, Jeff had been involved in a fight with a friend who had supposedly spread rumors that Jeff had herpes. It wasn't his first serious fight. Three or four months before that, Jeff had been involved in another fight, at a party, but his father had not learned about it until a few days later. After that incident, Conroy had sat with his son and told him, If anything like that happens again, I'm your first call.

Jeff vividly remembered his father's words when he was allowed to make his first call fourteen hours after he stabbed Marcelo Lucero. He grabbed the phone and told his father, Dad, I'm at the Fifth Precinct. Could you please come get me?

"Learning to hate is almost as inescapable as breathing," note Levin and McDevitt in their book.

> Like almost everyone else, the hate crime offender grows up in a culture that defines certain people as righteous, upstanding citizens, while designating others as sleazy, immoral charac-

ters who deserve to be mistreated. As a child, the perpetrator may never have had a firsthand experience with members of the groups he later comes to despise and then victimize. But, early on, merely by conversing with his family, friends, and teachers or by watching his favorite television programs he learns the characteristics of disparaging stereotypes. He also learns that it is socially acceptable, perhaps even expected, to repeat racist jokes and use ethnic slurs and epithets.[15]

It is not known if Jeffrey Conroy watched Bill O'Reilly or Lou Dobbs, and his father swears that there was never any talk against Hispanics at home. But it is a fact that when Jeff started going to school in 1996, Hispanic men, mostly Mexican, had begun to congregate around the 7-Eleven in Farmingville, not far from his house. By the time he got to high school, in the fall of 2005, Steve Levy had been elected Suffolk County executive.

Were Conroy and his friends paying attention? Perhaps not consciously, but even overhearing the anti-immigrant rhetoric that was prevalent in Suffolk County then, and indeed in the entire country, would have had an impact on them. "Young Americans are frequently targeted as the primary audience for the culture of hate, especially its films, music, and humor," observe Levin and McDevitt. "Partially because they lack diverse personal experiences, young people are generally unprepared to reject prejudiced claims coming from sources they regard as credible."[16]

Conroy once told a filmmaker that there "was more negativity coming out" of Levy's mouth in the newspapers his son took to the bathroom to read every morning than in anything that his family had ever said regarding immigrants.[17]

Prejudiced feelings were a fact of life in the local high school in Medford, the same school that the young men from the so-called Patchogue 7 attended. In 2008, there were three thousand registered students in Patchogue-Medford High School, including four hundred self-described Hispanics.[18]

Clarissa Espinoza, Julio Espinoza's youngest child, was one of them; she was a sophomore in the fall of 2008. Born in Patchogue, Clarissa is perfectly bilingual and bicultural. With her fair skin and flawless accent, she blended with the general population of the school and doesn't remember being the target of discrimination, but that does not mean she was blind to it.

"I didn't like high school," she says softly. "There was racism everywhere. The school was very divided."[19]

The division was stark and visible even to casual observers. Students who were learning English, mostly Hispanics, were placed in ESL classes, as mandated by the state. English-as-a-second-language classes are meant to teach English to newcomers, but in a school setting they can also create a barrier between native speakers and foreigners. In less politically charged circumstances, such a program can make a school more inclusive and international. This was not the case in Patchogue-Medford High School, where all four ESL classes were contained in one hallway with twelve classrooms. There was little interaction between ESL students and the rest of the school, and when there was, it wasn't productive or positive.

A few days before the end of the school year in 2009, the year Jeff and most of his friends would have graduated, two students from the Graduate School of Journalism at Columbia University—Tamara Bock and Angel Canales—conducted a series of interviews with Patchogue-Medford High School students for a documentary, *Running Wild: Hate and Immigration on Long Island*. The documentary aired on PBS; the transcript of their original interviews paints a dismal picture of high school life there.

A boy named David, sixteen and born in El Salvador, narrates how "the other people," the white, non-Hispanic kids, would throw food at the Latino students who huddled together at their own tables during lunchtime. "Like they would say that we immigrants [should] go back to Mexico," David recalled.

"And what do you do?" one of the filmmakers inquired.

"Nothing. Most of the time we remain quiet," David replied.

"So, when you are eating and someone shouts 'Go back to Mexico,' what goes through your head? What do you think and how do you feel?"

"I feel very [long pause] ashamed because we are in a country that is not ours, you know."

"Has there ever been a moment when someone has said something demeaning to you in the school hallways? And have you had a problem with someone who dislikes immigrant students here in school?"

"Yes, sometimes we are walking and they come by and push us with their arm and we can't do anything because, you know, we don't want to get in trouble with them," David said.

Students on their way to the gym would mumble under their breath, "You Mexican, go back to your country," whether the student was Mexican or not. Or, they'd yell, "Talk English!" and rush off to class. Other times, they would threaten the Latino students, saying that, if they complained, they'd call "la migra," immigration authorities. The list of insults was long, another student said. "You hear 'spic.' You hear 'Mexican.' You hear 'dumb-in-a-can' [for Dominican]. You hear 'beaner.' 'Border hopper.' There is a lot. The list can go forever. You hear 'alien,' 'illegal,' or 'II' for 'illegal immigrant.'"

Another teen, a boy named William, said, "You can't walk in the hallway without looking back." Angelica, seventeen, who was born in New York City but moved to Patchogue when she was nine, said she had heard "nasty comments" about Puerto Ricans and Dominicans. This is how she analyzed the behavior of some of her classmates:

I don't think that they're racist or anything. Like, I think it's what they hear at home. Like when you're hearing stuff on the news saying that, oh, like, Mexicans are crossing the border and Hispanics are coming over here and they're trying to take over our jobs. I think it's their parents telling them all this stuff and it gets implanted and embedded in their head. So they come to school with this hatred towards Hispanics, when, like, they're not the only immigrants coming to this country. But, like, I think the kids, they hear it at home, and then they come over here and they think they know everything but they are really ignorant.

She went on: "Everywhere. It's everywhere. If you walk down Patchogue on Main Street, you hear people in the street. If a Hispanic man is riding his bicycle or something down Main Street, you hear people, like, making nasty comments. Always, everywhere."

One teacher who spoke to the filmmakers, Craig Kelskey, a physical education instructor who had been working at the high school for thirty years, said the school was a reflection of the community. "Whatever problems are going on in the community, those problems get brought into the school," he said. "I mean, I'm sure that there's things said to certain kids during the course of the school day and of course you would be scared. I think that is only human nature."

The resentment toward Hispanics was fueled, in part, by the mistaken assumption that the Patchogue-Medford School District had had to cut sports programs in the high school to pay for ESL classes. About five hundred of the district's eighty-five-hundred-plus students were taking ESL classes then. They hailed from forty-three countries, two-thirds of which were Spanish speaking.[20] Parents and students alike thought the trade-off unfair, even if there never was any such trade-off. High school sports were sacrosanct and school board members always instructed the school superintendent, Michael Mostow, to "figure out" how to continue the program, even when there was no money left in the budget, even if they had to use old equipment. He did, taking money from here and there to keep all sports afloat and the voters happy.[21] Still, even if sports were not sacrificed, the animosity continued. Why should the taxpayers pay for the education of the children of "illegals"? many asked openly.

Community blogs were replete with anti-immigrant commentary, some thoughtful; some virulent. "Not my problem if ESL classes are crowded, hard to get to or there's not enough of them or because of budget cuts. My tax money shouldn't be funding these programs to begin with!! If I go to Mexico are they going to pay for and send me to classes to learn Spanish? Don't think so." So read a message posted on Medfordcommunity -watch.com in November 2008 and signed by "Dana." Another post read, "The problem is on the Federal level of government with their failure to take control of the immigration problem.... Americans are tired of paying the way for people who don't belong here and our sense of fairness is being pushed to the limit. I believe this anger would exist against any nationality that would take advantage of us in this manner. If the governments of these other countries aren't taking care of there [*sic*] own people why should we be expected to foot the bill for their care?" This one was signed "DG."

Even earlier, in a 2005 Long Island political forum, someone signing herself or himself "PM REALIST" wrote: "WHY DIDN'T THEY CUT THE ESL CLASSES? LET THESE KIDS LEARN ENGLISH LIKE OUR FOREFATHERS AND MOTHERS!!!"[22]

In many ways, the school was a microcosm of what was happening in the community. The district went from 4 percent to 24 percent Latino in five years. Three of the seven elementary schools in the district were 50 percent Latino in 2008.[23] A week before Jeffrey Conroy and his friends set out to hunt "beaners" in Patchogue, a swastika and some anti-black comments were found scrawled in a stairwell at the school, the same week that Barack Obama was elected the first black president of the United States.

Economic difficulties exacerbated the situation. On December 1, 2008, the National Bureau of Economic Research announced that the United States had entered an economic recession, which had really started in late 2007, when more than three hundred thousand jobs disappeared in November alone.[24] Banks failed, businesses declared bankruptcy, homes lost value, and even birthrates plummeted.

Experts agree that immigrants are often blamed for economic woes and that, in tough economic times, hate crimes increase in frequency and violence. There is something else the experts agree on: hate crimes have been part of the fabric of American society for a long time.

On August 11, 1834, a raging anti-Catholic mob carrying signs that read "No Popery" and "Down with the Cross" broke into the Ursuline Convent in Boston, Massachusetts, and set fire to it. The attack on the convent, which had been built in 1818, was the result of tensions between Boston's Protestant natives and newly arrived masses of Irish Catholics. This event is described by historian Ray Billington as "the first act of violence resulting from nativism" in the United States.[25]

Ten years later, riots erupted between Protestants and Catholics in May and July 1844 in Philadelphia and the surrounding districts of Kensington and Southwark. In the end, thirty people died, including an eighteen-year-old Protestant boy; hundreds were wounded; and dozens of Catholic homes were burned to the ground.[26]

If hate crimes then were mostly about religious differences, ethnicity later came into play, and practically no one was spared: nineteen Chinese massacred in Los Angeles in 1871;[27] eleven Italians lynched in New Orleans in 1890;[28] thirteen hundred Greeks driven out of Omaha, Nebraska, in 1909 by an angry mob;[29] hundreds of Mexicans beaten and injured in a ten-day riot in 1943 Los Angeles;[30] Vietnamese fishermen attacked in Galveston, Texas, in 1981;[31] and a forty-nine-year-old Sikh born in India shot five times and killed in Mesa, Arizona, as part of a post-9/11 rampage by a white aircraft mechanic from Phoenix.[32]

The first recorded instance of violence against Latino immigrants came during the California Gold Rush, when miners decided that "none but Americans" would be allowed to mine in certain areas.[33] Mexicans, Chileans, and Peruvians were ordered to leave the area around Sutter's Mill at Coloma.[34] In December 1849, a confrontation between Chilean miners and natives left two Americans dead, three Chileans shot, and eight flogged. In the end, all Spanish-speaking miners in the locality were banished.[35]

In the early twentieth century, violence and abuse of power were primarily directed against Mexican immigrants.[36] A century later, the same can be said, although not all the victims are Mexicans, even if the perpetrators set out to attack them.[37] Because immigration from all countries in Latin America greatly increased in the second half of the century, it is impossible to distinguish visually who is from Mexico and who is not. It is equally difficult to tell who was born abroad and who is a US-born, bilingual, and bicultural child of immigrants. There was no such confusion right after World War I, when thousands of destitute Mexican workers arrived in US cities desperately seeking jobs in a recession. In Denver, in 1921, public hysteria over the massive number of jobless Mexicans converging on the city culminated in local authorities incarcerating hundreds of Mexicans on loitering charges and detaining them in jail cells without trial dates.[38]

Competition for jobs was at the root of most instances of abuse, but greed was often a factor as well. In December 1927 in Stanton, Texas, police deputies C. C. Baize and Lee Small promised work to three Mexican men. The officers brought them to a bank and told them to wait at the entrance while they went inside, supposedly to arrange employment. The deputies then came out firing guns, killing two of the men, and claiming they had caught the Mexicans trying to rob the bank. Their incentive was a $5,000 reward offered by the Texas Bankers Association for anyone who apprehended bank robbers. The surviving Mexican told the true story.[39]

Through the years, the incidents pile up—the beating of a farmworker in Phoenix, Arizona, on May 9, 1912;[40] the clubbing to death of a fieldworker in Rio Hondo, Texas, in May 1921 because he called out to a young white girl in Spanish;[41] the attack on a couple in Luling, Texas, in 1926—the wife was raped—by a soldier from Fort Sam Houston, who was simply transferred from his base.[42]

By the second half of the twentieth century, the harassment was institutionalized, and later still became law. In 1954, Operation Wetback—a "paramilitary operation to remove Mexicans from several southwestern states"—led to the deportation of more than fifty-one thousand Mexicans and Mexican Americans from California alone.[43] Between 1954 and 1959, approximately 3.7 million Latinos were deported, most of them without due process. The roundups and deportations were based on visual assessments of Border Patrol officers. Thus, many US citizens and Latinos from places other than Mexico ended up deported to a place they had never been to.[44]

Forty years later, Proposition 187, also known as the Save Our State Initiative, passed in California in November 1994. (It was later declared unconstitutional by federal courts.) The ballot initiative, the first time a state stepped on federal ground to pass an immigration law, was to establish a citizenship screening system, and it aimed to prevent undocumented immigrants from using health care, public education, and other social services in the state. After its passage, there was a 23.5 percent increase of hate crimes against Latinos in the Los Angeles area.[45]

On June 11, 1995, arsonists torched the home of a Latino family in Palmdale, California, after spray painting on the walls: "Wite [sic] power" and "Your family dies." "Mexico" was painted on the wall with an "X" through it.[46]

In 2004, in Dateland, Arizona, Pedro Corzo, a Cuban-born regional manager for Del Monte Fresh Produce, was gunned down by two Missouri residents who traveled to a remote section of southern Arizona with the specific intent of randomly killing Mexicans. The young ringleader was later tried as an adult and received two life sentences for the murder; his accomplice was sentenced to life.[47]

Similar encounters, though not all deadly, took place in California, Tennessee, Texas, New Jersey, Georgia, Utah, Alabama, Louisiana, Kentucky, Maryland, Wyoming, Missouri, Nebraska, Florida, and Washington, DC, according to a report compiled by the Southern Poverty Law Center that included cases from 2004 to 2007.[48]

One of the most horrible and senseless crimes of hatred against Latinos took place in a suburb of Houston, Texas, on April 22, 2006, when David Ritcheson, sixteen, was attacked by racist skinheads at a house party after he supposedly tried to kiss a twelve-year-old girl. David Henry Tuck broke Ritcheson's jaw in knocking him unconscious, while screaming, "White power!" and calling Ritcheson a "spic" and "wetback." Keith Robert Turner joined in, and the two attackers burned Ritcheson with cigarettes, kicked him with steel-toed boots, attempted to carve a swastika into his chest, poured bleach on him, and finally sodomized him with a patio umbrella pole. It took thirty surgeries before Ritcheson, confined to a wheelchair and wearing a colostomy bag, was able to return to school. Tuck was later sentenced to life in prison. Turner got ninety years.

A year after the attack, Ritcheson, who until then had not been identified in press accounts, spoke at a hearing of the US House of Representatives Judiciary Committee. In a wrenching testimony, he recalled the horrific experience for lawmakers deliberating over strengthening federal hate crime laws. "With my humiliation and emotional and physical scars came the ambition and strong sense of determination that brought out the natural fighter in me," Ritcheson testified. "I am glad to tell you today that my best days still lay ahead of me." Tragically that was not the case. Less than three months later, he committed suicide, jumping from a cruise ship into the Gulf of Mexico. He was eighteen years old.[49]

Closer to Patchogue, on April 29, 2006, in East Hampton, New York, three Latino teenagers were lured into a shed by a neo-Nazi skinhead and his friends and then threatened and terrorized with a chainsaw and a machete. The Latino youngsters were held for ninety minutes while their attackers yelled, "White power!" "Heil Hitler!" and other insults.

"This is how you run across the border," one of the skinheads shouted as he chased the Latinos around with the running chainsaw. The attacker, fifteen, was later charged as a juvenile with reckless endangerment.[50]

On September 10, 2006, in Hampton Bays, New York, Carlos Rivera, a construction worker from Honduras, was stabbed multiple times outside a bar by Thomas Nicotra and Kenneth Porter, who yelled racial epithets during the attack. Nicotra and Porter, who were known to have insulted bar patrons before, were charged with felony robbery and assault as hate crimes. Porter was sentenced to one year in Suffolk County Jail for first-degree assault after testifying against Nicotra, who was sentenced to nine years in state prison.[51]

Almost two years later, on the night of July 12, 2008, in the coal town of Shenandoah, Pennsylvania, several high school football players were coming home from a party when they came across Luis Ramírez, twenty-five, an undocumented Mexican immigrant. An argument broke out, with some of the football players yelling ethnic slurs at Ramírez. Two of them—Brandon Piekarsky and Derrick Donchak—began fighting with Ramírez, who was knocked out after a punch in the face. When he was down, prosecutors later charged, Piekarsky gave him a kick to the head. Ramírez died two days later from head injuries. The following year Piekarsky and Donchak were both acquitted of all serious charges against them, but later, indicted on federal charges, they were found guilty of a hate crime and each sentenced to nine years in prison.[52]

Ramírez was the first Latino victim of a hate crime to become a national story in 2008. The second was Marcelo Lucero, in Patchogue.

By the time Jordan Dasch drove his 1996 red SUV into Patchogue, the village was quiet and few were walking the streets. The library, the hub of activity in the evenings, had long closed. The lights of the theater were off and only the cleaning crews remained in the restaurants on Main Street.

Suddenly the group spotted a man walking down the street. Kuvan thought he was Hispanic and yelled, "Stop the car! Stop the car! Let's get this guy." Jordan stopped the car fifty to seventy yards in front of the man. Kuvan, Anthony, Nick, and José jumped out of the car and ran toward the man. Jeff, Jordan, and Chris also got out of the car but stayed near it.

The man the group had spotted was Héctor Sierra, a fifty-seven-year-old waiter at Gallo Tropical, a popular Latin restaurant on Main Street owned by a Colombian family. He had come to the United States legally in 1973 and had lived in New Jersey, Queens, and Manhattan before settling in Patchogue, a place he thought was safe and quiet.[53] A naturalized US citizen, he had lived back and forth between Patchogue and his native Colombia for years. At the time, he had been working at Gallo Tropical for seven years and had risen to the position of headwaiter.[54]

That day, he had started his shift at 10:00 a.m. and had worked until 11:30 p.m. to accumulate a little overtime. He was tired and decided to leave the restaurant through the back door to shave off a block from his seven-block walk home. It was foggy and dark in the streets, almost midnight, and Sierra walked fast. He had little on him: a watch, a cell phone, and a wallet with a few dollars in it, but he had heard about groups attacking Hispanic men in the streets, so he was cautious. He wore a baseball cap, put his hands in the pockets of his coat, and walked with his head down.

Out of the corner of his eye he noticed a reddish, perhaps brown, SUV making a left turn and passing him slowly, as if whoever was in the car was watching him or knew him and wanted to stop and say hello. Sierra didn't know anybody who owned an SUV. He walked faster. He couldn't tell how many people were in the car but heard voices and knew immediately that, were anything to happen, he would be outnumbered.

The car stopped in front of a building. It was the only car around, and the streets were deserted. Sierra heard a noise from inside the car, three or four popping sounds, one after the other. To him, it sounded like a small-caliber gun. Then he saw four young men get out of the car—two from the right side and two from the left. They are young, he thought. Very young. Still, there were four of them and he was alone. Whoever was still inside the car kept the motor running. Not a good sign.

Then the four young men started running toward him. They were fast. Sierra recalled that a couple of his coworkers had been beaten up recently by youngsters. He was afraid the same was about to happen to him. He couldn't run forward. He couldn't stay in place. So he turned around and started running away, as he would later testify, "like hell."

"It's weird," he would later recall, "because as I was running away from them, you know my mother passed away like a couple of months before that ordeal and, as I was running from them, I was praying to my mother's soul. I don't know, it was like a short movie. It runs through your mind so fast and I was praying to my mother and to take me away from these wolves because I didn't know them, I didn't know who they were. I didn't know what their purpose was, so it was very scary."[55]

The young men caught up with Sierra from behind. They

punched him on the ears and kicked him. Afraid to get his face hurt, Sierra tried to keep his head down and didn't turn around to face them. He kept running, despite the blows, but eventually tripped and fell. He ripped his pants and cut his knee. Eerily, the young men were quiet as they attacked him, never yelling or insulting or even asking for money, as he had feared.

Sierra stood up, afraid that if he stayed down they would hurt him even more. He started moving in a zigzag way to avoid and confuse them. He got to a house where he thought Hispanic residents lived, but he tripped again and the young men chasing him began to kick him from behind. Sierra dragged himself on the lawn, trying to reach the porch of the house. He was now yelling for help.

He managed to reach the porch but no one was coming to his aid. "There were people up there and they never came out there. They were afraid to open the doors or something. I felt so defenseless, so lonely."[56] Desperate and trying to get away from the hard blows and relentless kicks, he started pounding on the windows. One cracked but didn't break. He kicked the front door. Hard. He was somewhat embarrassed that he too had become an aggressor, but he felt he had no choice.

The light of the porch went on but the door remained closed.

The light may have scared the attackers who backed up a few steps, enough time for Sierra to turn around and take a look at them. To him, they were simply "white kids." Two were right behind him; two others were farther away, staring. The teenagers ran away toward the SUV, and Sierra walked to the street to see where they were going. They got in the car quickly and made a left on Thorne Street.

Sierra realized that, although the attackers were gone, he was still screaming. His throat felt parched and raw, his mouth dry. A man in a car waiting for the light to change saw him and asked why he was screaming. Sierra finally realized the ordeal was over and he was no longer alone. He told the man what had happened and the man urged him to call 911. Sierra tried, but his phone wasn't working; it had been damaged in the attack. The man drove him to a nearby 7-Eleven, hoping to find a police car along the way or maybe even parked there. But the 7-Eleven was deserted. It was close to midnight. Exhausted, in pain, and afraid, Sierra gave up trying to find a phone or a cop, and he walked home without telling anyone what had happened to him that night.

If he had, if his phone had been working, if someone had called the police, if the Hispanics in the house with the porch and the light had offered help, perhaps the young men in the car would have given up on their evening entertainment and driven home. But no one stopped them.

The SUV took off fast. A few blocks away, Jordan parked in a parking lot near the library, and the seven young men inside the car tumbled out. They were pumped with adrenaline and started walking down Railroad Avenue, toward the train station. They were going to end the night as they had started it—by the train tracks.

Suddenly they saw two men walking out of a parking lot and down Railroad Avenue. The men, brown-skinned and with short black hair, appeared to be Hispanic. The teenagers couldn't have known their names then, but they were about to confront Angel Loja and Marcelo Lucero, best friends who had known hardships and poverty but never violence.

As Jeff would later tell police, "Everyone was pretty amped up and it was clear what we were going to do."[57]

CHAPTER 6

UNWANTED

On the early afternoon of November 8, 2008, Angel Loja was lounging on his couch, mindlessly watching television, feeling the tension of the week ebb away. The windows of his tiny second-floor apartment were open and a balmy breeze wafted in from the bay. Loja was feeling lazy and unencumbered.[1]

It was a Saturday, the first day of a nonworking weekend, and Loja had every intention of savoring his time off. No one was waiting for him. His last girlfriend had left him so depleted and heartbroken that he hadn't dared to even look at a woman in a long time. He felt as if this was the state that God intended for him: alone but at peace. He was free of the drugs he had dabbled in years earlier. He no longer woke up in the harsh light of the morning wondering where he was, startled that once again he had slept on a park bench. For eight years now, he had been living in Patchogue, and he had a stable job where on a good week he could make as much as $520.

Every weekday and some Saturdays, from 7:00 a.m. to 3:30 p.m., he sawed and hammered and nailed pieces of wood together, building house frames for a construction company. On his days off, like today, he could afford to do nothing, letting his shoulder muscles relax, his callous hands rest, and his thoughts wander aimlessly, muffled by the sound of the television.

The phone rang and Loja considered not picking it up, but the screen showed the name of his old friend, Marcelo Lucero.

Lucero sounded anxious and a little rushed when Loja answered the phone with a tired hello.

¿Qué más? What are you doing? Lucero asked.

The call startled Loja but did not really surprise him. For several years now, ever since they had found each other on the streets of Patchogue, Lucero often called on Loja to accompany him on shopping errands, to work out in the gym, or to dine together. Both single and unattached, they had an easy camaraderie born out of their similar circumstances: friends in a foreign land, pining for home while hungry for the promise of a better life.

Both had found their way to the United States after separate but equally harrowing journeys. They knew what it was like to search for jobs while trying to communicate in broken English. They were baffled by the intricacies of the rules in their new country, afraid of the police, and even more afraid of those who seemed to fear them: Long Island nativists who saw in the newcomers from Latin America a threat to their way of life.

Dark and athletic, Lucero and Loja were both highly spiritual, seeking otherworldly reasons for events or circumstances that others would see as coincidental. Once, when Lucero took a picture in the dark, the photo revealed an unexpected streak of light. Lucero thought he saw an arm, bent at the elbow. Loja did too. A spirit, they decided.

The unexplained world of spirits and saintly visions was not an abstract thought for them. In their world—an experience common to most Latin Americans of humble means and little formal education—nothing was more important than the word and the will of God. If things went well, it was God's will. If they didn't,

that too was God's will. Whatever happened, the answer was un-
questionable acceptance.

I'm here, just hanging out, Loja said, reaching over to lower the
television volume so he could hear his friend over the phone.

Let's go out—I'm bored, said Lucero, who had just left his
midday shift at a dry cleaner's in Riverhead, where he worked
ironing other people's fine clothing. In a previous job, also in a dry
cleaner's, he had lost all his fingernails to a fungus that thrived on
humidity. Ironing was a more tiresome but less painful job than
exposing his hands to the soap, water, and brush used to attack the
ring around the collar of the hundreds of shirts Lucero handled
every week.

Aren't you going to take a shower first? Loja inquired, trying
to buy some time because he really didn't feel like getting up from
the couch just yet.

No, no, I don't even want a shower. I just want to go somewhere, Lucero answered.

Resigned, Loja grabbed a sweater and walked out the door,
not even bothering to turn off the TV. To get his blood flowing
and sound more alert, he skipped steps as he went downstairs to
meet Lucero, who was at the wheel of his green Nissan Sentra,
a fourteen-year-old car that he drove every day to work, about
twenty-five miles each way. As always, he was dressed impeccably,
even though he had just come from work: nicely creased khaki
pants, a light-colored T-shirt, new Skechers shoes, and a Levi's
jean jacket.

They drove to a nearby park in Holbrook, a town about six
miles away, and decided to take a walk. Though it was fall, the
temperature hovered in the upper fifties, and the trees that had
yet to cede their leaves to the onslaught of winter were bursting
with life. Lucero noticed some worms inching along the trunk of
an old tree. This is life, he said joyously. So much life.

Loja chuckled, thinking Lucero was acting a little strange,

but before he could ask him about his mood, Lucero launched into one of his usual monologues. He counseled Loja on how to be a good man, a man who fought for his rights, who worked and saved, who knew how to eat and how to behave on all occasions. Lucero, who could easily spend $1,000 in a shopping spree at the local mall, drilled Loja on the need to have the right outfit for each occasion. If it's raining, don't wear sneakers, wear rain boots, he would tell Loja.

Lucero liked to cast himself as Loja's older, wiser brother, though the two were practically the same age. Lucero was thirty-seven, and Loja was thirty-six, but Lucero recognized that Loja had felt lost in America. He knew about the drugs and about the two relationships that had left him broken and despondent. He also knew that Loja was an angry man, who had walked away from jobs out of pride.

When he had been mistreated at his first job when he arrived in New York, the exchange had left Loja weary and a little scared. If this was his welcoming, what else could go wrong? What else should he be prepared for? For a young man who believed in premonitions and signs, Loja's first experience in New York had not been a good omen.

In time, his feelings hardened. No one seemed to have a soul here, he thought. There is no time for spirituality or even for kindness. Money, money, money, was all everyone thought about. The one thing he didn't lose, the dream that he kept tucked away in his heart, was his desire to go home. But for that too he needed money.

Often, as he did that day in the park, Lucero would remind Loja of an aspect of his own childhood. Your mother knew how to dress you; you always had the best clothes, Lucero would tell Loja. Lucero said it as a fact, a statement without bitterness or pain, but Loja knew why Lucero always mentioned that particular detail of his childhood, and why he was so exacting about clothing. As a child, Lucero had seldom worn new outfits. Other boys, cruelly, would make fun of him. Because he was the older boy, he always wore new pants but had to take good care of them. His younger brother, Joselo, was waiting to inherit them.[2] Sometimes, Loja knew, Lucero hadn't even had shoes to wear, which was ironic because the town of Gualaceo had once built its fleeting wealth on its reputation as the shoemaking capital of Ecuador. Everyone in Gualaceo, it seemed, could stretch a piece of leather over a wooden last and make a beautiful shoe.

Lucero had grown up poor, the oldest child of four—two boys, two girls—in a home ruled by a mostly absent shoemaker-father and supported by a short, stout woman who cooked for a living and kept her children under close supervision. Despite their poverty, or perhaps because of it, the boys had a carefree childhood, picking peaches and pears from the trees, and racing homemade wooden cars down the narrow streets that surround Gualaceo's main square.[3]

When Lucero was eight, in 1979, his father doubled over his worktable and died suddenly of a heart attack. His twenty-nine-year-old widow, Rosario, had to work nonstop to support the family, while keeping a vigilant eye on her children, particularly Lucero, who was overly attached to her. When she cleaned the house, he walked with her, holding on to the hem of her skirt. When she stayed up late at night sewing their torn clothing, he went to sleep at her feet. Doña Rosario, as everyone called her in a customary sign of respect for married or widowed women, was a stern disciplinarian. If the children misbehaved, she hit them. Lucero hated it when his mother turned her ire on him. He would run away, but his mother would run after him and bring him home.[4]

At the end of sixth grade, Lucero, who had never liked school, refused to continue his education. As the oldest son, he felt it was his duty to take care of the family, but in Gualaceo the options were limited. At first, he started helping in the kitchen, pounding on the corn mixture his mother prepared to make the pastries the family sold in the open market next to the church. Later, as a teenager, his mother found him a job selling locally made silver jewelry—much admired all over the country—in Quito, the capital, and other towns and cities, but his heart wasn't in it. What he wanted was to follow his friends to the United States.

At sixteen he tried to leave for the first time. As always, he turned to his mother for help and he asked her to borrow money from her acquaintances to fund his trip, but Doña Rosario, fearing the journey and the separation from her firstborn, didn't ask anyone for help. She lied and told him no one had wanted to lend money to such a young man supported by a single mother. What were the chances that they would ever get their money back?

At the time, the family lived in a small apartment. The girls slept with their mother in one bed, the boys bedded together in another. They shared a bathroom with three other families. A lightbulb in the courtyard was always on, which bothered Lucero and didn't let him sleep through the night.

I have to leave this house, Mama, he announced one day, and she understood that she couldn't hold him back much longer. What am I doing here? he would ask and look around with mournful eyes, as if searching for the friends he knew were already living in the United States and doing well.

The evidence was all around them. Their neighbors, the parents of his friends, were building houses two and three stories high. Young men in the United States were sending torn pages from magazines to their parents and pointing to the features they wanted to see in their new houses. An entertainment room, a formal dining room, a rooftop terrace, multiple bathrooms, marble counters, light-colored tiles on the floors, large television screens. The men sending their dreams home, one paycheck at a time, often slept in stables in eastern Long Island, next to the horses they tended, or crammed into basement apartments in Queens and elsewhere. They lived for the future, and the future began with a safe, elegant, and clean house that would bring all family members together.

Before the massive exodus of Gualaceños, few homes in that town had more than one bathroom, more than one floor, or a bedroom for each child. But once the town's youth started to go north, Gualaceo changed its character. It doubled in size, and the stark differences between the haves and have-nots became even more pronounced.

Lucero's family belonged to the have-nots. Sometimes there was not enough food in the house to eat. A paternal uncle would often come to the rescue, and the family would rally until they ran out of money again. Instead of helping his mother by getting a job, Lucero became depressed, getting out of bed at 11:00 a.m. or later and moaning all day about how he was wasting his life and not fulfilling his role as the oldest son.

One day, he got his siblings together for a meeting. "We have to have a better future. Mom, she's not going to work forever," he told them. "We have to sacrifice; we have to go over there to reach for the American dream."[5]

His opinion was important to his siblings, who looked up to him and had considered him the man of the family since he had been nine. All of them, including Doña Rosario, hung on his every word. What would Marcelo say? What would he do? How he felt tended to change the atmosphere of their household and to color their moods.

A sister, Catalina, knowing well how desperate her brother was and how afraid her mother remained, counseled their mother to let him go. This time, Doña Rosario listened. A woman in town loaned the family $5,500, a little boy offered $20, and others pitched in as well.[6] With the money in hand, the family set out to find a coyote, someone who would accompany Lucero on his journey through South and Central America and deliver him in one piece on the other side of the US-Mexico border. For fifteen days they planned his departure. Finally they found a coyote, gave him the money, and set a date.

Lucero left home on November 2, 1993, around 8:00 a.m.,

with $1,000 in his back pocket and two sets of clothing in a small backpack. His sisters and brothers lined up to hug him good-bye. He bent slightly and lowered his head in front of his mother, asking her for a blessing. Everyone, including Lucero, was weeping.

He took a bus to Cuenca and another from there to Guayaquil, where he boarded a flight to Tecumán, Guatemala. But as soon as he arrived at the Tecumán airport, the authorities there detained him: there was a problem with his travel visa, and he would have to be deported. On the way back to the plane that would take him home, Lucero asked for permission to use the bathroom. Permission granted, Lucero took off running for the door, and kept running through the streets of Tecumán until he realized no one was following him. Having lost contact with the coyote, he set out to make his way alone through Guatemala and Mexico. It took him almost two months, but eventually he made it to Texas and managed to call his family. I'm alive, he told them. And I'm on my way to New York.

"I don't know how, but he did [make it]," his brother Joselo once told a documentary filmmaker. "He would say, I'm going to make it there no matter what. I'm not returning home alive."[7]

Lucero arrived in New York on December 28, 1993. Somewhere along the way, the $1,000 in his pocket had been stolen. He was twenty-two years old.

When Doña Rosario found out her son had made it, her first thought was to wonder who would launder his shirts. He was so particular, she thought. Who is going to help him?

For a while, no one did.

After a short stint in New York City, Lucero moved in with six other young men he knew from Gualaceo, living in a big green house with five bedrooms and two bathrooms in Patchogue, near city hall and Main Street. He started working at a dry cleaner's. While the other men played basketball in the park and cracked jokes in their living room after work, Lucero kept his distance. He was fastidious about his things and his space. He kept his bed made and his night table in order, and he demanded respect from the others, who thought he was a little stuck-up. After about three years, Lucero moved on.[8] He rented a room on his own and began writing letters to his family that spoke of his loneliness, his hard life, and his yearning to see them soon. He complained that everyone in America was "addicted" to work.

"Everything here is always the same," he wrote in Spanish on December 28, 1996. "I'm tired of being in my apartment, and tired of the same thing every day, every month, every year. All I do is work and work, and I look at myself in the mirror and I see that I look tired, and that I'm growing old."[9]

On August 17, 1995, he sent what may have been his saddest letter. He had just had hernia repair surgery, and he found himself so alone that he despaired.

"This was so hard for me," he wrote.

> I was alone in the clinic. I went to sleep, and when I woke up I was in such pain that I felt the doctors had taken away half my life. All I could do was howl in pain. The worst part was that no one came to pick me up when it was time to go home the next day. To go up to my room, I had to drag myself up the stairs on my knees. Then I went to bed and I couldn't get up. I couldn't move. I was alone, locked in four walls, half moribund. I got very melancholic and I realized that in my journey in this life, I was alone. It was the most difficult experience in my life. I'm a little better now, taking small steps, but pale because I've lost a lot of blood.

He stopped writing four years later, after he bought a cell phone. In the last letter he sent to his family, in 1999, he wrote, "I'm a bird with broken wings," and he drew the picture of a wingless dove. When Doña Rosario received her son's letter a week after he wrote it, she wept at the sight of the drawing. Because she is illiterate, her daughter Isabel always read the letters to her. But she didn't need anyone to explain the message her son had sent this time. She immediately understood that helping him leave had been a mistake.

One day, when he was driving down Main Street, Lucero thought he spotted a familiar face and stopped the car at the curve. He lowered his car window and shouted, Angel! What are you doing here?

Though the two had known each other for a long time, they hadn't been close friends. In the land of soccer and volleyball—the sports Lucero and most Ecuadorian boys played—Loja was an anomaly. When he was thirteen, a man named Serafín Orellana had returned to Gualaceo after a few years in New York, where he had become a fan of NBA basketball. The man gathered a few boys, created a team, and taught them the intricate rules of the NBA. Loja was hooked. From 1988 to 1993 he played basketball every day with the team Orellana built, winning game after game in all local scrimmages. But before the team could move on to regional competitions, most of the boys and young men left Gualaceo and moved to Patchogue.

Lucero remembered Loja's performance on the basketball court. Though not nearly tall enough to dunk the ball effortlessly, as those in the NBA seem to do, Loja managed to do it by jumping very high. That was his signature, his specialty: jump more than a meter off the ground, surprise the opponent, and dunk the ball. That jump, he was often told, had saved the team on many occasions, and it kept Loja off the streets and focused. He was an athlete, and he carried himself with the grace and assurance of the best of them.

Lucero admired Loja's tenacity and game, and he remembered that as Loja approached his car on Main Street with a tentative smile. Loja felt a warm feeling overcome him, as he realized that, in the absence of family, an old acquaintance might just do. From that day on, the two often spent time together, shopping, and eating at the home of a woman who cooked and sold the dishes they missed from home. They also became gym buddies, sometimes spending three or even five hours a day in the gym. However, Lucero would never play basketball with Loja for he knew that some of the boys who years ago had made fun of his raggedy clothes and naked feet in Gualaceo were now Loja's basketball-playing friends in Patchogue.

The park outing and the sober talk about life and character and responsibility ended when Lucero suggested they go shopping at a mall in Smithtown, about ten miles away. They stopped at Express, one of Lucero's favorite stores, where he bought a pair of pants for $90 and a few T-shirts, including one for which he paid $60 and which made him look as if he fit in. Maybe that was the point of all this shopping, Loja thought. Lucero wanted to blend in. If people were going to look at him because he spoke broken English and had a brown face, they might as well look at an elegantly dressed man. Loja bought some items too. Lucero seemed happy, more relaxed than when he had picked up Loja earlier in the day.

Let's go home and eat, I'm hungry, he said, and Loja followed.

After stopping at Loja's to drop off his purchase, they went to Lucero's place, a second-floor studio with a small kitchen and a bathroom. His bed, as always, was made, and his Bible rested on the night table. A US flag dominated the wall behind the bed.

Come here, he said to Loja. I want to read you something I just found.

He picked up the Bible and tried to read Psalm 31, but inexplicably he stumbled over his words and handed it to Loja, who read out loud: "I'm scorned by all my enemies and despised by my neighbors—even my friends are afraid to come near me. When they see me on the street, they run the other way. I am ignored as if I were dead, as if I were a broken pot. I have heard the many rumors about me, and I am surrounded by terror. My enemies conspire against me, plotting to take my life."[10]

Loja was not surprised by his friend's chosen passage. Where they came from, death—even untimely death—was as common as life. It was another stage, a final one but one that everyone they knew was intimately familiar with. Lucero's father had died young. Loja had lost an older brother, a twenty-four-year-old medical student, to a mysterious ailment of the throat that no one ever fully explained. As far as enemies, the men knew they had many.

To lighten their mood, Loja turned on the TV and the two started watching a National Geographic documentary about African mammals. Lucero opened two beers and Loja went to the corner deli and bought fried shrimp, for about $9, and more beer. Later he went back to get more shrimp and more beer before the deli closed. The owner, who was almost done for the day, didn't charge him the second time. If Loja didn't take the shrimp, he would have had to toss them anyway, but Loja took the gesture as he always did: proof that good things happened to him, another sign that God was looking out for him.

After dinner, the two friends smoked marijuana. It had been a good day, a relaxing day, and now Loja thought it was time to leave. Lucero offered to drive him home. Loja declined. The two had been drinking and all they needed was a police officer stopping them and smelling their breath. He decided to walk home alone. After all, it was only seven blocks.

Two blocks from Lucero's home, Loja stopped to get a light for his cigarette from a passerby. Suddenly he felt a hand on his right shoulder and he jumped back, startled. It was Lucero, who had followed him.

What are you doing here? I already left you home, Loja said.

But Lucero wasn't done for the night. He wanted to go to the train station where he had met a pretty girl a few nights before, he told Loja.

Let's go, man, he pleaded. It's still early.

Loja knew it was past 11:00 p.m., not a good time for two Latino men to be walking in the streets of Patchogue, but he reluctantly agreed to accompany Lucero because, once again, he felt his friend was anxious and needed some company. There was no one at the train station. The parking lot was empty and eerily quiet. A fog had descended on the balmy night. Lucero suggested they go to a nearby bar. Loja didn't like the idea because he knew the bar was a hangout for the kind of white men who could spell trouble for brown men like them.

Not daring to leave his friend alone, Loja remembered that another friend, Elder Fernández, lived in a house behind the train station. Fernández was home watching TV and invited them over when Loja called.

As they made their way to Fernández's house, Loja spotted a handful of young men approaching them from a side street. He counted them. Seven. They looked young. All but one were white. At least one wore a hoodie. When they were close enough to look them in the eye, Loja didn't like what he saw. These boys are angry, he thought to himself, and he whispered to Lucero, Be careful.

Loja took two steps back to assess the situation. They were standing essentially in a cul-de-sac. To their left there were houses and a street blocked by the attackers. To their right, the train station. They could run back, but they would have to run very fast to find a way out for their exit was blocked on either side by either houses or the station. If they ran ahead, they might get to the alley where Loja's friend lived, but they would have to be faster than the teenagers who were closing in like hunters on prey.

The group of young men was now upon them, breathing hard and bouncing on the balls of their feet, pumping their arms, laughing, and bumping into each other unself-consciously, the way teenagers do. Were they joking? Were they high? Drunk? Loja could practically smell their breath.

There was nothing to do but to stand their ground and fight. Loja turned to Lucero and yelled, Watch out!

CHAPTER 7

A MURDER IN THE SUBURBS

When they spotted the men, Kevin "Kuvan" Shea was almost joyful, like a father finding his child's favorite toys under the bed. "There you go. They are right there," he said. Taking large steps, he approached Lucero and Loja, with Anthony and José at his heels.[1]

Loja noticed that the teenagers had separated into two groups, as if to block any possible escape. The attack didn't seem random but coordinated. They've done this before, he intuited, and started looking for a way out. This was not a fight they could win.

Then Loja thought he heard one of the attackers calling them "niggers."

"I said something like, 'Come through, nigga,' which is a term we use to call someone out to fight," Kevin told detectives later, in the early hours of November 9. "All of us were talking shit."

Loja, who had already noticed that one of them was black, shouted back, "Who are you calling a nigger? You are the ugly nigger!"

Anthony, José, and Kuvan began to taunt the men to get a

fight going. Yelling insults had worked in the past: get a lonely, drunken man angry and who knows what could happen? Get two powerless and possibly drunk men angry and the fun surely could be doubled. Nick asked, "What's good, Beaners?" "Beaners" was one of their favorite insults. "Fucking Mexicans" was another. Except for Jeff and Chris and possibly Jordan, the rest began to hurl insults: "Fucking illegals! You come to this country to take our money! You get out of this country!"

Loja and Lucero replied with the only insults they could think of. They called their attackers "faggots."

Anthony asked them if they had any money.

"No!" Lucero yelled back. "Why don't you guys go to work like I go to work, so you can have your own money?"

Lucero took his denim jacket off, ready for a fight. Kuvan put his right hand into the waistband of his pants, as if he were going to pull out a gun, and said, "Cut the shit, motherfucker." Lucero didn't move. Kuvan got even closer and punched Lucero hard on the face, at the upper edge of his mouth, cutting his lip open. Lucero started bleeding, from his mouth or his nose or both, and Kuvan mocked him, "You're already bleeding, that's all I had to do." Anthony threw a punch at Loja but missed.

On instinct, honed through years of jumping to dunk a basketball, Loja jumped so high he managed to get out of their reach and run toward the alley, where his friend Elder Fernández lived. Lucero ran in the opposite direction, with four of the teenagers closely behind.

Despite all the yelling and commotion, the streets were quiet. No one was at the train station. A train had left about an hour earlier, at 10:42 p.m.; the next one—the last train of the day—was not scheduled to come by until 11:59 p.m.[2] They were alone and there seemed to be no time to pull out a cell phone and call the police. Everything was moving too fast and too slow at the same time. Loja could see movements as if in slow motion, and he could hear the insults and the blows as if he were under water.

His head felt stuffed with cotton, but his senses were alert and his skin felt prickly and sweaty. The only thought in his brain was to escape—if possible, unhurt and with his friend.

Out of the corner of his eye, Loja could see that Lucero had fallen. Four young men were yelling and kicking him as if he were a football. For a moment Loja remembered the documentary of the African mammals he had watched earlier that evening with Lucero. This is what they are doing to my friend, he thought. Tearing him apart like hyenas.

At the sight of the blood, the rest of the attackers who had at one point encircled Loja felt emboldened and ran to aid the others with Lucero, who had already managed to get up and was swinging his belt over his head, forcing the gang to move toward the parking lot. At first, Kuvan thought Lucero had a nunchaku; Anthony thought it was a chain with a lock on the end, but Jeff realized it was a belt. A belt seemed less dangerous than a martial arts weapon, and they must have thought that seven young, agile men could easily handle two dazed men, especially with one hurt and bleeding, even if he was swinging a belt. Kuvan gave an order: "Surround them!"

The tone of the fight had changed. This was no longer a one-sided fight, like the one the teenagers had just had, kicking the back and legs of Héctor Sierra while he folded his body, covered his head, and took the blows while screaming for help. In Lucero, they had found the angry man they had been looking for—an opponent who was as fearless as they were reckless. Except for Jordan, who was afraid to hurt his back, the others obeyed Kuvan's command and crowded around Lucero in a half circle. But Jeff got too close and the buckle of the swinging belt hit him on the head. He quickly touched his forehead, enraged, then took out his pocketknife and approached.

Loja had enough time to pull his belt from his pants to try to help Lucero, but he realized the situation was too dangerous. Too many of them moving around, trying to squeeze in between the swinging belts. If the attackers managed to grab the belts, their one chance was over. Loja headed back toward the driveway where he had been standing seconds before. He fell to the ground and looked back, searching for Lucero, who this time was trying to follow him, swinging the belt as he walked backward, while keeping an eye on his attackers. Loja got up and ran toward the alley, momentarily losing sight of his friend.

Lucero swung at whoever was closest to him. It happened to be Nick. Jeff noticed and lunged toward Lucero with the open knife in his right hand. Lucero's back was toward Jeff, but he turned around suddenly, as if he could sense the danger. Jeff, who was about four or five feet from Lucero, continued to run toward him with his arm outstretched—the hand with the knife leading the way. It's impossible to know if Lucero saw the weapon, if it glinted in the light from the lampposts. Loja knows he didn't see it. Except for Lucero and Jeff, no one else seemed to have noticed the moment when Jeff plunged his knife beneath Lucero's right collarbone, close to the shoulder.

When Loja turned around toward the attackers, he saw that Lucero had fallen. He called out to him but Lucero didn't get up.

Suddenly the fight stopped. Jeff said to Nick, "We really gotta go." The others were still near Lucero, and Jeff yelled to them, "Let's go!" Kuvan must have detected a sense of urgency in Jeff's voice because he too called out for everyone to leave, and they all began to walk away.

Jeff, Chris, and Kuvan walked ahead of the others. When they turned a corner toward Main Street, Jeff said, "Oh, shit. I'm fucked. I stabbed him," and he showed them the blood on the knife. Chris urged him to get rid of the knife, but instead Jeff cleaned it in a puddle, trying to wash the blood from it, folded the blade, and put it back in his pants pocket. Jeff also told Nick that he had stabbed the man who had been bleeding. That explains it, said Kuvan, noting that all the blood on the man's shirt couldn't have been caused by his solitary punch to the face. Anthony, who had heard Jeff's hushed confession, told him he "had his back" and offered to take the knife and make it disappear, but Jeff refused and kept walking toward the car with the others.

Some of them thought they might just be able to get away, but then they noticed a camera on a building and realized that was a dangerous sign. If the camera was on, sooner or later they would be found. But before they could even articulate their fears, they heard the siren from a police car.

From his relatively safe spot, Loja called out again: Marcelo Lucero come, come this way. Loja kept calling out to him as the young men walked away. The fight was over. He thought that maybe someone had called the police, but no one was there. They were still alone. Only about five minutes had passed, but to Loja, shaking and pumped with adrenaline, it had seemed like hours. Still hovering over by the alley, Loja once again called out to Lucero, who had gotten up and was staggering like a drunk toward his jacket on the ground. He picked it up and went to join Loja. As Lucero approached, Loja heard the sound first, a hissing, like that of a half-opened garden hose: *pshshsh*. Then he noticed the blood, an ever-expanding stain on Lucero's shirt. By the time Lucero reached him, the blood had drenched his shirt and pants, down to his mid-thighs. Loja had never seen so much blood before. Instinctively he reached for his friend and asked what even then sounded like a silly question to him.

"Marcelo, are you all right?"

"No. Call an ambulance," Lucero managed to say before the gurgling sound of his own blood drowned his voice and he slumped over in his friend's arms.

Loja pulled out his phone and, with fingers sticky with blood, dialed 911.

The operator answered on the first ring, but then Loja's phone, which had been running out of charge, went dead. That first failed call, the police would later reveal, was made at 11:52 p.m. The operator called back, and the phone came alive momentarily, but again it died before Loja could utter a word. Desperate, he dragged Lucero's limp body onto the driveway and placed it halfway under a parked car, hoping to afford his friend some protection in case the attackers came back. He left Lucero momentarily and ran to the small, white-painted house where Elder Fernández lived. He pounded on the door and Fernández, who had been waiting for them, came quickly to the door.

"Elder, help me. They just stabbed my friend and he's bleeding a lot. Please call 911."

He did. The call came in at 11:55 p.m. Within a minute, it seemed, two police cars arrived. Suffolk County police officer Frank Munsch was in one of the cars. When he got out, Loja told them what had happened and lifted up Lucero's shirt so he could see the gushing wound.

"There was significant blood loss," Officer Munsch would later testify.[3]

Lucero was breathing rapidly, lying faceup in a pool of blood. His hands and feet shook, but he was conscious and his eyes were open.[4] At 11:59 p.m., the officer called for a "rush rescue." Under oath in court more than a year later, Munsch said that he applied pressure on the wound while making the phone call.[5] But Loja has maintained from the beginning that when he showed the officer Lucero's wound, the officer went to his car, retrieved a rag, and threw it on Lucero but didn't do anything else except question Loja for a description of the attackers. Short of breath and in broken English, Loja told him what had happened and described the young men as well as he could. Munsch had seen those teenagers walking in the area earlier, and he put out a description over his police radio.[6] The other officers asked Loja to go with them. Another police crew had already stopped seven suspicious young men at the corner of Main Street and Ocean Avenue. Would he help identify them? Reluctantly, Loja got in one of the police cars and was driven away. As he looked back, he noticed the ambulance had not yet arrived.

Christopher Schiera, a dispatcher for the Medford Fire Department and a volunteer with the Patchogue Ambulance Company, had just gotten home in Holtsville when he received the call: an adult male was bleeding by the train tracks in Patchogue, about five miles south. The call came in at 12:01 a.m. on November 9, exactly forty-six minutes after he had finished his six-hour shift.[7]

The Patchogue Ambulance Company, founded in 1934 by a small group of volunteer firemen from the Patchogue Fire Department, answers approximately twenty-four hundred calls per year, twenty-four hours a day, seven days a week.[8] At the time, Schiera was the company's assistant chief, which meant that he was in charge of staffing the ambulance and overseeing personnel, who were, with one exception, volunteers.

Schiera had been certified as an emergency medical technician of critical care, or EMTCC; he also had an advanced cardiac life support certification. As an EMTCC he had been qualified to attempt resuscitation, perform the Heimlich maneuver, and use an automated external defibrillator—commonly found in public buildings, police cars, and ambulances. In addition, he could have started an IV, administered drugs, performed an EKG, and intubated patients. At the time of the attack, though, Schiera's EMTCC certification had lapsed. While he was enrolled in a refresher class to get back his license, he wasn't supposed to perform any of the advanced life support techniques necessary when a patient has lost a lot of blood. He could drive, however, and when the call came over his portable radio for an ambulance driver, Schiera volunteered. Along with his girlfriend, who was also a volunteer, he drove toward the company headquarters to pick up the ambulance and crew that was already in-house. But halfway there, the dispatcher called again. The police department needed the ambulance immediately. The dispatcher said the man bleeding near the tracks had been the victim of a stabbing.

Schiera knew who was on call at the Patchogue Ambulance Company that day: two people who were certified to administer basic help but not to drive an ambulance. Under certain circumstances—when a patient is in critical need, for example—the company allows drivers not officially qualified to drive the ambulance to do so. This was one of those circumstances. Schiera asked the crew—Stephanie Mara and Gabriel Salerno—to drive the ambulance themselves and told them he would meet them at Funaro Court, where the man lay bleeding.

The ambulance got to Lucero at 12:12 a.m., two minutes before Schiera did.

There were several police cars near the entrance to Funaro Court, a street that to Schiera initially seemed like the driveway of the white, two-story house he saw there. The lights from the cars had attracted some people, who milled around competing for a chance to see the bleeding man on the ground.

Mara and Salerno were already attending to Lucero, whose name they did not yet know. They took his vital signs: his respiratory rate was 28 and labored—a normal rate wouldn't be above 16 or 20, at the most; his pulse rate was 46—a normal one is 60–100 beats a minute; and his level of consciousness was rated as reacting only to pain. EMTs rate four levels of consciousness: "alert," which means that the patient is alert and talking; "voice" or "verbal," which means that the patient is confused but talking; "pain," which means that the patient does not respond except to some form of tactile stimulation, such as being moved, or to having a flashlight shone in his or her eyes; and "unresponsive," which means just that. Lucero was one level away from being unresponsive.

Mara and Salerno got a long backboard to stabilize Lucero, holding his head in such a way to keep it in line with his spine. But Schiera thought the board wasn't necessary. The man lying on the ground before him had gone into shock. He was very pale, he was sweating profusely, and his breathing was short, rapid, and labored. He was not speaking and his eyes were closed. Shock is often described as the transition between life and death. He was bleeding from the wound in his chest, and half his body was still under the parked SUV where Loja had left him.

Schiera noticed bloody gauze on the ground and took a closer look at Lucero's chest. He asked one of the crew members to grab the oxygen tank and a mask and apply it to the victim. Vital signs were taken again, three minutes after the first check. Lucero's respiratory rate was not recorded because at that point he had an oxygen mask on; his pulse had lowered even more, to 40 beats per minute; and now his level of consciousness had dropped to "unresponsive."

Lucero's breathing was so labored that the oxygen mask didn't help him. Schiera asked for a device known as an Asherman chest seal, a dressing used when a punctured lung is suspected. He had no idea how deep Lucero's injury was or what had caused it but he assumed the worst and reasoned that the chest seal would help him by allowing air to escape from the chest while stopping the bleeding. But then, as they attempted to move Lucero, he began to bleed again, more profusely this time, and the seal washed right off his chest. They put Lucero back down and inserted a plastic device in his mouth to keep the airways clear. They also applied another oxygen mask and a bulky dressing to stanch the bleeding. At 12:25 a.m., thirteen minutes after the ambulance had arrived but twenty-nine minutes after Fernández had called 911, Lucero was finally placed in the ambulance and driven away from Funaro Court, leaving behind a trail of blood.

Six or seven police cruisers convened at the area known as Four Corners in the Village of Patchogue, the intersection of Ocean Avenue and Main Street. Seven teenagers had their hands up, their hearts in their throats, and their bodies pressed against the glass windows of a real estate office.

A cop named Richardsen began to frisk the teenagers for weapons. When he got to Jeff, he patted him once and didn't feel anything, but then Jeff said, "Can I speak to you in private?"

The officer pulled him aside. "I got the knife on me," Jeff said.

"Where?"

"In the waistband."

Richardsen lifted up Jeff's sweatshirt, found the knife, and opened the blade.

"There's blood on it," he said.

To which Jeff replied, "I stabbed the guy."[9]

Just then, Loja arrived on the scene in a police car. His attackers were lined up against the wall. Loja could see them all clearly, except for the one he knew to be black, José Pacheco, though he didn't know his name. He told the police that one was missing, the dark-skinned one, and they brought him forth so Loja could take a good look. They shone a flashlight on José's face. That's him, Loja said, and stayed put, legs shaking, looking at the group for a few more minutes. He watched as the police took them away. Then he too was driven to the Fifth Police Precinct.

The emergency crew wanted to take Lucero to a helicopter landing zone at Briarcliffe College, a few blocks away from Funaro Court. The crew thought that his condition was critical and that he needed to be airlifted to Stony Brook University Hospital about fourteen miles to the north. As a level-one trauma center, the hospital has a trauma team that includes a surgeon, nurses, anesthesiologists, and aides on standby twenty-four hours a day, seven day a week. The team can perform surgery right in the emergency room, without losing precious moments moving a broken body to another area. Brookhaven Hospital, which is the closest hospital to Patchogue, not even five minutes away, has doctors on call who are trained to handle trauma, but they can't perform surgery in the emergency room—it is not a level-one trauma center.[10]

At 12:28 a.m., the ambulance arrived at the college, ready to transfer Lucero to the helicopter, which hadn't yet arrived. At that very moment, the crew noticed that Lucero's heart had stopped beating. An air ambulance is not supposed to transport patients who've gone into cardiac arrest. The crew decided to take him to Brookhaven Hospital after all. On the way there, they began administering CPR, compressing his chest and trying to help Lucero breathe with an oxygen mask. They also used an external defibrillator. Police cars blocked off intersections and stopped traffic for them, but they had to make one more stop to pick up a medic from the Holbrook Fire Department. The medic had been called because, unlike the others in the ambulance, he was trained and certified at a more advanced level.

Brookhaven Hospital was so close that all the medic had time to do was to check the electrical output of Lucero's heart with an EKG machine. The situation was dire. They arrived at the hospital at 12:34 a.m. As Schiera was pulling the patient from the back of the ambulance, he took a look at the EKG monitor. It showed a heart rhythm known as "pulseless electrical activity"—a medical term for a heart in its final stages of life, producing electricity that resembles a heartbeat but it is not.

Medical personnel, who had already been alerted to the severity of Lucero's condition, met them at the door. But it was too late. Lucero was pronounced dead at 1:09 a.m. on November 9, about an hour and a half after he was stabbed. The medical examiner would later confirm the obvious: the cause of death was a four-inch-deep stab wound to the chest.[11]

"Is this going to be a problem for the wrestling season?" Jeffrey Conroy asked homicide detective John A. McLeer of the Suffolk County Police Department. It was about 3:30 a.m. Five minutes earlier, McLeer, accompanied by another detective, James Faughnan, had gone into the room where Jeff sat handcuffed. He was wearing blue jeans, a black, gray, and gold Patchogue-Medford Raiders basketball sweatshirt with white piping, and black sneakers. At some point, McLeer would have to ask Jeff to take off his clothes. They would become evidence.[12]

McLeer introduced himself and took off Jeff's handcuffs, which were connected to a chain that was attached to the desk. McLeer and Faughnan had the task of finding out what had transpired at Funaro Court. But first they needed to respond to Jeff's question.

"Jeff, we're from the homicide squad. Forget about wrestling. It's the least of your problems right now. That's the least of your concerns," McLeer said.

And just like that, Jeff's transformation from star athlete to murder suspect began.

The interview room in the Fifth Precinct detective area was small and square, just over nine feet by nine feet. The concrete block walls were painted off-white. The floor was tiled and sparsely furnished—just a desk and chairs. From the one window in the room, blocked by bars, one could see the outside. A solid wooden door separated interviewers and interviewees from the rest of the precinct. A desk, old and chipped, was against the wall with the window. Faughnan sat at one end, opposite Jeff. McLeer sat in the middle. They asked Jeff some basic information—name, date of birth, address, phone number—and then read him the Miranda rights.[13]

After each sentence, Jeff wrote his initials, indicating he had understood his rights: "You have the right to remain silent." (He didn't remain silent.) "Anything you say can and will be used against you in a court of law." (Everything he said was used against him—immediately and also in court.) "You have the right to talk with a lawyer right now and have him present while you are being questioned." (Jeff did not call a lawyer; he didn't even ask to call his parents.) "If you cannot afford a lawyer and want one, a lawyer will be appointed for you by the court before any questioning. If you decide to answer questions now without a lawyer present, you will have the right to stop the questioning at any time until you talk to a lawyer." (Jeff talked for hours, not stopping until his father—whom he eventually called—told him to.)[14]

With the legal stuff out of the way, Detective McLeer asked him how he had ended up at the Fifth Precinct.

"I already told the big cop what I did, and he's got my knife," Jeff said. The "big cop" was Michael Richardsen, who had already turned in the knife, now tucked away in McLeer's gun locker.

McLeer, who had been a cop for twenty-one years and a detective for the last thirteen of those, wanted more information and asked the question differently. Later, in court, he explained his interviewing method: "A good interview is ideally a conversation, and ideally the person you're talking to is doing most of the talking, giving you information."

That he did. Jeff remained calm and was cooperative. If he was afraid, he didn't show it. He was subdued and chatty as he related the events of that night: from his visit to Alyssa's house earlier in the evening to the get-together in the Medford train station and the park and eventually the decision to go "fuck up some Mexicans."

As McLeer teased information out of Jeff, he studied him carefully. He noticed a red spot—a fresh injury, it seemed—on the top of his head and saw that his knuckles were slightly swollen and bloody, as if he had been in a fight.

"Hey, Jeff, did you hit the guy?" McLeer asked.

But Jeff said his swollen knuckles and bloody hands were the result of his roughing around earlier that evening with his friend, Felicia, at the train station. He said he must have scraped them on the ground. On his right index finger, there was a Band-Aid. Jeff had an explanation for that too. On Friday, he said, he'd had a fight with one of his best friends, Roman.

"Hey, Jeff, why would you be fighting with your best friend?" McLeer asked.

"Same reason I'm here now, because I'm a fucking asshole."

McLeer directed the conversation back to the stabbing. "How did you wind up down in Patchogue? Again, how did you wind up with me here this morning?"

So Jeff explained about getting into Jordan's car and heading for Patchogue, and how Kuvan and Anthony had started to hit "the guy"—at that point Jeff didn't know the name of the man he had stabbed. He mentioned the swinging belt and said that he had been hit by the buckle. Since he didn't want to get hit again, he took his knife out and stabbed the man.

"I stabbed him once in the shoulder, I think," he said.

He described the knife. He said it was black and that he had found it in a hotel room and that his parents knew he had it.

McLeer asked if he had ever been arrested before. Jeff said "almost," and "for the same shit," which he described as "Mexican hopping."

McLeer pressed him for details, and Jeff revealed how on Monday of the week that had just ended, accompanied by Kuvan, Anthony, and José, he had "knocked out cold" a Hispanic man on Jamaica Avenue. On that occasion, it was José who threw the punch, Jeff said. The cops had arrived, but the victim refused to press charges.

"Jeff, do you and your friends just go around kicking the shit out of Mexicans for nothing or beating the shit out of Mexicans for nothing?" McLeer asked. Jeff said he didn't, but Kuvan did and he added that he, Jeff, was "an asshole for getting involved."

He also admitted that he had gone "looking for Spanish people to beat up before," not just a week earlier on Jamaica Avenue.

That first part of the interview lasted forty minutes. At 4:05 a.m., the detectives put the handcuffs back on Jeff and stepped out of the room to take a break and to share with their immediate supervisor the confession they already had. In less than ten minutes, they went back in. Once again, they took off the handcuffs and this time asked Jeff if he would be willing to give them a written statement. Once again, they read Jeff his rights. Jeff waved them off and signed his initials, indicating that he understood he didn't have to say anything and that he had rights. And he kept talking.

At 4:15 a.m., the detectives began composing Jeff's "written statement" out of the notes they had taken from the initial interview, with additional information asked, as needed. The detectives asked him to read and initial any changes. Toward the end of his statement, Jeff said something curious: "I don't blame the Spanish guy [Lucero] for swinging the belt at us. It was obvious he wanted to get the fuck out of there. He was ready to defend himself, but we just didn't back down." It is clear that, for the briefest time, in the heat of their fierce and uneven encounter, Jeff had felt something akin to admiration for a man he knew only as a "beaner."

Once Jeff signed his confession, McLeer went to his gun locker and retrieved the knife, which was inside a latex glove to preserve DNA and fingerprints. He showed it to Jeff, who recognized it as his. At 6:50 a.m., they were done. The handcuffs went back around Jeff's wrists and around the chain that kept him tethered to the table. Then the detectives left the room. Six other teenagers needed to be interviewed.

By that time, McLeer and Faughnan had already spoken to a shaken Loja, whose first question had been, "How's my friend?"

"I'm sorry," one of them told him. "Your friend passed away. He's dead."[15]

When Loja heard the news he felt angry, but then, more than anything else, he felt sadness. Overwhelming sadness. Just a few hours before, he had gone shopping with Lucero, they had shared a meal and drinks, they had talked about the future, about life and work and home. Now, sitting alone under the unnaturally bright lights of a police station in a town where he felt he was no longer welcomed, Loja pondered how he could go on when the very color of his skin, the language he spoke, the slant of his eyes, and the texture of his hair had turned him into the victim of a hate crime.

Everything he had ever suspected or feared about the United States had just come true in one terrible, terrible moment in which he had lost not only his innocence but also his best friend. He thought of his journey of eighteen days from Gualaceo to New York, the hours of thirst and hunger crossing the desert, the nights when he thought he couldn't possibly survive such perilous conditions. He also thought of what his life had been since he had left home: a succession of poorly paid jobs, abusive comments from insensitive bosses, and resentful stares from some people who hadn't adapted to the idea of seeing Latinos walking down Main Street. Did they belong there? Did he? Did he really belong in a place so far from home? Perhaps it was time to give up the American dream.

All he knew that night as he contemplated his callous hands— still red with Lucero's blood—was that his friend was dead and that his own life had changed. He would no longer be an anonymous immigrant trying to make a living in a New York suburb. From now on, he intuited, he would be known as the man who was with Marcelo Lucero the night he was killed, the man who had been unable to keep Lucero alive.

"Kuvan and I probably started the whole thing," Anthony Hartford, who was a big seventeen-year-old at about six foot one and 175 pounds, told detectives during his confession. "Kuvan hit one of them in the face and he started bleeding a lot. I swung at the other guy and missed."

Anthony said that he and Kuvan had been hanging out together since the early evening of November 8, along with another friend named Bobby. Jordan had later joined them and given them a ride to the Medford train station. On the way to the station, where they met the others, they had stopped at a gas station by the Long Island Expressway and bought an eighteen-pack of Budweiser.

He also said that the last time he had been out "jumping beaners" had been five days earlier. On Monday, November 3, he, with José and Kuvan, had attacked a "beaner" on Jamaica Avenue. José had punched the man so hard he "knocked him out," Anthony said, and he added a chilling thought: "I don't go out doing this very often, maybe only once a week."

Kuvan's confession closely mirrored that of Anthony. Both of them referred to Christopher Overton as "a kid named Chris," making it clear he was not a part of their group. Kuvan too took responsibility for the events of that night, saying that it had been he, Anthony, and Nick who had started talking about "looking for people to fight." He said they had been looking for "beaners to fuck up," and he readily acknowledged that, later that night, he had been the one who threw the first punch, the punch that made Lucero bleed. But he also said that, after the punch, he had started to walk back toward the parking lot. It was then he had realized that the "Spanish guys" had taken off their belts and that one of them—the one he had "snuffed"—was swinging the belt over his head.

If he had been thinking of leaving, seeing the swinging belt made him change his mind, because Kuvan said he then yelled to the others "to surround the guy and try to control him." Kuvan also told detectives that he had seen Jeff run toward the guy he had punched, but, like Anthony, he didn't see the actual stabbing. All he knew was that the fight stopped shortly after that.

"The guy was walking back into the street and he had a lot more blood on him, far more than when I punched him in the mouth," Kuvan said. "As we walked towards the SUV I thought we might get away, but Chris pointed out a video camera and within seconds a police car rolled up on us."

Kuvan was candid about his participation in past beatings of Hispanics. "I have been involved in beatings like this before but no one ever used a knife. We would just beat people up." As Anthony also did, Kuvan described the beating of a Hispanic man the Monday before, on Jamaica Avenue. But, unlike Anthony, he said that Jeff had been there as well, along with three other young men who had not been mentioned before. He was clear on one detail: on that occasion, "Anthony, José and I knocked out a Spanish guy."[16]

The "Spanish guy" who was knocked out on Jamaica Avenue was Octavio Cordovo, an immigrant from Mexico who had arrived illegally in the United States only a few months before the attack. He lived in Medford and worked sporadically in construction. Like so many other immigrants in Medford, every morning at dawn he stood at a corner near a 7-Eleven, waiting for someone in a truck to stop and offer him work for a day.

On November 3, 2008, he had worked from 7:00 a.m. to 4:00 p.m. and had then gone home. Sometime later, at about 7:30 p.m., he had left the house to walk about four blocks to a CITGO gas station to buy coffee with a friend named Adrián. Two young men had approached them. He noticed that one was white and the other was black. Cordovo also noticed that other young people were milling around in the park next to the gas station and walking toward them as well. As he passed the two young men, the white one asked if they had any cigarettes.

"We simply told them, 'We don't have any,' " Cordovo would later testify in court.

What happened next was a blur. The young men pushed Adrián. One—Kuvan or Anthony—hit Cordovo on the shoulder and pushed him hard on the chest. Cordovo heard young girls yelling for the attackers to stop. "No, no, don't do it!" they said. That's the last thing he remembers. He was knocked down with a punch to the mouth, not unlike Lucero, and started bleeding, but luckily for him he passed out. Unlike Lucero, he didn't have the chance to fight back.

In his confession, José did not talk about the attack on

Cordovo, but he corroborated his friends' account of the attack on Loja and Lucero, and he added a new detail. Before Kuvan threw the first punch, "the shorter of the two Spanish guys said he didn't want no trouble." The shorter one was Lucero.

José also told police that later, as he saw the cops pulling up next to them, he had taken a small white folding knife from his pocket and thrown it in a garbage can. He said that Jeff had given him the knife earlier that day, telling him he should have it in case he ever needed it.

Nick confessed not only to the attack on Loja and Lucero but also to a different one that same day. On Saturday morning, he said, at around 5:00 a.m., along with Jordan and another young man also named Nick, they had come upon a Hispanic man and begun to insult him, hoping for a fight. The man had broken a glass bottle and gone at them. Nick, who carried a pellet pistol, had fired it at the ground three times and then driven off with the others. He had then thrown his pistol in the woods, thinking the loud noise and the commotion would attract cops. In fact, police stopped Jordan's SUV near a bodega, but no one was arrested. Later, Nick had gone back to the woods to retrieve his pistol.

Jordan gave the same version of the events as the others, and even corroborated Nick's account of the earlier attack, adding that he too had fired his BB gun at the man with the broken bottle. Like Nick, he had thrown the gun into the woods by the train tracks. When the police came and questioned them, they lied and said they hadn't done anything. The police took their names and told them to go home. Later, Jordan went back to the woods to get his BB gun. As he spoke to detectives that night, the gun was still in his car.

Chris gave the shortest statement of all seven. His version of events matched that of the others in all but one point: he was the only one in the group who said he had never hunted "beaners" before.

• • •

Six and a half hours after he left Jeff alone in the interview room, McLeer went back in and asked Jeff if he would be willing to draw a sketch of the events surrounding the stabbing. Jeff agreed and drew a childish and chilling portrait of the killing. He used two stick figures to indicate where the attack had started and where it had ended. The last stick figure has an explanatory note: "got stabbed by me."

After Jeff finished the drawing, McLeer asked him if he would allow them to videotape his statement, with a district attorney, not a detective, asking questions this time. Jeff agreed to that too, but then he seemed to have doubts and asked McLeer if he thought it was a good idea. McLeer understood Jeff was asking him for advice. It was the first time that night when Jeff had shown a degree of vulnerability. He seemed to be asking for the guidance of an adult. McLeer wouldn't advise him, and so Jeff finally did what his father had so many times before drilled him to do: he asked McLeer if he could call his dad.

On Sunday morning, Bob Conroy was worried. A couple of hours earlier, Matt Cleary had called to say that Jeff had not spent the night in his home, as he had been supposed to do. What do you mean he's not there? Conroy had asked, a surge of panic seizing his body as he remembered that he had fallen asleep without having heard from Jeff. Well, where could he be? Cleary had no idea, and, what's more, his sons had texted Jeff the night before and had not heard from him either.[17]

Conroy called his wife, who had gone to church, and asked her if Jeff had called her. He had not. Conroy called three local hospitals and the police station, where, unknown to him, his son was still being interviewed. Whoever answered the phone told him that there was no one there by the name of Jeff Conroy. Worried, Conroy's wife came home, and Conroy went outside to smoke a cigarette. That's when the phone rang.

We have Jeff in custody, Detective McLeer said. He's charged with manslaughter.

From the shock of hearing the news, Conroy fell and almost fainted. He was confused and angry and wasn't even sure who was calling him or who had died. Conroy couldn't comprehend that his son had been charged with killing a person. He placed his hand on his chest, near his heart, and willed himself to remain calm and coherent. Then he asked the detective to let him speak with his son.

At Jeff's request, a phone had been brought into the interrogation room, where the detectives remained, listening to the one-sided conversation.

"Dad," Jeff said.

"Jeff," Conroy said.

Conroy pressed the speakerphone button so that his wife could listen in.[18]

Jeff told his parents that he was under arrest and explained that he had stabbed a guy, that the man was dead, and that he was being charged with manslaughter.[19] Later, Conroy would swear that his son never said he had stabbed a man. "A father would remember something like that," he told me. Conroy advised Jeff to stop talking.

Listen to me, Jeff. They are not your friends, Jeff. Keep your mouth shut.

Jeff refused to allow the videotaping after that.

Conroy hung up and called a lawyer. Then he drove to the police precinct and begged and pleaded to see Jeff. But the police wouldn't let him, and Conroy, his chest hurting and his anger boiling, had to leave without his son.[20]

It would take Jeff thirty-one hours to get out of the precinct, and when he did, he didn't go home.

CHAPTER 8

A TORN COMMUNITY

Mayor Paul Pontieri was reading the paper in his backyard when he received the call at about 10:30 a.m. It was a fine Sunday morning. Yellow and red leaves from nearby maple trees fluttered in the breeze. The sun was peeking from behind the clouds, and the temperature hovered around fifty degrees. As had been his habit for the last thirty years, Pontieri had already gone to seven thirty Mass at St. Francis de Sales, a Catholic church on Ocean Avenue. Afterward, as was also his habit, he had bought some knot rolls, Italian bread, and coffee, and had visited his mother and one of his sisters, who lived nearby. They had coffee and a quick chat.[1]

He went home after that, expecting to have a relaxing day. His children were grown, his wife, a busy woman who worked for the Southampton school district, always had things to do, and there was nothing on his mayoral agenda for that day. The elections were over—just five days earlier, 53 percent of the county had voted for Obama—and Pontieri himself had been easily reelected since he had run unopposed. All that awaited him this morning of November 9 was the paper and more coffee. Then the phone call changed the course of his day and, as he would soon find, the course of his mayoralty.

There has been a death in the street, someone from the county executive's office told him. The news startled Pontieri because there had been no murders in the village since he had been elected in 2004. He could recall one or perhaps two murders over the prior twenty-five years.[2]

Pontieri hung up and set to work. Not having dealt with a murder before, he did what any citizen would do: he called the police. The dispatcher told him that there had been a fight and some kids had been arrested. That was all he knew. After the call, Pontieri tried to go back to the paper but couldn't concentrate. Restless and unhappy with the scant information he had gathered, he drove to the police station, about five minutes from his house, and spoke with a detective, who gave him a very brief description of what had happened and told him he would know more once they were done with the investigation. Some of the young men involved had not yet been interviewed.

One thing was clear, the detective told him: six of the seven alleged perpetrators were white, and the victim was a Latino man who lived in Patchogue, a few blocks from the house where Pontieri had grown up and where his mother still lived. Not one of the young men under investigation for the killing lived in the village, but they lived nearby, close enough so that Pontieri was sure that people he knew were bound to know who they were or at least know their parents. Close enough so that some kids in the village surely had played baseball or football with at least one of the attackers. Close enough, Pontieri thought, to create the perception that Patchogue was a dangerous place.

Pontieri went home and began calling the village trustees. There was nothing to do and seemingly nothing to prepare for, he told them. He was simply alerting them so that they wouldn't be surprised when they watched the evening news or read the next morning's paper.

At around 4:30 or 5:00 p.m. he finally got the call he was expecting from the county executive's office, and that's when he learned that detectives were treating the case as a hate crime. Pontieri was an educated man, an educator himself, and a baby boomer. He had been a young man during the civil rights movement, and he was familiar with the term "hate crimes." But his idea of a hate crime was something that happened elsewhere, to other people. He couldn't understand it, and then he remembered the call he had received just a few days before from Jean Kaleda, the librarian.

This, he realized, was what Kaleda had been talking about. This was the type of attack the immigrants in the library feared. The crime the night before had not been an aberration after all. A young man had killed Lucero, but he knew the entire village would soon be implicated in the crime. How could I not have known that this was going on? Pontieri berated himself. Something else was bothering him as well. It was inconceivable to him that when he had heard the name of the victim, Marcelo Lucero, he had not recognized it. He took pride in knowing virtually everyone in town—not because he was the mayor but because Patchogue was his home. It was clear to him then that he hadn't been paying attention. He should have realized that the streets had not been safe for some residents, those more vulnerable to abuse and attacks precisely because they were newcomers, unknown to most, unknown even to him. He resolved to change that and to bridge the gap with people he previously hadn't really noticed.

Days later, when a reporter from the *New York Times* called, Pontieri was already steeped in his new role as the conciliatory mayor, the mayor for all—especially those whose names he didn't know. "It is imperative that we bridge the divide," he told the reporter, "and realize that the things we have in common far out-number those that divide us."[3]

But his urging was premature, and his hope for unity was far too idealistic for a village that had suddenly become the new ground zero in the immigration debate.

On Sunday morning, Denise and Warren Overton were frantic with worry. They had driven around all night looking for their son. They kept calling his cell phone number and getting his voice mail. Their hope was that Chris had found a girl he liked and was with her, turning off his phone so his parents wouldn't interrupt his romance. It was uncharacteristic but possible, they reasoned.[4]

Eventually the Overtons drove to Alyssa's home and asked about their son. She didn't know where Chris was and didn't know where Jeff Conroy lived, but she had the phone number of a cousin of José Pacheco. That led to a conversation with José's aunt, and an address for the Conroys. But when the Overtons got to the house where they thought Jeff lived and where they hoped they would find their son, no one answered the door. They walked around the house, kicked a basement window, banged on the door, and yelled out their son's name. Nothing. They had the wrong house.

For some reason, it never occurred to them to call the police. Sometime around 3:00 p.m., as she was talking on her cell phone with the equally worried mother of José, the Overtons' home phone rang. It was the police saying that her son was at the Fifth Precinct. There had been an altercation, she was told. No, no, no, no, no, Overton's brain was practically screaming, not again, as she ran out the door and sped to the police station, a one-story tan brick building framed by Doric-style columns. A detective met her at the entrance and told her what Overton was not prepared to hear. There had been a murder last night, he said, and Christopher was implicated. Overton dropped to her knees, sobbing and yelling that her son was innocent. He didn't do anything! I know he didn't!

The police said she was not allowed to see her son, and so Overton, dejected and in so much pain that she felt as if she had been flayed, went home and waited for the call the detectives had told her she would soon receive from her son. She didn't have to wait long.

Chris called and told her not to worry. All was well. Jeff had killed a man, but he, Chris, hadn't done anything. No, he told her, he didn't need a lawyer. He would be coming home the following day. I'm here only as a witness, he told her.

Overton called a lawyer anyway. It would prove to be a sound decision.

"My son has not been home since," Overton told me, tears running down her cheeks, during an interview in her cozy home in the early fall of 2012, overlooking the marshlands in East Patchogue.

The Reverend Dwight Wolter woke up on the morning of November 9 somewhat tired and with a lot on his mind.[5] He had gone to bed late but content after a peace concert in his church, the Congregational Church of Patchogue. Billed as a "World Peace Party," the event had featured a drummer and high school kids who had built their own drums. They had sat and played in a giant drumming circle in the church, joined by members of the congregation and the community.[6] This morning, Wolter had to deliver a sermon at 10:00 a.m., which he had titled "A New Heaven, a New Earth, a New Community, and a New Life." Based on Revelation 21: 1–6, the sermon included prescient passages:

> We need reminders that generations of our predecessors sacrificed and worked hard to make life easier for us. But over time, we have come to assume that our lives are (or should be) predictable and secure, and that our cherished routines

should never be interrupted. We open the front door in the morning and the newspaper is always there.

But no matter how secure we try to make our existence, something eventually comes along to remind us just how tentative is our grasp on life as we know it. We are only one phone call, one lab test, or one news event away from the bottom falling out of our world. And chaos is always looking for an opportunity to threaten creation. Not one of us is completely safe. No one is immune to death.

As a single father of a twelve-year-old boy and the leader of a congregation of more than 360 members, Wolter was busy. In church by 9:00 a.m. most days, he didn't really follow a routine. He worked seven days and two to four nights a week, though not all day or all night. His days were long but varied. A sick patient to visit, a concert to organize, a school meeting to attend, a fundraiser to launch.

Staying busy was soothing for Wolter, fifty-eight, because for years he had led a troubled and painful life. A rare childhood syndrome had required him to use a wheelchair or a pair of crutches for the first five years of his life. His mother, herself disabled, blamed him for her inability to walk, and his father berated him constantly. Both his parents were alcoholics, and Wolter, though talented and ambitious, turned to alcohol and pills in his youth and dropped out of college. For twenty years, he lived in Manhattan and made a living as a maître d' in restaurants such as Tavern on the Green and as the writer of six self-help books—three of which are on the topic of forgiveness. In his books, he has described his harrowing childhood and his path to recovery, as well as the lingering emotional scars of those early years.

He grew up without religion. The first time he entered a church he was thirty-four and couldn't even understand the service, confused about what book to follow: the Psalter or the hymnal. In 1986, when he was thirty-six, he found a spiritual home in the Unitarian Church of All Souls on the Upper East Side of Manhattan, one of the largest and most influential congregations in the United States. The pastor there, Dr. Forrest Church, the son of former senator Frank Forrester Church III, must have seen through Wolter. After reading Wolter's books, he suggested he enter the ministry. Wolter resisted at first, but soon came to understand that the message of self-empowerment that he preached in his books would be best expressed from the pulpit of a church.

Wolter finished his long-abandoned bachelor's degree and then, three years after receiving his pastor's advice, became a student at Union Theological Seminary in New York City. Upon graduation he was baptized as a Christian and ordained at the Riverside Church, a city landmark with a long history of social activism. Soon after, he became the pastor of a church in Florida.

When the opportunity to work in Patchogue came, he accepted the offer. After ten years in Florida, he was ready for a change. He had visited Patchogue in the spring of 2006, during the interview process, and was intrigued by what he had seen. In the shuttered downtown businesses he saw suburban blight. In the faces of people strolling Main Street in work clothes he saw the changing demographics of America. Patchogue would be a challenge, he knew, but also an opportunity to distance himself from very sad memories.

The previous year, his six-year-old daughter, Maya, had died in a car accident in Florida. When Wolter got to the hospital and saw his daughter's body on a gurney, he fixated on her open blue eyes. Her beautiful eyes were among the few body parts not damaged by the crash. He ended up donating them along with her heart valves. A move to New York would allow him and his son, Casey, of whom he had custody after a divorce, to continue healing away from the sites that constantly reminded them of Maya's death.

Wolter began his ministry in Patchogue in September 2006, and for more than two years Patchogue delivered exactly what Wolter had been looking for: some peace and healing but also the challenges of ministering to a mostly homogeneous congregation in a changing town.

He was proud of his church—the oldest in Patchogue, built in 1793—and of his congregation, which had been founded in 1773, three years before the Declaration of Independence was adopted. The church was made of brown stone, and some of its many stained-glass windows are rare, original Tiffany windows. In the afternoons, when the sun filtered through the windows, the walls of the church and of his office took on the colorful hues of the glass panes: pinks and blues and mauve mixed together with the blond wood of the altar and the benches. It was so beautiful that Wolter, who has the soul of an artist, saw the hand of God behind his move from Florida. Who, if not God, could have brought him to this place of beauty?

Yet certain things troubled him about his new home. For a man accustomed to enjoying the arts and a somewhat cosmopolitan life, Patchogue did not offer much. One of the most popular businesses on Main Street was a spanking new laundromat. Wolter had never felt farther from the city in his adult life. Paradoxically, he had felt closer to his idea of New York when he lived near Tampa or Daytona, in Florida, than now when he lived an hour's drive from Manhattan.

He knew there was diversity in Patchogue. He could see a constant stream of Hispanics just by peering outside his office, but none were knocking on his door. He couldn't understand how the village had not been altered by their presence. Where were the *empanadas* he liked to eat? The activities for and by Hispanics? Where did they live? It was as if two realities coexisted in Patchogue, one superimposed over the other, never really touching, never interacting. He figured things would have to change soon, but he wasn't sure how.

Once, he had come up with an idea to hold an event in his church where people from all nationalities and creeds were invited to share a plate of food and a story. Wolter thought he would need about $3,000 for the event. He went around asking for money and got legislator Jack Eddington to commit to it, but to access public funds Wolter needed to find an organization that would allow him to use its tax-exempt 501c3 status. He couldn't find any takers. Wolter concluded that Patchogue was just not ready to accept its own multicultural reality. Where do they think they are living? he wondered as he observed white ladies in their sweater sets and coiffed hair walking past his church and not even glancing at the workers walking alongside them. Whatever idea they had of Long Island, and, in particular, of their corner of the world in Suffolk County, Wolter knew the reality was something else. He feared that one day that reality would finally hit everyone in the face with such force that no one in Patchogue would be able to deny it anymore.

The day came sooner than Wolter could have anticipated.

Still in his pajamas in the early morning of November 9, Wolter poured himself a cup of coffee and turned on the television to watch the news. A news item stopped him: a Latino had been killed in Patchogue the night before. He didn't know why, but his intuition told him that there was more to the story than what the reporter was saying. The assailants were already in custody, the reporter said, adding mistakenly that the seven were white.

White against brown, Wolter thought.

Without really thinking about what he would do next, Wolter grabbed a pair of pants and put them on over his pajamas. He got in the car and drove around, expecting the worst. If seven teenage Latinos had killed a white man, he knew, the streets would be burning already. He wanted to know how Patchogue was reacting to the news and he wanted to try to figure out who the murdered man was, where he lived.

But the streets were quiet. Where is everybody? he wondered. His phone rang. It was a friend who had more information than he did and directed him to the street where Lucero used to live. Wolter had never heard of the street, but he found it as soon as he turned a corner and noticed the news vans with their satellite antennas.

Reporters were milling around, and a group of Latino men crowded the sidewalk. One stood out among the others; his face was ashen and his eyes were red-rimmed. Wolter figured he was related to the victim and approached. He tried to get a conversation going, but, not knowing Spanish, he felt like an intruder. When a television camera began to trail him, he thought it was time to leave.

Back at the church, Wolter easily managed to work the events of the day into his prepared text, in which he reflected on the first sermon he had delivered in Patchogue. That first sermon was titled "Traditions and Transitions," and in it he had explained how the best way to get through a transition was to root it in tradition. This time, he reminded his flock that their church, now his as well, had a long tradition of helping others in times of trouble. And the community was afflicted now, in need of help. Latinos were part of the community, everyone knew that, but did anybody in the church know any of them? Did they know their neighbors? The idea of lily-white Long Island was gone, he said, adding that he anticipated that the killing of the immigrant—Wolter didn't know his name yet—would be a momentous event in the life of the village. His sermon also opened the door wide to the possibility—indeed, the necessity—of change:

> Many people, even right here in church, see this as mere wishful thinking, the stuff of dreamers. They look around this pain-filled world and realize we have been waiting for shalom for over two thousand years and with a sigh they close the book on God's promise to us. The chance of the dream coming true is simply too remote to get worked-up about.

But every new reality begins with a dream and a prayer. And so don't talk to me about the statistical likelihood of success. There are too many awesome examples of lives, families, and communities transformed into places of peace. Despite strong opposition from some people, despite what we have been through, and despite awareness of how difficult spiritual work can be; many people simply will not abandon their dream. It is within the reach of the Congregational Church of Patchogue to build the church of our dreams, and to play an active part in the spiritual transformation of our church and community.

No one had mentioned the phrase "hate crime" to him yet, but to Wolter the hate portion of the crime was obvious. He had felt it brewing for a long time; it was almost predictable. Though he was sure he had never heard about another Latino being attacked in Patchogue, even in Florida he had known about Farmingville and the animosity the events there had created in the entire region.

Later that day, he called Mayor Pontieri and told him he wanted to be helpful in any way he could.

Wolter wasn't the only one who felt compelled to help, to do something, anything. The moment the live satellite trucks arrived on the morning of November 9, nearly everyone in Patchogue understood that they had only two options: hide from the glare of the cameras and go on with life as usual or face the cameras—and the world—and help the media shape a more complete, nuanced narrative of Patchogue. Most people were torn, but many chose the latter. It was as if a brutal action, such as the killing of a man because of his ethnicity, deserved an equally strong and physical response. But what to do?

Lola Quesada, a patrol officer in the Third Police Precinct, the precinct that covers some of the towns bordering Patchogue and Medford, thought she knew what to do when she read about the murder in the news. First, she sat down her boys—ages twenty-two, twenty, and nineteen—and asked them if they had ever been bullied or taunted or discriminated against because of their ethnicity. You know, she told them, this could have been you. They said they had seen others being bullied because of their poor language skills, but not them. Born in the United States, her children felt comfortable and untroubled by their own mixed background: Quesada is from Ecuador, and her husband's grandparents were Mexican, Puerto Rican, Honduran, and English.[7]

The family lived about a fifteen-minute drive from Patchogue, but she had no idea that fellow Ecuadorians were being harassed in a place she considered idyllic to raise a family. It wasn't as if she were naive to the perils of being an immigrant. When she had been pregnant with her first child, she and her husband had started looking for a house to buy. The broker kept taking them to see houses in low-income neighborhoods. The houses didn't look right, Quesada remembers thinking. Aren't there nicer houses for sale somewhere on Long Island? Then it dawned on her that they were being the victims of housing discrimination. She ditched the broker and found the house she wanted, brand-new and comfortable in an eastern Long Island town, where the majority of the residents are non-Hispanic whites and solidly middle class.

Quesada arrived in the United States legally with her family in 1970, when she was nine, and settled in Queens. Before leaving Ecuador the family had contemplated a choice of three states, California, Texas, or New York, and ultimately chose New York because they had family in New York City. Her father was a lawyer but didn't have a license to practice in the United States, so he became a social worker for the city of New York. Her mother worked as a seamstress. Quesada married young, at twenty-one, and became a nurse, but in her late thirties she had a change of heart. She decided to become a police officer. Her decision was based both on practical and sentimental reasons. She thought she would make more money and have better benefits, and she also thought becoming a cop was the right thing to do, a way to give back.

There was something about the discipline and rigor of training for the police officer's exam that appealed to her. "My father always said I was capable of doing anything I wanted," she told me when we met at a coffee shop on Main Street in Patchogue in January 2012. "And he thought it [police officer] was the most honorable job in the world." Quesada worked hard with a friend who trains athletes for the Special Olympics, and at forty became a police officer. When asked about her ambitions in one of her tests at the police academy, she wrote that some day she wanted to be an inspector, a rank just below chief in the police nomenclature.

For six years, she had worked as a cop, patrolling the streets of her precinct. Then Lucero was killed, and the shock of his death jolted Quesada out of her routine. She felt she had to do something radical. She read in the newspaper that Levy, the county executive, was looking for a liaison to the Hispanic community. She had experience and credibility in her community, where, she said, "she had her ear to the ground." Quesada wanted that job. "I needed to be part of the change," she told me.

Still distraught over Lucero's death, she went to visit her mother who had moved back to Ecuador. She was with her when the inspector called with the news she had been waiting to hear: the job was hers.

Julio Espinoza heard about the murder at home, before he went to work that Sunday. Someone called to tell him, and Espinoza immediately recalled the quiet man who often came to his shop to buy a telephone card to call his mother in Ecuador. Espinoza got in touch with some friends and customers, and little by little started piecing together the story. By Sunday evening, it was clear that Lucero had been killed because he was Hispanic. What gave him away? Espinoza wondered. Was it the shade of brown of his skin? His accent? Had he even spoken to his attackers? Was it the way he walked: head down and hands deep in his pockets to avoid unwanted stares?[8]

Espinoza was in despair. He had two children in the same high school where, he had heard, the attackers were students. What if his children became a target too? How could he protect them from people who pounced without provocation? His children had told him for years that the school was divided, with Hispanics often being the subject of taunts and even harassment. But he never thought it would come to violence, much less a murder. For the first time since leaving Ecuador he questioned whether leaving home and building a life in a town so far from everything familiar to him had been such a good idea.

For now, the only thing to do was to go pay his respects to Marcelo Lucero. Since no funeral or religious services had been announced yet, Espinoza drove straight to the morgue. But he couldn't get in, and the last thing he wanted now was to attract attention to himself. Espinoza drove home—carefully.

By Monday morning everyone knew what had happened, even those who had been out of town, like Jean Kaleda, the librarian. She was on the deck of the New London ferry, coming back from a trip to Cape Cod with a group of friends, and enjoying the last hours of a relaxing long weekend when she heard about it.[9]

Her friend Sally Rein, a forty-year resident of Patchogue, had received a call from her husband who told her that an Ecuadorian man had been killed by a group of teenagers. It was all over the news. Ashen, Rein relayed the news to Kaleda. Did you know a Marcelo Lucero? Rein asked Kaleda, who suddenly felt sick. This is it, she thought. This must be connected to what the English learners at the library had told her just a few days before. Her stomach lurched at the thought that it had come to this. She was stunned at the audacity of teenagers harassing a grown man simply because he was Latino, and horrified that the harassment had resulted in murder.

The rest of the trip home, Kaleda stayed on the deck, thinking long and hard about what had transpired and how it connected to her fears about the world in general and her sense that humankind never really learned from past mistakes. She also wondered if any of the friends she had made in Patchogue from Gualaceo knew Marcelo Lucero or maybe even were related to him. And she asked herself, though she knew the answer, whether she could have done anything to prevent his death.

As Kaleda was returning home, Gilda Ramos, the Spanish-speaking librarian who had been so instrumental in reaching out to the community, was arriving at work. In the morning, she had watched the news and heard about the killing. In her car, she learned more about the story on the radio. Now she had the victim's name and a possible motive for the murder: hatred. When she got to the library everyone wanted to know what she, as a Hispanic herself, thought. Ramos gave everyone the same answer: unbelievable.[10]

She looked for Kaleda but then remembered she was on vacation. She called Kaleda at home and on her cell phone anyway. Just leaving the message made her feel she was accomplishing something. She thought, with sadness, that steps should have been taken earlier to prevent this murder. Her students had told her about the harassment, and what had she done? Nothing other than tell her supervisor, who, she knew, had told the mayor. A meeting had been scheduled, she knew, but now it was too late. Why hadn't anybody done anything about it? Why did it have to get this far? Now there was a dead man, and the whole country, if not the world, was looking at Patchogue as a place of hatred and intolerance.

Ramos was deep in thought when she saw the mayor approach. Pontieri was upset and worried and wanted to know what to do. What now? Ramos didn't know, but she told him she would help in any way she could to alleviate fears among Hispanics and to calm everyone else. The scheduled meeting with the community would have to take place, they agreed, but a week later, the following Wednesday, November 19. That would give them enough time to get through the difficult days immediately after the murder and to pay their respect to the Lucero family. By the way, did anybody know what was happening to the body? Was there a funeral, a Mass, anything planned?

No one knew. It was a tense and confusing Monday.

The next day, county executive Steve Levy called the murder "a one-day story" and added that the killing had received undue attention because he had been very vocal about his views on immigration. The implication was that Lucero's had been a routine death, if any violent death can be called routine.[11] Two days later Levy retracted his words. He wrote a letter to *Newsday*, the local daily, in which he said he had made a mistake. "The horrible incident is indeed more than a one-day story," he wrote.[12] He was right.

On November 12, Wednesday, Mayor Pontieri, accompanied by his wife, went to Gilda Ramos's evening class for English learners. With Ramos translating his words, he told the students that he was very worried about what had happened and that he would do what he could so that they would never again be afraid to walk the streets of Patchogue. Pontieri hoped that the fifteen students there would begin to spread the word that he cared and that Patchogue was safe.[13]

Earlier that day, Reverend Wolter was invited to speak at a community event in front of the middle school his son Casey attended. Several civic leaders and elected officials were invited as well, and some were very angry. Levy was not there. Eddington was, and he urged everyone to work together. He conceded that a "terrible incident" had taken place in their midst, but, he said, "Let it not define our county, our community and our town." He also appealed to the state to be "proactive" and not "reactive" by funding tolerance-focused educational programs in schools and additional social workers. Several others spoke, including Luis Valenzuela, a respected civic leader who was the executive director of the Long Island Immigrant Alliance.[14]

"This is indeed a tragic, tragic event. It is something that wounds the community. It wounds our humanity and yet we need to be mindful that there have been circumstances that promote a climate of intolerance here in Suffolk County," he said in a somber tone. Gathering steam as he went on, he issued a challenge that sounded more like a threat: "We challenge the legislators in this community not to ever introduce another anti-Latino bill."

Eddington, his hands folded in front of him and staring straight ahead, didn't seem to react to Valenzuela's words, as if he had not been one of the legislators who had introduced bills perceived as anti-Latino. There was loud applause, and voices from the audience asked, "Where is he?" Everyone knew that Valenzuela was referring to Levy. "Where is Levy?" voices went on. "He didn't show up!" someone yelled.

Valenzuela let the moment pass and went on to explain why the death of Marcelo Lucero had not been a surprise. "Fourteen months ago, right in this community, we had a demonstration, and the theme was hate speech equals hate crime," he reminded everyone, and he ended his talk with the most poignant of all battle cries: "Never again!"

Wolter knew that the angry tone of the rally was justified, but he thought that something more than anger was needed. He looked around and noticed that the majority of those present were Latinos. When his turn to speak came, he tried to change the tone from that of merely criticism and blame to empowerment and cooperation. He urged everyone to follow him in a four-word chant, "How can I help?" One way to help, he said, was to donate money to the Lucero family for the return of the body to Ecuador, which is what his family had requested. He had already begun calling civic organizations and asking them to make financial contributions to defray funeral and family expenses, which he knew would occur.[15]

"If you don't have the money right now, I'll wait two or three minutes," he said, and some on the stage and the audience chuckled.

Other community leaders addressed the crowd as well, but no one captured Wolter's attention like a young man who suddenly leaped on the stage and grabbed the microphone. He was wearing a blindingly white T-shirt, a dark denim jacket, large sunglasses that hid his eyes, and a checkered cap worn low over his forehead, but Wolter recognized him as the same man he had seen in the group of Latinos standing near Lucero's home. As Wolter would soon learn, he had been right in assuming then that the young man knew Lucero. He was Lucero's younger brother, Joselo.

When Joselo took the stage, everyone listened. He had a quiet dignity about him, the kind that comes from searing pain and from knowing one has been wronged.

"I'm going to take these glasses off so you can see an immigrant," Joselo said, and Wolter was riveted.[16]

For about five minutes, he talked about his color, his features—the immigrant in him—but he also talked about his loneliness and his pain. He said he had received so much support that he felt "among family." He described his brother as a hardworking man who was trying to make a living while helping the family he had left behind. "We are simple people," he said, and he pleaded with the audience to help to stop hate and to "try to live together."

About the young men who had attacked his brother, he said, "I don't hate them, but I want justice."

His message resonated with Wolter, who feared that the killing of Lucero would divide the community even further. In Joselo he recognized not only a young man in pain but also a potential leader, someone who could use the death of his brother to try to build bridges. Wolter had been following the news on television since Sunday, and invariably he saw white or brown faces talking about the crime, but he didn't see any mingling. He didn't see anyone crossing the aisle and standing with the other. Wolter thought he could be the white face among the brown faces.

When Joselo got off the stage, Wolter followed.

Joselo had not wanted to come to the United States. His mother had made that choice for him. She told him he was leaving four days before he was scheduled to leave. Joselo was in shock when he heard, fearing his "one-way ticket" would forever separate him from everything he knew, from his country and his family.[17]

In time he came to understand his mother's reasons. Shortly before he left, he had been kicked out of school for bad behavior, and he had been restless at home, hanging out with a group of fourteen friends. But, one by one, his friends had started to make their way to the United States. At the same time, Doña Rosario was worried that her son would get in trouble, or, worse, that he would be recruited to fight in a skirmish between Peru and Ecuador over border territories, which began in November of 1994, escalated into war in January of 1995, and ended a month later. The conflict, known as the Cenepa War, left a bloody trail: about five hundred soldiers dead from both sides.[18]

By then Joselo was gone. He arrived in Patchogue two years after his brother.

"In some ways she want to make me a better person," he told a documentarian shortly after his brother's death. "She want to, you know, help me grow up, you know. Cuz we don't have many hopes. We don't have many opportunities in my country. So I don't go to school. It was really a hard decision for her. Either way, she can keep me there and send me to the war or send me here."

At the beginning, living on Long Island was "like a nightmare," he said. His brother, whom he had seen as a father figure since the death of their father when Joselo was six, was working all the time. His friends, who were so excited to see him at first, were busy as well. Everyone worked, went to school, or had responsibilities. Everything was far. Joselo couldn't just walk outside and meet friends, as he used to do at home. All of a sudden he was alone in a place where he did not know the language. He was nineteen.

"I just see in the mirror myself," he said. "And I was like, uh, I don't know what to do."

He cried often. "Mom, this is not for me," he sobbed on the phone with his mother more than once. Not only did he miss his family but he also missed a young woman he had fallen in love with and had hoped to marry. For the first two weeks, he would dream about Gualaceo every night. He would wake up in the morning and wonder, "Where am I?" Slowly he came to understand that there was no way back, and that he needed to find work and grow up. After a year sharing a place with his brother, he moved out and began living on his own.

Still, Joselo saw his brother as his protector and guide. The two talked all the time and saw each other often. The Friday before Lucero was killed, they had talked for about forty-five minutes. They had gone out to dinner and then parked by the train station and continued talking. As he was getting ready to leave, Joselo, who sometimes called his brother "Loquito," as in little crazy one, said, "I'll see you tomorrow or later."

"Okay," Lucero replied.

Then, when Joselo was walking off toward his own car, Lucero surprised him with a shout: "Loquito! Take care of yourself."

That was the last thing Joselo heard his brother say. The next day, Lucero went to work and Joselo went out with friends. They didn't see each other or talk all day, which was not unusual.

On Sunday morning, Joselo was still in bed when he heard pounding on the front door. He jumped from the bed and looked out the bedroom window. There was a car outside, so Joselo went to the door to see who it was.

It was a detective, showing him his badge. Joselo was surprised because he had never been in trouble with the police in Patchogue. "Are you Joselo?" the detective asked. Joselo said, "No, I'm not Joselo." He had a weird feeling. He was scared and thought that whatever they wanted to tell him, he didn't want to hear, so he decided to lie. But the detective pressed on. "This is something really serious. Do you know Marcelo or do you have any relationship with Marcelo Lucero?" The mention of his brother's name made Joselo focus. "Yes, of course. He's my brother," he replied.

The detective then asked to come in. They needed to talk. He asked Joselo to sit down. At that moment, a cousin called Joselo and asked him if he was all right. Joselo had no idea why his cousin was calling, but thought it was related to the detective's visit. "I don't think so," he said. "I'll call you back." He hung up and expectantly turned to the detective.

"What I'm going to tell you is something really hard and I want you to take it in the calmest way possible," the detective said. "Your brother was murdered last night. Seven kids attacked him and stabbed him."

At that moment, Joselo would recall later, he did not believe the detective. "I simply said, 'No, this is not right. It's not true.'" He picked up his phone and called his brother's cell phone number, but of course no one answered. He called a second time. No answer. Then the detective said, "He's not going to answer. We have his cell phone."

"That was the worst moment of my life," Joselo said.

When he got off the stage, Joselo walked south on South Ocean Avenue. A group of Latinos were huddled on the corner waiting for him, but Wolter was not deterred. He felt as if God was taking him in that direction. Like a leaf in the wind, he let himself be guided. Out of habit, he reached in and pulled out his business card. Oh, great, he thought to himself. Another white guy with a business card. He put it away and approached the men, who seemed to have built a protective layer around Joselo. Wolter asked for their permission to speak, and to his surprise his first words to Joselo were, Where is your brother's body? Until that moment, he hadn't known what he was going to say or what his role in this tragedy would be.

Joselo appeared surprised and relieved at the question. His shoulders dropped, as if releasing tension. His face relaxed. Why? he asked. Because it's been a few days, Wolter said. What are you going to do with the body?

A brief discussion ensued. No one knew what to do, but Wolter knew that shipping the body of a murdered undocumented Latino to Ecuador would be a complicated, multistep process. There was no point in saying that to Joselo, Wolter reasoned, and changed the topic. Are you going to have a service to put some beauty and healing into this?

I don't know, Joselo said. Maybe at the funeral home.

A funeral home, it's not going to be big enough, Wolter said. Then he pointed to the tower of his church, the tallest structure in town. I'm Reverendo Wolter, he said, trying to reach out with a word in Spanish.

Oh, said Joselo. That's your church?

No, Wolter replied. That's your church. Then proceeded to offer it for the service. He gave Joselo choices: You can have the service in the morning, afternoon, at night. You choose the preacher, the language, the music. Whatever you want.

Joselo agreed and said he would call the funeral home.

But Wolter knew that too could be cumbersome for Joselo to handle alone. The body was still in the morgue. There was an investigation going on. You know what, he said, I'll talk to the funeral home.

Shortly after their talk, Joselo went to Wolter's church to plan the service for his brother. The Reverend Allan Ramírez, a local Ecuadorian-born pastor and an advocate for immigrants, would play a role in the service. A friend of the family had offered to sing. The rest, Joselo said, he wanted Wolter to handle.

The first thing Wolter did was to make the decision to close the service to the media. He wanted the service to be solemn and memorable. The idea of photographers focusing their lenses on Lucero's corpse repelled him. He also feared that, as rattled as everyone's nerves were, the memorial could turn into a forum to air differences. Already Wolter had felt the sting of criticism. Several of his parishioners and others in the community had criticized him for offering the church for the service. Was he siding with the Latinos? Whose side was he on anyway?

The night before the funeral service, Wolter had attended a community meeting at the local synagogue. Several civic leaders and elected officials were there, and some spoke. But the meeting had deteriorated as many began to hurl insults at legislator Jack Eddington. They criticized him for introducing legislation, mostly unsuccessfully, that they described as anti-immigrant.

Eddington, who was trained as a social worker and had been taught to solve problems, didn't perceive his attempts at improving the Patchogue-Medford area as anti-immigrant. He viewed them as practical solutions that could benefit all in the community, including immigrants. If, for example, Eddington was concerned that there were too many accidents at a particular intersection and a study revealed that the accidents were caused because cars stopped to pick up immigrants looking for work, the obvious solution to him was to prevent the laborers from standing in the streets soliciting work. To him that seemed logical. To many in the community, that seemed racist.[19]

Eddington deeply resented being called "racist." Born in 1947 and raised in a housing project under the shadow of the Queensboro Bridge in Long Island City, he had been the victim of black and Latino bullies who singled him out for being white, red-haired, freckled, and Irish. His body still bears the scars from being shot with a zip gun—a crude homemade weapon—when he was about ten years old. "I couldn't understand why they were attacking me," he told me the first time we spoke in 2010. Later he understood. "They were doing to the whites what the whites had done to them," he said, referring to the African American kids who had terrorized him. In an unpublished memoir that he wrote a few years ago, he described how he viewed the world when he was young: "It can be a hostile place. A place where you must always be prepared for an attack. Where you must always be vigilant and armed for defense."

He had found no respite at home. If he misbehaved, his father would hit him with a contraption he called "cat o' nine tails," a foot-long wooden stick with nine two-foot-long strips of rawhide. "It would leave welts on my back and often break the skin. And the strange thing about it is that I never thought to tell anyone or complain to anyone or seek help. Who would I go to?" He writes that he was beaten once or twice a week with that instrument of torture.

Eventually, after a four-year stint in the navy, he became a clinical and school social worker and an educational consultant with the US Department of Education and the New York State Department of Substance Abuse Services. He got into politics, as a member of the labor-backed Working Families Party and later as an Independent because he figured his training as a problem solver would help him find solutions to issues in his community. Instead, he said, he found very little willingness to compromise and even less common sense among his fellow legislators. He was first elected to the Suffolk County legislature in 2005 and was reelected twice. Most of his time in office, he was the chairman of the Public Safety Committee, which means that many of the complaints against immigrants landed on his desk.

"No one wants you to be fair," he told me often. "They want you to be on their side."

The complaints varied, but mostly he heard from people who, like himself, worried that Hispanic immigrants, who remained stubbornly monolingual, hadn't been able to assimilate in the community as quickly as earlier waves of immigrants. And why is that? he pondered. Eddington didn't know, but he did know that advocates for immigrants spent all their time and energy criticizing those they perceived as anti-immigrants, such as him, and yet no one was helping the new arrivals. Why can't they teach them how to properly dispose of the garbage, for example? Eddington wondered. Why do they keep parking their cars on the grass? Why do they sit on the lawn drinking beer? Why can't they live in families, like everyone else, instead of having twenty-seven single men living together in a house meant for four? Why haven't they been told that it is not a good idea to play volleyball in the backyard until the late hours of the night? Those games had become noisy, unlicensed businesses where food and beer were sold, while everybody else on the block tried to sleep. During his years in the legislature, he had personally shown up with the police at several volleyball games to stop them.

These immigrants, Eddington concluded, "were not following the rules." But the social worker in him could also see that the Hispanic immigrants probably didn't know any better. Unlike earlier immigrants, who had migrated with their families for the most part, the immigrants from Ecuador or Mexico or El Salvador settling in Suffolk County tend to be men who had left their families at home, poor and with little or no formal education.

When Eddington was running for reelection in 2008, there was not a community meeting or activity he went to where someone didn't stop him to ask, What are you doing about illegal immigrants? Eddington told them what he always said to such requests, Let me see what I can do. In fact, he had already done plenty. In 2006, he cosponsored a bill to require companies doing business with the county to certify that they had verified that their employees were authorized to work. In other words, hiring of undocumented immigrants was not allowed. The bill became law. He had also on occasion referred to Hispanic immigrants in ways that, he could now see, had been interpreted at best as insensitive, if not racist.

So Eddington was an easy target.

The night before Lucero's funeral, as Eddington stood in the middle of a circle at Temple Beth El, many in the audience blamed him for contributing to the atmosphere that had turned average teenagers into killers.

Undaunted, he attempted to communicate who he was and what he stood for. "Very few people here know Jack Eddington," he began. "They don't know me. They know the legislation. . . . I have not given up trying. I want to let you know that the people who are pointing the finger at me [have] not reached out to me."[20]

At that point some shouted, "Baloney!" To which Eddington replied, "When I do try, I get shouted down."

He kept talking, and the shouts subsided as he told the audience about his service in Vietnam and about his hope that everyone in Patchogue and Medford would get together to create a safer environment so that no one would be afraid to walk the streets at night. He ended his three-minute speech by quoting an Irish blessing that he had learned from his grandmother: "May God give you for every storm, a rainbow; for every tear, a smile; for every care, a promise; and a blessing in each trial. For every problem life sends, a faithful friend to share, and for every sigh, a sweet song and an answer for each prayer."

The next day, he did not attend the memorial service for Lucero. Levy did not attend either. The *Times* reported that Pontieri had asked Levy not to come.[21]

People had been lining up outside for hours before the Congregational Church of Patchogue opened its doors shortly after 5:00 p.m. on November 15, a week after Lucero's murder. The service crammed 1,452 people inside the church; 420 were able to find seats, but the rest stood in the aisles and around the back, while a few hundred more remained outside.[22]

Though emotions were high, it was a subdued event, with music—there were two choirs and a folk singer who sang in Spanish—and some deeply felt speeches by people who had known Lucero from Gualaceo. Joselo, dressed in a simple black suit jacket with a large silver cross dangling from a chain on his chest, stood by the casket embracing mourners. Dark circles framed his brown eyes.[23]

Wolter, who explained that he was speaking on behalf of Joselo, said that Lucero was a talkative man who relished a good debate. "If you held up a black stone," Wolter said, "he would claim it was deep blue."

Before the service, Wolter had arranged for a private viewing for the family who had yet to see the body. Almost two years later, Wolter would describe those forty-five minutes with Joselo and some friends and relatives as "very, very difficult."

"I heard howls of pain, emptiness, and horror gurgle up from the throats of the family as they looked upon the body of the young, Latino, undocumented, murdered Marcelo Lucero," Wolter wrote in a published essay.[24]

Once the service began, the coffin remained open near the altar: Lucero was dressed in a dark gray pin-striped suit, crisp white shirt, and gray- and blue-striped tie. He lay with his hands folded in a white-lined coffin piled with bouquets of flowers.[25] Next to the coffin, there was a painted framed portrait of him dressed in white and surrounded by a green-and-gold halo—as if he were a saint—with the Ecuadorian flag to his left and the flag of his hometown on the right. Copies of that image were printed on the offering boxes at the front of the church. Lucero's older sister, Catalina, who lived in Queens, sat in the front pew, along with Joselo. Representative Nydia M. Velázquez, a New

York City Democrat, sat next to Catalina and consoled her as she sobbed when people approached the casket to kiss her brother's forehead.[26]

"Perhaps what Marcelo accomplished in death is far greater than he might have been able to do in his life," Wolter said in his sermon. "What he has done for this community since his spirit left this earth is that he can possibly be the source of healing, hope, and reconciliation for a town that can reform itself."[27]

The Reverend Allan Ramirez took the pulpit as well, with a mixed message: he urged forgiveness but not without accountability first. "As believers, we also must be ready to extend forgiveness, even for Mr. Levy," he said, referring to Steve Levy. "For that forgiveness can only happen—it can only take place—when Mr. Levy can take responsibility for the way in which his legislation and his views may have influenced a climate of racial hatred."[28]

The mourners listened intently, their arms draped around each other, occasionally wiping away tears. At least one man appeared to have come straight from work—he was wearing dirty jeans and a hooded sweatshirt. A woman with a long braid wore a red-and-gold necklace, a traditional ornament among the Quechua Indians of Ecuador.[29]

After about an hour and a half, the service was over. It took more than thirty minutes to carry the casket from the front of the crowded church to the funeral home's car waiting outside. So many people approached to touch it one last time. When the casket was finally placed inside and the door was closed, many who knew him in life sighed in relief. Marcelo Lucero was finally going home.

CHAPTER 9

A LITTLE PIECE OF HEAVEN

The body of Marcelo Lucero arrived in Gualaceo on November 19, a Wednesday, in a gun-metal coffin draped with the yellow, blue, and red flag of Ecuador. It had arrived in Quito, the sprawling capital of the country the night before and traveled in a hearse overnight two hundred miles south to Lucero's hometown. Gualaceños congregated at the town's entrance to receive the hearse at about 9:30 a.m. Some held handmade signs that said in Spanish, "No to Yankee Racism," "No Human Being Is Illegal," and "Ecuador Is a Country of Peace."[1]

The coffin was carried through town by some of Lucero's friends. Two of them held up a sign made of flowers that spelled TUNAS, an acronym in Spanish for Everyone United, No One Walks Alone, noted *Newsday* reporter Bart Jones who traveled from Long Island to Gualaceo to await the arrival of the body. Hundreds of people—including children in school uniforms (girls in blue or red sweaters and plaid skirts, and boys in yellow shirts and black pants)—accompanied them in a procession that took them to City Hall "for a brief ceremony under a blazing sun."

The mayor declared three days of mourning. Flags were flown at half-staff and public employees were given the day off to attend the services.

"Some schoolgirls held hands and raised them in salute as the coffin passed. Others waved small white flags that said 'Paz'—'Peace.' Other people threw flower petals on the coffin as it went by, while some mourners watched from balconies. Lucero's mother and sister walked arm-in-arm behind the coffin as hundreds of mourners followed," Jones reported.

Finally the body lay at rest on the first floor of the house that Lucero's labor in New York had built, a house he so cherished that it had been carefully built to his specifications. It took two years and about $100,000 to get it built. His mother had been able to move in on Mother's Day, 2005. In phone calls and letters to his family, Lucero had detailed his vision: one space downstairs for a family business or shop, along with a two-bedroom apartment and a patio; one main floor with three bedrooms where he would live with his family; and a third floor for a two-bedroom apartment with a terrace to rent. From afar, he had chosen the light beige and rust floor tiles, the dark caramel wooden kitchen cabinets, the intricately carved wooden door for his suite off the living room, the paint colors for the walls with tones that complemented each other, and all the furniture—elegant but comfortable.[2]

The entertainment center had to be custom-made because the television set he wanted was too big to fit in any of the furniture available in the local stores. It was to occupy a prominent place in the living room, and, had Lucero moved back home, it would have been the first thing he saw as he opened the door of his bedroom. A portion of his ashes, inside a small box adorned with an angel and a copper image of the Virgin Mary, now rest on a shelf of the entertainment center, just above the television set. The bedroom that would have been his remains locked. No one likes to go in, but Doña Rosario, frail and deeply sad, indulged me when I visited in July 2010.

A large TV dominated the room, which is kept dark and cool by heavy, gold-colored curtains tightly closed against the sun. A queen bed was in the center of the room covered with a burgundy-and-gold duvet. For the flooring, Lucero chose warm wood, instead of the cool tiles more typically used in South American homes. The walk-in closet had nine shelves for clothing and shoes. A gray stuffed bunny sat on top of the unopened bags of clothing that awaited his arrival.

With a deep sigh, Doña Rosario left the room and returned the key to the pocket of her apron after locking the door behind her.

Marcelo Lucero's death was especially shocking to Gualaceños because murder is almost alien to their way of life and because it shattered their ideas about the United States as the land of prosperity and opportunity.

In their pretty, compact city there is hardly any violent crime, but there are plenty of social ills that most agree have been brought about by the emigration of hundreds of men, many of whom have left behind wives and children. Undoubtedly, those families lead more prosperous lives than they would have if the head of the household had stayed home. Yet, behind many of the attractive facades of the newly built outsized houses of Gualaceo, there is a lot of sadness and despair.

Divorce is rampant: men and women have sought lovers in their loneliness and created other families in Patchogue or in Gualaceo. Some children who long for the missing parent have turned to alcohol and drugs, and bitter relatives resent the success of those who left and think that they too ought to benefit from emigration. Especially worrisome for some here is that young people, assuming that everything that comes from the United

States must be good, have started to sport American garb: jeans torn at the knees, pants that fall perilously below the hips revealing checkered underwear, and nose rings and other facial piercings.[3]

When I visited Gualaceo, my first impression was that I had stepped back in time to a gentler, slower era. It's no wonder that Lucero thought he was working too much and that Angel Loja resented the way he was treated in the United States. I paid ten dollars a night for the no-frills but perfectly adequate and clean hotel where I stayed. I took a walk by the river and around the pretty central plaza, and I visited the church and the local weekly newspaper, the same that had helped immigrants find their way to Jean Kaleda and the library in Patchogue.

Even an outsider can clearly see that the connection between Gualaceo and Patchogue is like an overextended umbilical cord, nurturing both Gualaceños who left home and those who pine for them and want them back but depend on them for their survival.

There was a farmer's market on one side of the Catholic church, where a disproportionately large and beautiful cabbage went for fifty cents and a Sponge Bob cake cost thirty dollars. On one block alone I counted fifteen shoe stores, a sign that the shoe business is thriving again in this part of the country. Another store carried dozens of T-shirts with logos in English; most had the stars and stripes of the US flag. There were fragrant flowers everywhere—hibiscus, callas, and bougainvilleas. Indigenous women squatted on the uneven sidewalks, roasting *cuyes*, or guinea pigs, a local delicacy that often finds its way to Long Island, packed in ice.

Several small businesses in town serve as direct links between Gualaceo and New York, sending packages and receiving money for a fee, and a spacious office on the main thoroughfare helps Gualaceños with all sorts of migration issues, from visas and death certificates to tracking down relatives who have not been heard of since they left for the United States.

I visited a food market, lodged in a cement-and-brick building, with such variety of meats, potatoes, and fruits that it was
overwhelming to the senses: gorgeous, impossibly yellow and fat
bananas; several varieties of eggs, including goose and ostrich;
a row of four roasted pigs, with eyes closed and open mouths;
and at least a dozen sacks of potatoes, each different in color and
texture. The air smelled of ripe fruit; spices like thyme, paprika,
and cinnamon; raw and sizzling meat; human sweat; and women's
perfume combined with the occasional whiff of fresh, dewy air
from the mountains. It seemed impossible that anyone would
starve in Gualaceo or even feel the urge to leave this lush land for
greener pastures. Yet about fifteen thousand Gualaceños have left
for the United States. Six thousand of them live in Patchogue or
nearby, according to an estimate of the Gualaceo mayor, Marco
Tapia, who, like most people here, has been both a victim and a
beneficiary of migration.

Two of his siblings live on Long Island, he said. His brother
left when Tapia was nine, and his sister left five years later. With
their economic support, he became a physical education instructor and, when I met him, his brother was paying for his law school
education. Tapia was thirty-one and lived rent-free with his wife
and children in the modest house of an uncle who has been in the
United States for twenty-five years.

Gualaceo, which in 2010 had about forty-seven thousand
residents,[4] is part of Azuay, the province that has sent the largest number of emigrants to the United States. Of the municipalities in Azuay, Gualaceo, which is known regionally as *el
jardín de Azuay*, or Azuay's garden, has had more of its people
leave for the United States than any other municipality, with the
exception of one, San Fernando, which is about sixty miles to
the southwest. In the elementary school that Lucero attended as
a child, about 120 of the 500 students registered in 2008 had at
least one parent living in the United States. María Cuesta Rodas,
a teacher there, told the *Newsday* reporter there was so much

sadness and suffering among the kids that the school had hired a psychologist to help.[5]

At the same time, Tapia, the mayor, estimates that at least 80 percent of the local economy is fully dependent on *remesas*, remittances from overseas—from the United States, certainly, but also from Italy, Spain, and Israel. That Azuay leads the nation in emigration makes sense given the characteristics of the region and of migrants everywhere. In his book *Portrait of a Nation: Culture and Progress in Ecuador*, former Ecuadorian president Osvaldo Hurtado explains that the people of Azuay are entrepreneurial, with a rigorous and uncharacteristic work ethic. Hurtado argues that well into the nineteenth century the rest of the country had not yet recuperated from the bad habits of colonial times: a toxic combination of racist Spanish conquistadors and natives who saw no benefit from hard work because, no matter how much they exerted themselves, the Spaniards were never going to accept them in their seriously stratified society. Hard work also seemed unnecessary because, for the most part, Ecuador is such a generous, lush land that survival was attained with very little effort.[6] But the people of Azuay had to contend with an irregular topography, with rivers, valleys, hills, glaciers, and mountains. Getting to Cuenca from Quito, for example, used to be a long and arduous project that involved riding horses up and down the frigid Andes. So the people of the Azuay region were mostly isolated and had to learn to use their "assiduous effort," their "intelligence and their arms" to survive and even thrive, Hurtado explains.

For decades, the local economy relied heavily on the straw-hat industry, which required only the cultivation of the plentiful *toquilla* plant for the straw and dexterous fingers to weave it into seamless, beautiful hats. When the hat business decreased, the workers were poised and had the contacts to follow the path north that their hats had forged. Then, in 1993, a landslide near Cuenca killed about three hundred people and destroyed the road that connected the city with the towns in northeastern Azuay. Many lost their jobs, which forced them to migrate, thus accelerating a process that had begun decades earlier.[7]

Those who study migration patterns would find that Gualaceo is not a rare case. In fact, emigrants tend not to be the poorest of the poor. To leave home, to travel to unknown lands without a safety net, family structure, or even language, requires a resourcefulness typical of those who have received some formal education, have access to capital to pay for the trip, and have an entrepreneurial spirit. Those characteristics are usually found not among the destitute but among a striving middle or lower-middle class. What most immigrants are looking for, then, is not a plate of food, a warm bed, or a safe roof. They have that at home. Instead they are looking for opportunities to prosper beyond the somewhat rigid social and economic structures of their native countries.

"Immigrants all have different skills and characteristics, so any claim about them is by definition a generalization," writes the British economist and journalist Philippe Legrain in his book *Immigrants: Your Country Needs Them*, before he offers a sweeping, but fitting, generalization: "Immigrants tend to be younger, fitter, more hard-working and more enterprising than local people. Why? Not because foreigners in general are more industrious and adventurous, but because migrants are a self-selected minority."[8]

Tapia, Gualaceo's mayor, is not a student of immigration patterns, but he knows enough about his people to want them to come back. He especially wants those with acquired skills, and those who left families behind. He said that he is worried about the kids who are growing up without their parents. His own sister-in-law left when her daughter was two and her son was five. They are now twenty-two and twenty-five. And Tapia remembers growing up without his brother. When he wanted a toy, his brother would send it from New York, but Tapia said he would have preferred to have his brother at home.

"We would have childhood memories now," he said.

His message to his people is simple, "Enough, Gualaceños. You've made enough money. It's time to come home."

The government of Ecuador agrees, and it has launched a program known as Plan Retorno, which allows migrants to return with all they need to set up a home or a business or both without paying taxes for items such as a new car or an industrial-size stove. According to figures cited on a government website, 3,279 Ecuadorians had taken advantage of the offer and returned to Ecuador as of March 2010. Tapia knew of at least twenty who had returned from Patchogue.[9] Some of them spoke to the *Newsday* reporter the day Lucero's body went home.

"When I heard the news," José Rómulo Ríos González told Jones, speaking of Lucero's death, "it was as if I had been stabbed myself." Ríos had once shared a house with Lucero in Patchogue. Unlike Lucero, he had made it home alive.[10]

When Doña Rosario saw her son's body inside the casket, she practically didn't recognize him. He had left a young, thin man with lush hair and a face scarred by acne. He had returned as a grown man, strong and thick, taller than she remembered him, and with a lot less hair.

All afternoon the day of the wake, mourners came to visit. A picture of Lucero wearing a baseball cap and tan overalls was placed on a chair near his coffin. His friends from TUNAS watched over him somberly. TUNAS was more than an acronym, it was the way to define a group of about forty men who had been friends since childhood. They shared memories of roaming around town together, swimming in the nearby rivers and playing *trompillo*, a kind of top on a string that is a popular game in Latin America.

As they got older, most of the members of TUNAS left for the United States, specifically Patchogue, where, the moment one landed, others would follow because they knew that, at the very least, they would have a helping hand and a place to stay. Indeed, when Lucero had arrived in Queens he had gone to live at the house of a TUNAS friend in Bay Shore. Later, in Patchogue, some of his roommates were TUNAS, including Ríos.

"An innocent man had to die so people would realize the racism occurring against Latinos on Long Island," said Juan Pablo Jadan, who, at thirty-eight, was the leader of the group keeping vigil next to Lucero's body. He too had lived in Patchogue. "A natural death is one thing. Dying because of violence, racism, and hate is another."[11]

At one point during the wake, Lucero's younger sister, Isabel, walked out of the house to face the television cameras and microphones and demand punishment for those who had killed her brother.

"We don't want the criminals who did this to end up laughing because they think it is a joke," she said. "We want justice to be done so my brother can rest in peace."[12]

The body was cremated the following morning. Later, around 4:00 p.m., Doña Rosario and Isabel, in a black dress, walked out of the house, each carrying a wooden box with Lucero's ashes. Once again, they were surrounded and followed by hundreds of people, many holding flowers in arrangements made to look like crosses. Together they walked a few blocks to the Catholic church in the center of town. The church bells rang as some six hundred people found seats on the wooden pews. The family placed the two boxes—one with a cross, the other with an image of the Virgin Mary—on a table covered with a purple cloth, surrounded by six candles.

In the homily, the Reverend Jorge Moreno denounced the "xenophobia" that he said had killed Lucero, but it was Isabel, speaking on behalf of her mother, who made everyone cry.

"Marcelo, my son, you will never be far from my heart, because the love of a mother is interminable," she said, as her mother wept from her seat in the front pew.[13]

At the end of the Mass, and surrounded by what seemed like the entire town, the family walked to the cemetery about a mile away. Toward the back of the cemetery, across a section with brittle and dry grass, there is a twenty-foot-high mausoleum made of concrete, painted white, and divided into two-foot-by-three-foot openings. The Lucero family located No. 150 and gently placed one wooden box inside. Doña Rosario pressed her head against the niche and began to wail.

"Why did they take my son?" she sobbed. "Why did they take you?"[14]

In Suffolk County the same questions were being asked, and although the pain was surely less raw than it was at the Lucero home in Gualaceo, it was equally tinged with anger. Immediately after the murder, there was a lot of navel-gazing and finger-pointing.

Teenager Jeffrey Conroy may have plunged the knife into Lucero's chest, but the culprit, it was almost universally believed, was Steve Levy, the Suffolk County executive who had managed to get overwhelmingly reelected in 2007 by recognizing and exploiting the insecurities of newcomers behind all of those white picket fences. He had expertly and cynically stoked their fears—of rising taxes, of aliens, of single unemployed men who drank too much, of Spanish, of a different culture encroaching on their little piece of heaven in suburbia, of rape, of diseases, of terrorism—and picked and picked at it as if it were a scab until it bled. When it did, the shed blood was Lucero's, but Levy's hands were tainted by the expanding, ugly stain of racism Lucero's murder had left behind.

Looking for guideposts in a situation he had never before faced, Mayor Pontieri, in the days following the killing, sought the advice of two people: his wife, who listened and offered support, and Rabbi Joel Levinson, of Temple Beth El, just one block north of Main Street. The Brooklyn-born rabbi had moved to Patchogue eight years earlier, and he was especially shaken by the attack because it had taken place on the eve of the anniversary of Kristallnacht—the night of November 9, 1938, when the Nazis in Germany and parts of Austria unleashed a series of attacks against Jews, killing ninety-one, sending some thirty thousand to concentration camps, and destroying thousands of their businesses.[15]

Rather than give Pontieri advice, Levinson validated the choices he had already made: to be the mayor for all by reaching out to the Latino community, to law enforcement, to educators, and to anyone else who could help them move forward. Pontieri kept those ideas in mind when, on the evening of November 19, as Lucero's body lay in the coffin in Gualaceo, he faced a crowd of 125 people at the Patchogue-Medford Library. The meeting took place just a few weeks after Jean Kaleda's alarmed call about attacks against immigrants, but to Pontieri and everyone there that night that seemed like a lifetime ago. Everything they thought they knew about their village had changed overnight. From the beginning, Pontieri set a conciliatory tone, but the meeting had moments of anger and tension.

"We are here to help and serve," Pontieri said, once again relying on Gilda Ramos to translate his words into Spanish. He added that Hispanic immigrants were as important to the community as his own family members were and as his grandparents had been. His grandparents, he emphasized, had come to Patchogue as the Ecuadorians had: without much, but looking for a better life.[16]

Deputy Inspector Dennis Meehan of the Fifth Precinct, who was transferred to another police precinct shortly after that meeting, told the audience that police wanted to "start now" to create opportunities to have an open dialogue with the community, and he encouraged those present to report incidents of harassment and abuse to police.

At that point, a man who spoke only Spanish said he had been chased, not by young thugs, but by plainclothes officers on a street near his home. They had caught him and beat him, and he had ended up with a broken arm, he said. Meehan seemed to be aware of that case but scolded the man for bringing it up, despite his opening the door to such reports just a few minutes before.

"This meeting is not the place for this," Meehan said, firmly ending that line of dialogue.[17]

Thus, the gathering ended on a confusing note. On the one hand, Pontieri had opened his arms to all with his "we are one community" assertions; on the other hand, a representative from the police said come to us with your complaints, just don't do it in public, where the media can hear you.

The following day, six of the seven teenagers who had attacked Lucero were arraigned in Suffolk County Criminal Court. They were charged with multiple counts of gang assault and hate crimes, not only for Lucero's death but also for other assaults prosecutors said they had committed against Hispanics, notably Héctor Sierra and Octavio Cordovo. The judge set bail for five of them at $250,000 cash or $500,000 bond. Chris Overton was denied bail because of his previous felony conviction for the 2007 burglary in East Patchogue.[18]

The teenagers, one by one, were led to a courtroom, where their parents and high school friends awaited. Lucero's relatives and friends were also there, and they wept openly as the prosecution laid out the sequence of events that had led to his death.

The seventh defendant, Jeff Conroy, was arraigned the following week and denied bail. He was charged with second-degree murder and manslaughter as a hate crime. Conroy was the only one charged with murder because, prosecutors said, the other teenagers did not know he had stabbed Lucero until he told them. Lawyers for the six defendants argued that their clients had been unfairly charged with a crime that others committed, and they took pains to point out that their clients could not possibly be racists because they had friends of all colors and races. To try to prove it, they pointed to the diverse group of young men and women in the courtroom.

All pleaded not guilty, but in the eyes of the prosecutors, the media, the Ecuadorians in Patchogue, and just about everyone who had been paying attention, they were already guilty. Suffolk County district attorney Thomas J. Spota sounded an ominous note when he spoke at a news conference after the arraignment.

"To them, it was a sport," he said. "We know for sure that there are more victims out there."

From the start, Bob Conroy said that the treatment his son and his friends had received from the media was unfair.

"Jeff was ostracized by the press," he told me the first time we met and every time I saw him after that. "He was used as a poster boy of everything that's wrong with this country about illegal immigration. It all fell on the back of teenagers, on my son's back."[19]

On November 25, a Manhattan-based advocacy group, Latino Justice/PRLDEF, wrote a letter to the US Department of Justice Civil Rights Division asking for an investigation of the Suffolk County police, which, they claimed, systematically violated the rights of Latinos by downplaying or ignoring constant attacks against Hispanics because of their ethnicity.[20] That same day, Suffolk police commissioner Richard Dormer announced that he was stripping Fifth Precinct commander Salvatore Manno of his command and appointing a Hispanic, Arístides Mojica, to take over the job. Mojica, who grew up in the South Bronx as the oldest of five in a Puerto Rican family, was the department's highest-ranking Hispanic member.[21]

In an interview with *Newsday*, Mojica acknowledged that he faced a serious challenge.

"You can't assume it's an anomaly," he told *Newsday*, speaking about Lucero's murder. "You can't assume it will never happen again. You can't assume that bad behavior is localized to Patchogue." He promised to earn back the trust of the Latinos in the area.[22]

To find out just how many silent victims and unreported crimes were out there, Reverend Wolter opened the doors of his church on Main Street on December 3 to Latinos who felt they had been victims of hate crimes. He invited them to share their stories. Their tales were recorded by a reporter for the public radio station WSHU, an affiliate of National Public Radio. Wolter invited the media, but at least one reporter, *New York Times* editorial writer Lawrence Downes, found the whole thing distasteful. He called it a "guilt fiesta" and questioned whether those who were being interviewed knew that their words were being recorded.

Downes quoted Pontieri, who told him the meeting should have been held in the library, the main gathering place for Patchogue's Latino population, and without reporters. But Spota, the district attorney, seemed to find the activity fruitful. He told Downes that he saw seventy-five to one hundred people filing through the church to tell their stories, and he was expecting to be able to gather a few useful accounts of unreported assaults.[23] In the end, Wolter said, fifty-three people spoke about having been attacked or harassed in Patchogue and other areas nearby. A week or so later, prosecutors showed up at the church with a subpoena for the recordings. They took away all the recordings. Wolter said he felt relieved.[24]

With so much media attention, people in Patchogue began to feel they were under siege. Reporters just would not go away (three separate documentary crews had started filming almost from the start). Latinos were emboldened, but also scared and outraged. Non-Latinos were defensive, and also scared and outraged. What had happened to their village and when would they get it back?

When would things go back to normal? The guilt and the shock took many shapes. County executive Steve Levy, in a surprise statement, referred to Lucero's assailants as "white supremacists," without any evidence to support his claim, just as earlier he had described immigration advocates as "communists."

Michael Mostow, the superintendent of Patchogue-Medford School District, called the attack "an aberration" and told the press there were no racial issues or divisions in the high school the teenagers attended,[25] but Manuel J. Sanzone, the son and grandson of Italian immigrants and the principal of the Patchogue-Medford High School, took precautions nonetheless. He mobilized a mini-lockdown at the school, which meant that backpacks were checked and extra security personnel patrolled the halls. Four days after the murder, he spoke to his students. "I told them that how they handle this, and what they learn from it, becomes a part of their character," he explained to a *New York Times* reporter, "and that even if they feel afraid for classmates who were involved in it, they should never forget that there was a victim here."[26]

About five weeks after Lucero's death, a school board meeting ended in a shouting match as parents and board members traded insults. At issue was the infamous hallway that housed English-as-a-second-language classrooms. It was here that Hispanic students tended to congregate. A girl who spoke in favor of the ESL classes was booed off the stage and had to leave the meeting.[27] The parents of white non-Hispanic students complained that after the murder the hall was "unsafe" for their children, as they, not the Latino students, were now the subject of harassment. But Mostow and other board members said the students themselves had not complained and assured the parents that their children were safe. At that point, a North Patchogue resident named Bill Pearson suggested that perhaps the best solution was to eliminate ESL classes. His suggestion provoked some anger, which led to the shouting match and to Mostow calling Pearson "a racist." Pearson demanded an apology, but Mostow shouted back, "Not to you, racist!" Pearson told a *Newsday* reporter he planned to contact a lawyer.[28]

In one of my meetings with Conroy, he mentioned that his daughter too was afraid to walk down the "Spanish" hall.

There were candlelit vigils in the dead of winter for Lucero and a lot of support for his family, while Loja quietly disappeared into the background. Reporters wanted to speak with him, but he shunned them all.

Jack Eddington and others started to organize a community soccer tournament where all ethnicities were invited. The Latino team lost in the first tournament, in 2009, but the event served to build some bridges and it felt good to be playing out in the open. A writer's workshop promoted writing as a way to fight hate in the community, bringing together Spanish-speaking and English-speaking women who had stories to tell.[29] An Ecuadorian filmmaker on Long Island made a short film inspired by the case, *Taught to Hate*, which was shown at the Long Island International Film Expo.[30] And a Stony Brook University student won an essay contest for writing an analysis of the articles about Lucero and his killers that appeared in major news publications. He received a full semester's worth of in-state tuition at the university.[31]

Diane Berthold, a local designer with myriad health problems but a can-do attitude, began a quilt project. She got together with several other women who also felt the need to create something beautiful and permanent. The Healing Hands & Mending Hearts Quilt Project was born, eventually yielding three quilts from different community groups. The quilts were unveiled in 2010 at the Patchogue American Legion Post.[32] Later they were displayed in an empty storefront on South Ocean Avenue, a stone's throw away from the corner where Jeff and the others were arrested.

The Lucero Foundation was launched to bring Latinos together in Patchogue. It held monthly meetings in an unheated room on the second floor of a building on Main Street. Schools began to offer Spanish-language classes for adults who wanted to learn the language to communicate with their neighbors. And the area where Lucero was killed—at the intersection of Railroad Avenue, Funaro Court, and Sephton Street—was optimistically and prematurely renamed Unity Place just two months after the Southern Poverty Law Center, an influential civil rights organization based in Montgomery, Alabama, released a scathing report titled *Climate of Fear: Latino Immigrants in Suffolk County, N.Y.* The report found that Lucero's murder was the result of "nativist intolerance and hate violence" that had been festering for years in Suffolk County. In particular, it blamed local officials for fostering such an environment and Steve Levy for minimizing the murder by calling it a "one-day story."[33]

The report also detailed thirty-five attacks against Hispanic immigrants in Suffolk County from June 1, 1999, to November 8, 2008. In 2008 alone, at least fourteen immigrants, mostly Ecuadorians, were attacked or harassed in Patchogue.[34] Yet few had dared to call the police, for two reasons: they worried about getting deported and they had been told by others who had already been through the same ordeal that the police never did anything because the youths were minors. After Lucero's murder, and until August 2009, seven other attacks were reported, two of them in Patchogue. The victims of the latter two attacks—two men in one incident and one man in the other—told police that they were attacked by teenagers. At least some of the teenagers told their victims that they wanted "to kill a Hispanic."[35]

The Ecuadorian consulate in New York encouraged immigrants to come forward to speak of their abuse and harassment, and hate crime reports increased nearly 30 percent in the county. The consulate also began a program to help Ecuadorians assimilate faster to suburbia, teaching them, among other things, about the illegality of littering and of drinking in public—the very kind of practical education Eddington had long been advocating for.[36]

In Gualaceo, Doña Rosario told reporters that she would like to come to New York to face her son's attackers, not to show any hatred—she felt none—but to show them that the man they had killed had a mother who loved him very much.

"I just want to see their faces," she told *Newsday*. "I don't want to hurt them. But I want them to see he had a mother here waiting for him. I want them to put their hand on my heart and feel the enormous damage they have caused this family."[37]

Margarita Espada, a Puerto Rican playwright, wrote *What Killed Marcelo Lucero?* which premiered in 2009 at Hofstra University. There were a dozen actors, most with no experience or training, in the play, which portrayed real events and characters surrounding the murder, including an anti-immigrant politician, day laborers, a white non-Hispanic family, and a Hispanic family. Much of the dialogue came from news accounts.[38] It played in different venues on Long Island until, one day in the spring of 2011, it came to Patchogue.

There were about two hundred people in the audience, which was white and Latino, young and old. The bilingual play felt more like a conversation starter than a work of art. It had no ending, and Espada said she had left it open because the ending was yet to be written. It was up to the people of Suffolk County to write it.

Bob Conroy sat in the sixth row to the right of the stage. He wore black jogging pants and a blue T-shirt with a red windbreaker and black cap that he did not take off. He chewed gum and watched intently as the events of his recent life unfolded on the stage. An actor representing a Latino worker riding a bicycle was attacked by kids with a bat. "Go back to Mexico!" they yelled, and they stole his bike. Thugs kicked a boy and emptied his knapsack. "I was half expecting to find a burrito," said one of the attackers before discarding the bag.

Except for his jaws furiously working the gum, Conroy didn't move. At the end, the actors gathered on the stage around a casket surrounded by all the flags of Latin America. They brought it down to the audience. Then Espada interrupted. "Stop!" she ordered, addressing the actors. Turning to the audience, she asked, "How can we create a dialogue?"

Luis Valenzuela, the immigration advocate, spoke first and reminded the audience that during the year that Lucero was killed, six anti-immigrant bills had been introduced in the legislature. One college professor said that after Lucero was killed, he had been afraid of being Latino, for the first time in his life.

A few other people spoke, and then Conroy asked for the microphone. Everyone turned to face him, and a hush descended in the theater. It was the first time he had publicly spoken since his son had been arrested. He cleared his throat.

"I'm sorry for what happened, but I felt that the problems of a nation fell on a seventeen-year-old child," he said, repeating the theme that seems to fuel his anger.

Then he went on, in a somewhat rambling but seemingly heartfelt talk.

"At seventeen you can't drink, you can't drive alone. He dated a Spanish girl. My first wife was Spanish. This has opened my eyes. You guys [actors] did a good job, but I take exception to one thing: it was not in the heart," he said, referring to the wound on Lucero's torso, which in fact had been closer to the shoulder than the chest. "It was considered a nonthreatening wound that wasn't treated for forty minutes."

Valenzuela interrupted him to say, "I support you one hundred percent in that it wasn't your son alone. This is society's issue."

Conroy said he was "livid" that his son had been described in the papers as a "ringleader." "It could have been any of your children," he said to the audience that remained riveted by his words.

"Absolutely," Valenzuela agreed.

"Know the facts before you label somebody," Conroy said before sitting down eight minutes after he took the microphone.

There was a smattering of applause, but a man in the audience got up and urged everyone not to forget that there was only one victim in the attack against Lucero, and that victim was not Jeffrey Conroy; it was Marcelo Lucero. Toward the end of the evening, Reverend Wolter, who had encouraged Conroy to attend the event, said he was pleased with the way it had turned out. "For the first time in this community everyone had a seat at the table," he said.

But not everyone was at the table that evening; the Lucero family did not attend.

On the evening of February 16, 2009, Doña Rosario arrived in New York City to see her surviving son, Joselo, and to attend hearings scheduled before the trials of the teenagers accused of killing her son. It was the first time she traveled outside Ecuador.

She arrived at JFK Airport, accompanied by her daughter, Isabel, and her grandson, three-year-old Isaac. Crying and shaking, she clung to Joselo, who was waiting with a bouquet of white roses and eucalyptus. The two were speechless for several minutes, but nearby reporters could hear Joselo's tear-choked whispers, "Mi mamá, mi mamá."

Joselo took off his black jacket and delicately draped it around his mother's small frame. The family left the airport in a car driven by Sgt. Lola Quesada, who now worked as a police liaison to the Latino community and had gained enormous relevance in the community in the days immediately following Lucero's death.[39]

Nine months later, in November 2009, Doña Rosario was back to mark the first anniversary of her son's death at an interfaith service in St. Francis de Sales Church in Patchogue. Surprising everyone in the church, Steve Levy approached the Lucero family in their front pew and spoke to them quietly. He said he was sorry for their loss and thanked Joselo for speaking out about his brother. Joselo just nodded. A picture taken by a *Newsday* photographer shows Doña Rosario bundled in an oversized dark coat, shaking Levy's outstretched hand. Officer Quesada is between the two, most likely translating. Joselo Lucero stares straight ahead with hands deep in his pant pockets.

When it was his time to speak during the service, Joselo addressed Levy directly. "You have a second chance to change, to do what you did wrong before, to now do better things." This time it was Levy who stared straight ahead.[40]

Afterward, Mayor Pontieri told reporters he had arranged for Levy to come to the service. He admitted that he should have alerted the Lucero family, but said he had not thought about it.

Joselo was fuming.

"I feel like I was ambushed here," he said. "There are people I don't want to talk to."

Two months later, the people's case against Jeffrey Conroy reached the courtroom of New York Supreme Court judge Robert W. Doyle in Riverhead, Long Island.

CHAPTER 10

TRIAL AND PUNISHMENT

The night before, the attorney laid out her new black suit, the one she had bought especially for this trial. After eighteen months of preparation, countless hours poring over documents, and entire weekends spent thinking up strategies and opening arguments, it had come down to superstition: Megan O'Donnell, an assistant district attorney in Suffolk County with twelve years of experience, always wore black the first and last day of a trial. She felt it brought her good luck. With the Lucero case, she needed it.[1]

Much more than the fate of a young man was at stake in this case. What would it telegraph to the world if in Suffolk County, Long Island, a bunch of kids could get away with the murder of an undocumented immigrant? With so much media attention surrounding the case, at times it seemed as if the whole world was watching, which was not entirely true. For the most part, the coverage was local, about half of it from Spanish-language media outlets, though reporters from as far away as Amsterdam had shown a fleeting interest in the story in the days after the murder. But advocacy groups—both local and national—as well as the federal government were certainly paying attention. On September 1, 2009, six months before the first day of the trial, the US Department of Justice Civil Rights Division and the US Attorney's Office for the Eastern District of New York initiated a joint investigation of the Suffolk County Police Department. O'Donnell, of course, was aware that her case was in the spotlight. Something Jeffrey Conroy had boasted to his friends right after the stabbing remained on her mind: "Imagine if I get away with this?"[2] She didn't think of Jeff and the other six who had been arraigned as young men who had made a mistake. Their behavior had been gang-like, she thought, and her job was to stop gangs from terrorizing the place she called home.

Megan O'Donnell was born in Patchogue. Her father, a banker, is an immigrant from Canada. Her mother, a legal secretary, is from North Carolina. When O'Donnell was seven, the family moved to Virginia. She became interested in law in eighth grade, when a teacher organized a mock Revolutionary War trial. O'Donnell played the lawyer representing the Americans. She lost her case but to this day thinks she should have won.

O'Donnell started college in Virginia, but midway through returned to New York and finished her political science degree at Stony Brook University. Her law degree is from Hofstra University, also on Long Island. She was ambivalent at first as to what role she would play as a lawyer upon graduation, but in the summer after her first year of law school an internship at the Suffolk County District Attorney's Office led to her decision to become a prosecutor. O'Donnell graduated in May, took the bar exam in August, and the following month began working in the Suffolk County District Court prosecuting misdemeanors.

Her first trial involved a woman who had been inappropriately groped in a restaurant kitchen where she worked, but O'Donnell quickly moved on to the Major Crimes Bureau, prosecuting felonies such as burglary, rape, and murder. After three years, she was assigned to the special investigations unit, prosecuting gun-related and gang violence. The assignment was random, but it became a passion for her, and she stayed for seven years. By her own account she is very focused, organized, methodical, analytical, and determined. In college, she took up running and is still at it, usually jogging at 5:00 a.m. four days a week.

It surprised no one when O'Donnell's boss, District Attorney Thomas Spota, assigned her Jeffrey Conroy's prosecution. At the time, she was one of 185 assistant district attorneys in the county, but one of only about twelve who could handle a homicide case.

As O'Donnell wrestled with the case, the biggest issue was not Jeff's culpability. Despite the fact that no one, not even Angel Loja, had seen him plunge the knife into Lucero's upper torso, the evidence pointed to him and so did his own confession. Age was not a problem either because in New York State anyone over sixteen can be tried as an adult. Jeff was seventeen at the time of the attack. If there would be any leniency in his case, it would have to come from the judge at the time of sentencing if Jeff were found guilty, not from the district attorney's office.

There was no question about the nature of the crime either. All the boys had confessed to attacking Lucero and Loja because of their ethnicity. During the confessions, the young men had not said why they had gone out that night to pick on Hispanic men, but during their interviews with prosecutors and with probation department officers they had revealed somewhat of a motivation. Their statements varied, but they all shared fears that immigrants were taking jobs away from US citizens, enrolling in schools, and therefore causing tax money to be used in programs such as teaching teachers to speak Spanish, and not paying taxes into the system. O'Donnell had heard it all before. Her sense was that the kids were mirroring what their parents believed, what they said most nights around the dinner table.[3] In an incident file report prepared shortly after his arrest, Jeff is quoted as saying that though he didn't consider himself a "white supremacist" and didn't belong to any such group, he followed white supremacist activities on the Internet and held "racist thoughts," having been "raised in a home where his parents held racist beliefs."[4] (Conroy vehemently disputes this and doubts that his son could have said any such thing.)

The issue then was intent. If Jeff intended to cause Lucero's death that meant he should be charged with murder, but if his intent was to harm him, albeit seriously, that would result in a charge of manslaughter. But O'Donnell and her colleagues did not have to decide. They took their case to a grand jury.[5] Ultimately, the grand jury charged Jeff with seven crimes. The most serious charges, the ones that could send him to prison for life, were murder in the second degree as a hate crime (meaning he intentionally caused Lucero's death by stabbing him), and manslaughter in the first degree as a hate crime (meaning that while the intention may have been to cause serious injury to Lucero, Jeff caused his death by stabbing him). The other charges were gang assault in the first degree, conspiracy in the fourth degree, and attempted assault in the second degree as a hate crime for the attacks on Héctor Sierra, Angel Loja, and Octavio Cordovo.[6]

It was, up to that point, the biggest case of O'Donnell's career. She was thirty-seven when she got the case and thirty-nine when it finally made its way to the court on March 18, 2010, a Thursday. On that first day of *People of the State of New York v. Jeffrey Conroy*, O'Donnell put everything aside—politics, media, pressure from advocacy groups—and applied all her focus and considerable energy to the one thing that really mattered to her: winning.

The courtroom of Judge Doyle was silent and expectant when O'Donnell rose from her chair behind a polished wooden table in front of the judge and addressed the court and the members of the jury—seven men, five women, and four alternates.

"Your Honor," she began, "madam foreperson, counsel, on November 8, 2008, the hunt was on." And then O'Donnell was off, describing in great detail how two separate groups of friends with different lives and separate plans collided at Funaro Court near midnight on that date with disastrous and life-altering results.

"Seven teenagers, one of which was the defendant, Jeffrey Conroy, wilding, roaming the streets of Patchogue for one purpose and one purpose only, to find a Hispanic person to randomly and physically attack," she said.

The jurors were riveted. Their facial expressions—horror at the description of the murder, or concern for the family of Marcelo Lucero—did not escape the hawk-like attention of Jeff's experienced attorney.

William Keahon, a former prosecutor who was sixty-five at the time, always came to court impeccably dressed in neutral-colored or black suits and neatly coiffed, with his thinning silver hair combed back and his face scrubbed red and completely devoid of facial hair. The *New York Times* described him as a "forceful, unpredictable litigator" who twice asked Judge Doyle to declare a mistrial on technicalities and who, during jury selection, argued successfully that a dark cloth that covered part of the defense table cast his client in an ominous light. He offered to bring in his own tools to remove the cloth if it was screwed in. But he didn't have to—the cloth was gone the next day.[7]

Keahon was famous for taking on tough cases and often winning acquittal for clients charged with horrific crimes. This is how a 2007 profile published in *Newsday* described him: "Keahon, after all, is the same guy who won Suffolk's first acquittal for first-degree murder in 1997, even after defendant Gairy Chang made a full confession to the crime. He is the guy who last year kept a jury out seven days in the Zachary Gibian case after presenting the seemingly far-fetched theory that Gibian's disabled mother—not Gibian, who eventually was convicted—was the one who killed Gibian's sleeping stepfather with a samurai sword." He was also the lawyer for Evan Marshall, who in 2007 pleaded guilty to dismembering a retired schoolteacher and keeping her head in the trunk of his car.[8] Yet in his opening statements on Jeff's case, Keahon didn't say much about his client or about the case. With the exception of a few pertinent names, his intervention could have been the same for any other trial. Later it became obvious that he had been saving his wild-card strategy for the end of the trial.

"Now, you've had an opportunity to listen and hear a very persuasive opening statement by the Assistant District Attorney," he told the jurors. "And, as Miss O'Donnell was speaking to you, I was listening to her, I was watching each of you, how you were reacting, and I saw on some of your faces almost an acceptance of what she was telling you about, almost an acceptance of the facts that she told you she would prove, almost as if you had accepted that it had been proven."

Jeffrey Conroy had been in jail for sixteen months. He was now nineteen, but despite the black suit he wore to court most days and the fact that his hands were cuffed as he entered and left the court, Jeff still looked like a sullen but scared teenager who appeared to not fully understand the gravity of his situation.

Nothing had been proven yet, but Keahon knew that in the press his client had already been tried. By the time the trial started, four of the teenagers had pleaded guilty to first-degree gang assault and conspiracy as hate crimes; two more would do the same before the year was over.[9] Many on Long Island and beyond, including several prospective jurors, knew the sordid details of the crime and of the restless evening that led to it.

Prosecuting crimes as hate crimes became possible in the state of New York after the Hate Crimes Act of 2000 was approved by a majority in the legislature, becoming law on July 10, 2000. Here's how the act reads in part:

> The legislature finds and determines as follows: criminal acts
> involving violence, intimidation and destruction of property

based upon bias and prejudice have become more prevalent in New York State in recent years. The intolerable truth is that in these crimes, commonly and justly referred to as "hate crimes," victims are intentionally selected, in whole or in part, because of their race, color, national origin, ancestry, gender, religion, religious practice, age, disability or sexual orientation. Hate crimes do more than threaten the safety and welfare of all citizens. They inflict on victims incalculable physical and emotional damage and tear at the very fabric of free society.

Crimes motivated by invidious hatred toward particular groups not only harm individual victims but send a powerful message of intolerance and discrimination to all members of the group to which the victim belongs. Hate crimes can and do intimidate and disrupt entire communities and vitiate the civility that is essential to healthy democratic processes. In a democratic society, citizens cannot be required to approve of the beliefs and practices of others, but must never commit criminal acts on account of them. Current law does not adequately recognize the harm to public order and individual safety that hate crimes cause. Therefore, our laws must be strengthened to provide clear recognition of the gravity of hate crimes and the compelling importance of preventing their recurrence. Accordingly, the legislature finds and declares that hate crimes should be prosecuted and punished with appropriate severity.[10]

Washington and Oregon were the first states to enact hate crime legislation, in 1981. Today forty-five states and the District of Columbia have penalty-enhancing hate crime laws, though the laws vary with regard to the groups protected, the type of crime covered, and the penalty for those who commit hate crimes. The exceptions are Arkansas, Georgia, Indiana, South Carolina, and Wyoming.[11]

According to a report by the National Institute of Justice—the research, development, and evaluation agency of the Department of Justice—the most common motivating factor in hate crimes reported to the police is race, followed by religion, sexual orientation, ethnicity, and victim disability. Only 11 percent of the hate crimes reported are motivated by ethnicity, while 61 percent are motivated by race.

It is safe to assume that most offenders probably don't know the difference between race and ethnicity. Part of the problem in defining a hate crime against a Hispanic is that, in the United States, the terms "Hispanic" and "Latino"—which for the most part are used interchangeably—have become racialized. In assigning the color "brown" to what is, in fact, a multihued ethnicity, it has become increasingly difficult to distinguish between ethnicity and race when discussing Hispanics—a US census category that defines a great number of people who can be of any race and were born in Latin America or trace their ancestry to that region. The category is self-assigned. In other words, anyone can claim to be Hispanic. There are fifty-two million Hispanics in the United States, not all of them immigrants, of course, and the numbers swell to almost fifty-six million if one counts Puerto Ricans, who are born US citizens, making Hispanics the largest minority group in the country.[12]

Among them, there are black Cubans and white Dominicans, Argentine Jews and Indigenous, born-again Christians from El Salvador. There are Mexican Americans who have lived in Texas for generations and consider themselves Hispanics yet don't speak Spanish, and there are newly arrived black Costa Ricans, descendants of Jamaicans, whose first language was English. Adding to this true melting pot are those who speak not Spanish but indigenous languages such as Mixteco, Nahuatl, and Chinanteco. And then there are Garifuna people from Honduras, Guatemala, and Nicaragua, who descend from West African, Carib, and Arawak people. They speak their own language in addition to Spanish and may or may not claim to be Hispanics in the US census. If one of them was attacked by hatemongers, would that action fall under the category of race or ethnicity? It would probably depend on the epithets the attackers called the victim during the attack. In the Lucero case ethnicity was the issue, but his attackers may have thought "Hispanic" labeled a race.

Where hate crime statistics draw even closer to the Lucero case is in what motivates hate crime offenders. According to the Bureau of Justice Statistics, part of the Department of Justice, 66 percent are "motivated by the desire for excitement." Those are called "thrill-seekers." Only 1 percent feel they are on a "mission"—that is, "so strongly committed to bigotry that they make hate a career."[13]

For years, the FBI has kept an exhaustive record of hate crimes reported by police officers. The year Lucero was killed, 7,783 hate crime incidents were reported. Of those, 51.3 percent were racially motivated and 11.5 were motivated by ethnicity or national origin; 64 percent of the crimes motivated by ethnicity or nationality targeted Hispanics. The offenders were overwhelmingly white (61.1 percent). Most of the crimes against persons involved intimidation (48.8 percent) or simple assault (32.1), but 18.5 percent were aggravated assaults, seven persons were killed, and eleven were raped.

One of the murdered victims in 2008, of course, was Lucero, but he wasn't the only one that year in New York. José Sucuzhañay, also of Ecuador, was beaten with a beer bottle and an aluminum bat a month after Lucero was killed. On December 7, 2008, Sucuzhañay, who had had too much to drink, was walking home with his brother, Romel, arms linked, in Bushwick, Brooklyn. Keith Phoenix, thirty, and Hakim Scott, twenty-six, mistook them for a gay couple and began yelling antigay and anti-Hispanic slurs. Scott smashed a beer bottle on José's head and chased Romel down the block, armed with the broken beer bottle, while

Phoenix grabbed a bat from the back of his SUV and attacked José, cracking his skull. Scott was convicted of manslaughter and assault and was sentenced to thirty-seven years. Phoenix was convicted of second-degree murder and sentenced to twenty-five years to life and an additional twelve years for attempted assault, both as hate crimes.[14] A few months before their case was tried in Brooklyn, Jeffrey Conroy became the first person to be prosecuted for homicide as a hate crime in Suffolk County under the state's hate crime law.

Jury selection in the trial of Jeffrey Conroy was a tedious but fascinating exercise for anyone interested in the mood of Suffolk County regarding issues of immigration. The judge revealed his own ignorance by repeatedly referring to Hispanics as "Spanish," as if the fifty-six million who self-identify as Hispanics could be reduced to a language many of them no longer speak or never did.

Perhaps because he used the term, or perhaps because they also didn't know any better, potential jurors kept using the same word when the judge, attempting to figure out their biases, asked questions such as "Do you know any Spanish people?" or "Do you have any Spanish friends or are they members of your family?" Some did know Hispanics, and their biases for or against Hispanics—mostly against—was enough to get them eliminated from the jury pool. More important, though, their comments in court were like an X-ray of the country, exposing some of the deepest fears of suburban America.

"Why are illegal aliens allowed to testify?" one prospective juror asked Judge Doyle. "That's okay in the eyes of the government?" When the judge prodded him further, he said he would question the credibility of a witness who was an undocumented immigrant, "considering he's not an American."[15]

Another prospective juror asked, "If these people are going to testify, are they going to be arrested after they testify, being that they are illegal?"[16]

Those two were quickly asked to leave the jury pool, as well as a young woman who said that her father "has a huge opinion about illegal immigration." Asked if that would interfere with her ability to be fair, she said her father's opinion had become hers.[17]

A man told the judge that his house had been broken into by illegal immigrants while he slept, which rendered him unable to remain impartial in the trial of a man accused of killing an undocumented immigrant. A young man from Riverhead revealed that, because he grew up in a racist environment in Pennsylvania, he could not be fair. Another man, a school bus driver, said he couldn't be fair either because he was a member of a union that had taken a position on the lack of federal immigration policy, adding that he had earned his job and salary the "old-fashioned way," legally.[18] Yet another man said he had had a number of bad experiences working with immigrants on landscaping jobs. "They weren't very truthful," he told the judge. A union electrician said he had an objection to people who are working without documents and without paying taxes.[19]

Reporter Manny Fernandez of the *New York Times* wrote at one point that the jury selection had the "feel of a call-in show on talk radio, as men and women sounded off on illegal immigration, hate crimes, their ethnic background and the American dream."[20]

In the end it took eight days to select the jurors, after four hundred prospective jurors were excused one after another. On March 18, the prosecution called its first witness.[21]

At first, Jeff's lawyer tried to blame Lucero's death on the delay in getting him to a hospital that was a mere three miles away. The *New York Times* asked a forensic pathologist not involved in the case to examine Lucero's autopsy report. The pathologist described Lucero's wound as a "survivable injury if promptly treated."[22] When the *Times* told Joselo what the pathologist had said, the information took his breath away. "We're not talking about 10 minutes," he said. "We're talking about 39 minutes. I don't even know how to describe it, this incompetence. We're talking about somebody's life."[23]

The folding knife used in the killing was displayed for the first time during the testimony of Officer Michael Richardsen, the one who had patted down Jeff and at first missed the knife. A large photo of the knife, blood still staining the blade, was shown to the jurors. The black handle was curved, and the blade had a thick, serrated edge.[24]

Although the defense tried to show that Jeff had a diverse and loyal group of friends, and therefore could not have harbored ill feelings toward any group of people, some of the most damning testimonies against him came from his oldest and best friends. First, Keith Brunjes, who had known him since the two were about eight years old, testified how one day in May 2008, when the two were watching the HBO prison series *Oz*, they decided to imitate the prisoners in the show and make homemade tattoos. Using ink purchased at an arts-and-crafts store, a needle, and thread, Brunjes said, he first tattooed Jeff with a lightning bolt and a star, and about six weeks later gave him another tattoo: an inch-square swastika on Jeff's right upper thigh.

Brunjes said he didn't know why his friend wanted to be so marked, but he also testified that it appeared as if Jeff understood the implications. "If I ever go to jail, I'm screwed," Brunjes said Jeff told him after he had finished the tattoo. Another friend, Alyssa Sprague, told jurors that when Jeff showed her his lightning bolt tattoo, she thought it was the Gatorade logo, but he corrected her. No, she said he told her, it was white power.[25]

The testimony of Angel Loja too was damaging for Jeff and difficult to listen to. His words brought the court to an even deeper than usual silence.

"I heard the blood rushing from my friend. It sounded like water from a faucet," he said, but Keahon focused on the fact that Loja hadn't seen the knife or his friend getting stabbed.[26]

Retired deputy chief medical examiner Stuart Dawson told the jury that when the knife had penetrated Lucero—"inserted all the way" to the hilt—there had been "some kind of twisting and turning." The stab wound was just below the right collarbone, not usually a terribly dangerous place for a wound, but the knife had nicked an artery and a vein. He repeated what others had said: Quick action might have saved Marcelo's life.[27]

Contradicting Loja's testimony, Dawson appeared to say that Lucero had not been beaten repeatedly. Other than the wound that killed him, his only other injury came from Kevin Shea's admitted punch to the mouth. Lucero's autopsy also revealed that he had low levels of cocaine and marijuana in his body and enough alcohol to be "right at the levels of intoxication or just short of it."[28]

Nicholas Hausch, the only one of the group to appear as a witness for the prosecution, painted a desolate picture of "beaner hopping." This is how he described it: "It's when you go out and you look for a Hispanic to beat up." In a packed courtroom, Nick admitted that before the attack on Lucero, he and two friends had gone "beaner hopping" as well. They had punched and kicked a Hispanic man who was riding a bicycle. Nick said he took the man's white baseball cap "as a trophy."[29]

Nick also made a comment that was a setback for the prosecution. After the stabbing of Lucero, he said, he had heard someone say, "Imagine if I get away with this," the comment that O'Donnell had attributed to Jeff. However, Nick said, it was not Jeff who uttered that remark. He didn't know who had said it.[30]

The most dramatic and unexpected moment of the trial came during its fourth week when Jeff took the stand in his own defense. It was an unusual and risky move. His lawyer later told reporters that in his twenty-five years as a defense lawyer, he had put his clients on the stand fewer than ten times.[31] The tactic can change the outcome of a trial. If the defendant is likable and believable, it can sway jurors to a not-guilty verdict, but if jurors don't believe the defendant, the results can be disastrous for the defense.

So when Jeff took the stand, his fate was in his hands. All the preparation and pretrial hearings and motions and posturing came down to the recollections and personality of a nineteen-year-old performing under the most stressful circumstance of his life.

He wore a white, open-collared shirt without a tie as he sat on the witness stand.[32] His testimony began simply enough, with answers to his lawyer's questions about his life, his age, whom he lived with, and what sports he played. Then the lawyer started asking him about the night of November 8, 2008, from his visit to Alyssa Sprague's home to the moment when the fight with Lucero was over and, he said, Chris Overton approached him.

"And what did he say to you?" Keahon asked.

"He said, 'Jeff, I think I just stabbed the guy in the shoulder. I really cannot get in trouble with this. Can you please take the knife? I only nicked him and I promise you he's not hurt.' And then, after that, I'm like, 'Why can't you get in trouble for this?' He says, 'Because I already told you that I was involved in a murder case last year and I still haven't gotten sentenced and I'll be screwed if I get caught. So can you please take the knife?' And then he's like, 'Look back. He's even walking away.' I looked back and the guy was walking away."

"Did you take the knife?"

"Yes."

"What did you do with the knife?"

>"I was holding it."
>"Did you see Nicky Hausch?"
>"Yes."
>"Did he say anything to you?"
>"Yes."
>"What did he say to you?"
>"He said, 'What happened?'"
>"And what did you say?"
>"I told him—I'm like, 'I stabbed the guy.'"

Just like that, composed and unsmiling, staring straight ahead, Jeff transferred the blame to Chris, a kid he had met the night of the killing.

When her time came, O'Donnell sounded incredulous as she asked Jeff how he could possibly take the blame for killing Lucero to protect someone he had just met.[33]

"I felt bad for him," he answered.

Jeff also told her he had gone along with his friends that night because he had needed a ride for a sleepover, not because he had any intention of going "beaner-hopping." He had never touched Lucero, whom he described as the aggressor in the confrontation, wielding his belt as a weapon against the teenagers. Lucero "could have walked away," he said. As to his confession the night of the murder, he admitted that he had told detectives that he had stabbed Lucero. However, he explained, the detectives also wrote down things that he had never said, particularly his admission that he was part of a group that hunted down Latinos for a fight.[34]

As Jeff's testimony dragged on for about three and a half hours, one could hear groans and guffaws from the packed courtroom.[35] "Can you believe this kid?" someone muttered loud enough to be heard by some of the hundred people that crowded the gallery,[36] among them Lucero's mother and sister, who had flown in from Ecuador and attended the trial for the first time that day, and his brother, who was present almost every day. Doña Rosario sat as she always did, stone-faced, inscrutable in her pain. In her left hand she held a tissue, with which she dabbed at the corner of her eyes. The Suffolk County district attorney, Thomas J. Spota, made a rare appearance. As always when he attended, he sat in the first row. A few rows behind him sat Denise Overton.

Asked afterward how she had felt when she heard the accusations against Chris, Overton told reporters, "It was horrible, absolutely horrible."[37] She said that Jeff had "no conscience whatsoever."[38] It wasn't the first time someone had tried to blame her son for a crime.

Chris was the only one among the seven young men who attacked Lucero to have been implicated in a murder before. Jeff's defense was not a novel one.

On May 8, 2007, exactly eighteen months before Lucero was killed, Christopher Overton had joined four other teenagers to burglarize a house in East Patchogue owned by Carlton Shaw, a thirty-eight-year-old Jamaican immigrant who worked three jobs to support his family. When Shaw confronted the burglars, one of them shot and killed him. His three-year-old boy, unharmed, was later found asleep on his chest.

Terraine Slide, then sixteen, was charged with second-degree murder. Slide's cousin, Levon Griffin, pleaded guilty to the same charge. The other three, including Chris, were fourteen and fifteen at the time. They pleaded guilty to first-degree burglary and pointed to Slide as the killer.[39] During his murder trial, Slide's lawyer argued that the young man had been coerced into confessing guilt for a murder he did not commit. Slide, who was the only one of the defendants to be tried as an adult, blamed Chris for firing the shot that killed Shaw.[40] The jurors did not believe Slide and found him guilty. However, the conviction was reversed by a state appellate court and prosecutors decided to retry him. In May 2011, Slide pleaded guilty to first-degree manslaughter instead of going to trial a second time. During questioning in court, Slide still maintained that Chris had brought the .22-caliber revolver used to kill Shaw.[41] But this time he admitted to having fired the shot himself.[42]

On September 6, 2011, Justice Doyle, who had presided over Slide's case, sentenced him to twenty-five years in prison.[43]

The jurors did not believe Jeff either.

On April 19, 2010, after four days of deliberation, at 11:22 a.m., the jurors read their verdict: Jeff was acquitted of the most serious charge—second-degree murder—but he was found guilty of manslaughter as a hate crime and of gang assault in the attack on Lucero, as well as attempted assault on three other Hispanic men. The verdict meant that the jurors did not think that Jeff had intended to kill Lucero, only to cause him serious physical injury.[44]

Jeff heard the verdict while standing next to his lawyer.[45] Keahon placed a hand on his back and felt him begin to tremble.[46] When the jurors were excused, and Jeff finally sat, he bowed his head. As he was about to be handcuffed and led away by court officers, Conroy turned to face his parents and seemed to give them an encouraging look.[47] His parents had sat quietly in the courtroom, but when they walked outside, Conroy began to cry, covering his face with one hand while his wife, who had attended the trial sporadically and had testified for about ten minutes on her son's behalf, remained stone-faced.[48]

Lucero's family arrived in court after the verdict was read, but in time for Joselo to praise the district attorney's office, saying that their work had restored his faith in the American justice system.

Steve Levy, who had switched to the Republican Party to run for governor, called the attack on Lucero "a heinous, reprehensible act." In a statement released right after the verdict, he seemed to urge the judge to deliver a tough sentence. "It is my hope that the sentence will properly reflect the brutal and blind hatred that was displayed on the night of the murder," the statement read.[49]

Not everyone was content with the verdict. Allan Ramírez, the Long Island pastor who hovered protectively around the Lucero family, said that a manslaughter conviction meant "our lives are not worth very much."[50]

The cameras trailed the Lucero family as they drove away from the courthouse and toward Funaro Court in Patchogue, where Lucero's blood had once left a 370-foot-long twisting path.[51]

Someone had placed yellow and red tulips on the spot where Lucero bled to death. Children's toys, including a blue plastic pool, were scattered on the pavement, along with a flattened Arizona Iced Tea can, several fans, an old computer, broken lamps, and an air-conditioning unit. Scraggly plants clung to life against a rusted metal fence. Twelve television cameras captured the scene as the family received hugs and kisses from friends and well-wishers.

In front of them all, on the sidewalk, stood Doña Rosario, who spoke of forgiveness, and her son, Joselo, who once again turned to the cameras to plead his case.

"This is the place where my brother broke the rules," he said, referring to the often-mentioned fact that Lucero had fought back. "He defended himself. He wanted to be treated like a human."

About Patchogue and hate crimes, Joselo appeared to have mixed but prescient feelings. At the courthouse he told reporters, "The hunting season is over, at least for now." But later, after praying softly at the site where his brother had been killed, he seemed to reconsider. Hate, he said, "is always looking for another place."[52]

EPILOGUE

The hunting season wasn't over. As Joselo Lucero had predicted, hatred simply moved elsewhere. On December 18, 2009, thirteen months after Lucero was killed, the *New York Times* quoted Thomas E. Perez, head of the Justice Department's Civil Rights Division, as saying that the department had dealt with more federal hate crime cases that year than in any other year since 2001. Twenty-five hate crime cases were filed in 2009, two more than in the year before. The higher number was not necessarily a reflection of an increase in crime. Rather, it was a change in prosecutorial attitude. After a downtick in prosecutions of hate crimes during the George W. Bush administration, Perez pronounced the Civil Rights Division of the Department of Justice "open for business."[1]

In 2011, the Bureau of Justice Statistics issued a report about citizen-reported hate crimes for the years 2003–2009. Almost ninety percent of the crimes in that period were "perceived to be motivated by racial or ethnic prejudice or both," and 87 percent of the crimes involved violence. In 2009 alone, "an estimated

148,400 hate crimes were reported to the National Crime Victimization Survey," including eight homicides. Yet only about 45 percent of the total number of crimes were reported to the police; 19 percent of those who didn't call the police explained that they had decided to remain quiet because the police "could not or would not do anything to help."[2]

Shortly after Lucero was killed, the Associated Press reported that there had been a surge in hate crimes since the election of Barack Obama as president.[3] If so, Lucero may have been the first victim of that surge, a mere four days after the election. However, there is no indication that Obama's election had anything to do with the attack on Lucero and Loja. They were hunted because they were vulnerable, and because the teenagers who attacked them must have felt that all Hispanics they encountered in Patchogue and Medford were Mexicans, and therefore illegally in the country. Their perceived immigration status rendered them somehow lesser human beings in the eyes of the teenagers.

Upon hearing about the case, many have expressed surprise that one of the teenagers—José Pacheco—was black and Hispanic, not only because he was a friend of Jeffrey Conroy and the other white young men in the group, but because he too had participated in repeated attacks against immigrants. How, I've been asked repeatedly, could he turn against his own people? Those who study the nature of bias know that one can be both an ethnic or a racial minority and a bigot. "This duality is common," wrote Touré, the author of *Who's Afraid of Post-Blackness?*, in a *Time* magazine column. "We give humanity to those we know, but the true test is, Can we extend it to those we don't?"[4]

Only three of the teenagers spoke to reporters after their arrest: Jeffrey Conroy, José Pacheco, and, briefly, Nicholas Hausch.

Jeff was said to be "reflective," "apologetic," "humble," and "hopeful" when he spoke to *New York Times* reporter Manny

Fernandez as he awaited sentencing in a Suffolk County jail in Riverhead. During the hour-long interview he spoke "of his love and concern for his family," and of the future he still hoped to have with Pamela Suárez, his on-and-off girlfriend since middle school.[5]

"I'm nothing like what the papers said about me," he said. "I'm not a white supremacist or anything like that. I'm not this serious racist kid everyone thinks I am."

He told an anecdote unheard until then: when he was in his junior year of high school, in October 2007, he had confronted two white men outside a convenience store who were about to steal the bicycle of a Hispanic man, possibly a day laborer. As for the swastika tattooed on his thigh, he said, "It doesn't mean anything to me at all."

From behind a Plexiglas partition and wearing prison greens a year after the attack, José told Sumathi Reddy, a *Newsday* reporter, that he had "nothing to do with this crime," claiming that he had been in the car that night with the other six teenagers because he had needed a ride home.[6] Because of his involvement in the case, he had been threatened by Latino gangs in jail; some inmates had spit on him. He said that he spent his days reading books his mother brought him and trying to learn Japanese. He played basketball, went to a prayer group, and called his mother every day.

"I'm innocent," he said. "I want the public to know I'm a good person. I'm not a monster."

Nick, in a brief interview with *Newsday*'s Andrew Strickler when he was out on bail, said that if he could do it over again, he "wouldn't go out" the night of the attack.[7]

Kevin has not spoken to reporters, but his father, responding to my inquiry for an interview, sent me a letter in March 2012 in which he said that his son would like to meet with me. "He would like you to see how he has matured and grown from his mistakes," Thomas Shea Sr. wrote. "I must let you know that I love my son and try to see him as often as possible," he went on. "What happened, how it happened, and what led up to this tragedy is impossible for us to answer, but we would like to show that this was not in character for Kevin."[8]

Though I followed up with both, I never heard back from them.

After the attackers were sent to prison—Jordan Dasch, José Pacheco, and Anthony Hartford each got seven years, while Christopher Overton got six, Kevin Shea got eight, and Nicholas Hausch got five—the Lucero family filed two separate lawsuits, one against the teenagers and their parents and another against the county, the village, and the police. The latter was dismissed on a technicality and is now on appeal, but the suit against the families is pending in Suffolk County Supreme Court. In it, the estate of Marcelo Lucero accuses the parents of the teenagers of inadequate supervision of their children's "dangerous and defective condition," which is described in the document as "a propensity toward vicious, violent, anti-social, criminal and assaultive conduct."[9]

On November 6, 2012, four years after Lucero's death, President Obama was reelected with overwhelming support from Hispanics, who punished Republicans for, among other things, their fury at undocumented immigrants and their reluctance to contemplate any kind of legislation aimed at legalizing them. Though not all of the estimated 11.1 million undocumented in the country are Hispanics, the majority of them, at 59 percent, are Mexicans, who live all over the country but tend to concentrate in Nevada, California, and Texas. In 2010, they represented 5.2 percent of the US workforce.[10]

Merely five months before the election, in a move that was widely interpreted by political pundits and analysts to be part of a strategy to win the Latino vote, President Obama issued a presidential order deferring the deportation of young undocumented immigrants who had been brought to the country illegally as children. The tactic worked. Latinos went to polls in droves—11.2 million Latinos voted—helping win Obama four more years in the White House.[11] Immediately after, the president promised to make immigration reform a priority.

In a piece that began with this sentence, "The sleeping giant has awoken," CNN reported that Latinos, who made up 10 percent of the electorate for the first time ever, had helped Obama win the election in key states such as New Mexico, Colorado, Nevada, Florida, and Virginia. "Latinos, the fastest growing minority, making up 16% of the nation's population, made their mark on election night as they voted for President Barack Obama over Republican Mitt Romney 71% to 27%, a lower percentage than Republican candidates have received in the last three elections."[12]

On November 8, 2012, the *Wall Street Journal* ran a post-election editorial with a headline in Spanish: "¡Estimados Republicanos!" The "Dear Republicans" headline—the first I've ever seen in Spanish atop an editorial in that newspaper—was attention-grabbing; the content of the editorial was even more provocative. The conservative, pro-business newspaper chastised Republicans for the "antagonistic attitude that the GOP too often exhibits toward America's fastest-growing demographic group." It called the antagonism "unnecessary," because immigrants—documented or not—are a "natural GOP constituency," with their belief in hard work and their conservative culture.[13]

The month after the election, national Latino leaders, emboldened by their show of power on Election Day, said they would "keep a report card" on the immigration debate expected to take place in 2013 so they could mobilize Hispanic voters against those who do not support "comprehensive immigration reform," a code phrase for legislation that would allow undocumented immigrants to remain in the country legally and on a path to citizenship.[14]

On April 17, a bipartisan group of eight senators introduced a sweeping immigration bill that President Obama characterized as "largely consistent" with his principles but that drew the ire of opponents who began to publicly discuss strategies to kill the bill. At issue is the fear among conservatives that a clear path to citizenship would encourage even more illegal immigration. The bill passed the Senate in late June. As of this writing, it is unclear if the House will pass a similar bill.[15]

Last year, one of my children wrote a letter to Vice President Joe Biden as part of a class project. Biden replied, or signed the letter that someone else wrote for him, addressing my son's question about undocumented immigrants but emphasizing the illegality of their status and placing the burden of solving their problems on the immigrants themselves.

"This Administration is working to protect our borders at points of entry with additional personnel, infrastructure, and technology," he wrote in the letter dated December 20, 2012. "The Recovery Act provided over $400 million in funds to accomplish this. While strengthening border control is an important pillar of reform, we are also removing incentives to enter the United States illegally by preventing employers from hiring undocumented workers. Enforcement, however, is not the only solution. We must also require current undocumented workers who are in good standing to come out of the shadows and follow a responsible path to citizenship."

The Obama administration has deported a record number of undocumented immigrants—as of August 2012, 1.4 million, more per month than George W. Bush did during his eight years in office.[16] And the border has never been more secure. Last year, Customs and Border Protection's budget reached $11.7 billion, 64 percent more than in 2006, when the Republicans had the White House. There are now 651 miles of fence, 21,444 agents, and nine drones protecting the US-Mexico border.[17]

All of that protection has paid off, and may have become somewhat superfluous as immigration from Mexico has tapered off. A report of the Pew Hispanic Center, released in April 2012, revealed that "the largest wave of immigration in history from a single country [Mexico] to the United States has come to a standstill. After four decades that brought 12 million current immigrants—most of whom came illegally—the net migration flow from Mexico to the United States has stopped and may have reversed." The researchers explained that the decline was the result of many factors, including the weakened US economy, stronger economic conditions in Mexico (coupled with plunging birthrates in that country), and the perception—rooted in reality—of the dangers of crossing the border, with its heightened security, risk of deportation, and the threats from organized crime.[18]

In Patchogue, people say things have changed, that immigrants no longer fear the police or the teenagers who used to harass them. It is no longer open season on Hispanics, they say, but it is all very anecdotal and very inconsistent.

After years without reports of attacks, a Hispanic man was assaulted and robbed in April of 2013 in the village of Patchogue. In the weeks that followed, and up to May 14, when *Newsday* published the story, there were other attacks in East Patchogue.[19] Mayor Pontieri said they appeared to be crimes of opportunity, not of hatred, and he was comforted by the fact that this time he was one of the first to hear about the attacks. "For me, the fact they came to see me first shows me we have made headway," he told me. "It's about trust."[20]

Julio Espinoza says he doesn't notice any racism, but then he never did. He is a busy man who spends his day rushing between his several stores—the business has grown to employ practically everyone in his family—and chatting with friends and clients who still come to him for advice and wisdom. The uncertainty he felt right after Lucero was killed has been replaced by the complacency that comes when one's immediate world remains untouched. His children are well and thriving, and the youngest has already graduated from the high school that Jeffrey Conroy and his friends once attended and that so divided the community with its separate areas for immigrants and natives.

Angel Loja, who practically disappeared after he testified in the trial and refused to speak to the press, breathes a heavy sigh when asked if things have changed. "*¡Ay, señora!*" he tells me every time I ask, as if he were dealing with a persistent but naive child who can't quite comprehend the ways of the world. Racism permeates everything in Patchogue, says Loja, who has moved from the village and found a job driving a school bus. He is in a stable relationship and seems less sad than when I met him in 2011, but he remains angry at elected officials in Patchogue and in the state, and at the way he knows many people regard him because of the color of his skin or the slant of his eyes. He is trying to save $1,500 to pay the expenses related to the residency status he hopes to acquire soon.

The Justice Department has not yet issued the final results of its investigation of the Suffolk County Police Department, but on September 13, 2011, it did release some preliminary observations and recommendations, which were highly critical of the police department.[21] Among other things, the twenty-eight-page letter pointed to a lack of follow-up after bias crime reports as well as inconsistent reporting and tracking of hate crimes. It also criticized the department for inquiring about immigration status during investigations, and mentioned language barriers as possible obstacles to building relationships with members of the Hispanic community. In addition, the letter pointed to signs that preceded Lucero's murder and that the police chose to obviate. "The tendency to brush off attacks as 'just kids being kids' fails to recognize the severity of criminal conduct in which minors may engage," the Justice Department stated, adding that "bias-driven behavior, even if it does not rise to the level of a hate crime, can be significant, and it should be addressed. Unchecked, it can develop into serious hate crimes, as evidenced by the events preceding the death of Marcelo Lucero."[22]

When the letter was released, some changes had already taken place in Suffolk County. Lola Quesada, the police officer so often standing by the side of the Lucero family, was promoted to special assistant to the police commissioner for minority affairs, a new position. As such, she shed her uniform and became a full-time community relations officer to the Latino community. Among other things, she teaches what she calls "street survival Spanish" at the police academy for new recruits. The report lauded her work as well as the fact that police officers are encouraged to learn Spanish and to interact even more with the Latino community.[23] In 2011, Quesada was promoted to the rank of detective in the Hate Crimes Unit.

There were some other positive signs in Suffolk County. Mayor Pontieri, who has never visited his parents' native Calabria and rarely leaves Patchogue, traveled to Gualaceo in the summer of 2010 at the invitation of Marco Tapia, Gualaceo's youthful mayor. The four-day visit was informal and generated a lot of publicity for the mayor, who told reporters he was making a "goodwill" trip. The Lucero family, still reeling from Pontieri's decision to invite Steve Levy to the memorial a year after Lucero's death, refused to meet with him. But Pontieri met with local officials, danced with Gualaceñas, and gave a brief speech in which he said that he didn't want to focus on the past but to acknowledge it and move on. As always, he established a connection by dwelling on his immigrant roots: "When the ambassador for Ecuador visited Patchogue, after the tragedy of Marcelo Lucero, I showed him a picture of my grandfather and the men who worked for him. . . . They were strong young men with shovels who were building the roads of Patchogue. Not much has changed from now and then. We still have strong men with shovels building roads, except then they were from Italy. Today many are from Ecuador!"[24]

He got thunderous applause for that. Skillfully, as he has

learned to do, Pontieri skirted the immigration debate by repeating his mantra that such talk was above his pay level. His job is to make sure that Patchogue is safe and prosperous for all its residents, no matter their immigration status or nationality. That kind of forward-looking, safe talk has served him well. Pontieri has traveled to several cities in the United States spreading a message of tolerance and integration, he has written about his experiences in Patchogue, and he was the indisputable star of a one-hour PBS documentary titled *Not in Our Town: Light in the Darkness*, about the Lucero case, which was released in the fall of 2011.

Pontieri and Quesada were not the only ones to earn accolades or promotions or both after the Lucero case. Megan O'Donnell, the prosecutor, was promoted to deputy bureau chief, and in early 2013 she left the district attorney's office for a job at the Suffolk County Attorney's Office, handling civil matters for the county in federal court. The Patchogue-Medford Library received the 2010 National Medal for Museum and Library Service from the hands of First Lady Michelle Obama during a White House ceremony on December 17, 2010. The medal is the highest honor conferred to museums and libraries for outstanding community service; in this case, it honored the library's ongoing work with immigrants.[25]

Three months later, Gilda Ramos received the Paralibrarian of the Year Award, given by *Library Journal*. She, along with Jean Kaleda, is widely believed to have spearheaded the community outreach efforts that earned the library national recognition. The library has become the indispensable institution for Ecuadorians in Suffolk County, an incredible turn of events that speaks volumes of Kaleda's tenacity and warmth. She too has visited Gualaceo. She spent ten days traveling through Azuay in March 2011. When I asked why, she replied, "Because they are my patrons! I have to know where they come from." But of course, it is more than that.

Nationally, immigrants too are getting some kind of delayed recognition and acceptance. A generation ago, California voters approved a ballot initiative to keep undocumented immigrants away from public hospitals and schools, but now "more California residents than ever before say that immigrants are a benefit to the state," the *New York Times* reported in February 2013.[26] In Arizona, where Mexican ethnic studies were once banned, a federal judge has ordered that courses that reflect the history, experience, and culture of Mexican Americans can be taught in the classrooms.[27]

A study released in October 2011 by the Fiscal Policy Institute, a nonprofit research organization in New York, found that immigrants, no matter their legal status, are important contributors to the economy on Long Island and are a relatively affluent group, with a median income for a family with at least one immigrant adult of $98,000, compared with $110,000 for families headed by US-born adults. The report stated that in Nassau and Suffolk Counties, two of the country's fifty most affluent counties, immigrants represent about 16 percent of the population and add about 17 percent of value to the economy through their work.[28] In an interview with the *New York Times* about the study, Steve Levy, the Suffolk County executive, contended that the study had been done by a "left-leaning" group that had not drawn a distinction between documented and undocumented immigrants. "No one is denying that legal immigration contributes to our culture and our economy," the *Times* quoted Levy as saying. "It looks like selective data was put into this study omitting the drain on services that come about from the illegal population."[29]

Once again, Levy was wrong. While economists agree that the cheaper labor of undocumented immigrants helps lower the wages of adult US workers without a high school diploma, they also agree that the net impact for everyone else is positive. Immigrants—documented or not—benefit the economy and contribute about $15 billion a year to Social Security through payroll taxes. They can be a drain on services in areas where they congregate in great numbers. However, the dollars they bring to local economies outweigh the costs of the services they receive.[30]

• • •

Perhaps nothing has had a bigger impact on Suffolk County than a major restructuring in the political front. Jack Eddington, bruised from the accusations of racism lobbed his way, retired from politics, saying he was tired of the partisanship, the bickering, and the whole game of politics.

Levy "abruptly ended his bid for a third term in March 2011 in a deal to end a 16-month criminal investigation of his political fund-raising," the *New York Times* reported. Levy, who had amassed a campaign war chest of $4.1 million, agreed to turn over the money to the Suffolk district attorney's office. In return, Thomas J. Spota, the district attorney, closed the investigation, which he said had begun in the summer of 2009. Spota said little about the investigation, but he indicated that there was no evidence that Levy, who up to then had enjoyed an impeccable reputation on matters of finance and ethics, had personally benefited from his campaign funds.

Ironically, some of that returned and unclaimed money—$17,500—ended up in the hands of the Workplace Project, an immigrant rights organization, after the Reverend Allan Ramírez, now retired, asked Spota for a portion of Levy's funds.[31]

In January 2012, Steve Bellone became the new county executive in Suffolk County. Bellone wasted no time in delineating the differences between him and his predecessor during his inaugural speech. "For those who are willing to work hard and are looking for a better life, regardless of where you came from—we want you in Suffolk County," he said.

He told a story about his Irish immigrant grandparents and the tiny apartment in Manhattan's Washington Heights they once shared with his mother, aunts, and uncles. He said he had gone back there recently with his mother, in her first visit to the old neighborhood in nearly fifty years, and they were welcomed by a Dominican family. "We are stronger together," he added.

According to a *New York Times* editorial, "[A] good share of his [Bellone's] speech was devoted to the importance of immigration, a tacit attempt to reverse Suffolk's reputation as a place riven by anti-immigrant sentiments and violence."[32]

In his first few months in office, Bellone appointed Luis Valenzuela, for years an important immigrant rights activist on Long Island and a pillar of strength during the tumultuous months after Lucero's murder, as a member of Suffolk County's Human Rights Commission. He was confirmed unanimously by the legislature. Bellone reached out to the community in other ways. He was grand marshal of Brentwood's Puerto Rican Day Parade, and on November 14, 2012, he signed an executive order requiring county agencies to translate essential public documents and forms into six languages besides English—including Spanish, of course—and to provide translation services for residents who don't speak English.[33]

Undaunted, Levy continues to wave the anti-immigrant flag, even from the sidelines. When asked about Bellone's appointment of Valenzuela, he said that Valenzuela was an "articulate gentleman. But he is as far left as they come in the illegal immigration lobby. Steve [Bellone] said my opposition to illegal immigration was divisive, but in his quest to be liked by everyone he is capitulating to those who want to surrender on the issue."[34] Bellone declined to comment on Levy's portrayal of his policies.

It is impossible to gauge how non-Hispanic residents feel about immigration now. Feelings of racism and discrimination can't be legislated away, but actions can. People in Patchogue may still despise or fear their Hispanic neighbors; they just don't talk about it or seem to be acting on it. Other words, other phrases, have been substituted for harsher comments about immigrants. Expressed concerns about public housing, drunkenness, and overcrowded houses continue to be used in not-so-subtle reference to the larger issue of immigration.

In May 2012, Pontieri held a live online chat with residents, facilitated by *Patchogue Patch*, a local web publication. Some of the questions reflect a lingering anxiety regarding Hispanics. They are transcribed here as they were written:

Comment from S & L: Mr. Mayor, regarding overcrowded rentals in the Village of Patchogue, why are they allowed to do this?

Paul Pontieri: They are not allowed. We have very strict housing codes that are enforced, but like most things it is imperative that residents who live near these overcrowded homes advise the Village that they are so. What I will guarantee to you [is] that if you feel there is a home within your neighborhood that you can identify by address that we will investigate it, give out violations as needed, and close if we must.

Comment from Luke: Why is there a bodega next to an elementary school on Bay Avenue? This is on the Village side. There are MANY vagrants/drug addicts/criminals that linger around there EVERY MORNING! what is being done about this?

Paul Pontieri: Luke, I appreciate the comments, I will contact the Suffolk County PD and work with them to move them away from the school.

Comment from Tino: Mr. Mayor, Thank you for this honor of a "live chat" I have a question, about how many of the many rentals in patchogue would you say rent to "section 8?" being someone who rents in the village, i'm not against it, but i'm also not a fan of section 8 living next door and across the street

Paul Pontieri: Tino, I don't know the number of it, but Section 8 vouchers have been frozen by the federal government and whatever is in the Village now, it will never get any greater than it is.

The Patchogue-Medford Library too has received a number of messages from patrons who can't understand why librarians are reaching out to Hispanic immigrants. One such letter, dated September 7, 2010, calls undocumented immigrants "criminals." "Over the past several years I have noticed that the *Patchogue-Medford Newsletter* is partially printed in Spanish. I am wondering why since we live in the United States of America not in Mexico or some place south of the border," the patron wrote, adding, "Have you looked at Main Street in Patchogue? I don't know whether I am in America or in some third world Mexican village."

Another village resident sent a succinct e-mail: "We live in AMERICA NOT IN MEXICO." Yet another wrote: "It seems that the only reason the PM Library exists is to assist these 'hard-working undocumented immigrants.' I choose to call them what they really are CRIMINALS." And another: "Step outside the door of your Library. Notice that smell in the air, no not the beans and rice or the beer or the stink of urine, it is the smell of change."

In January 2011, a seemingly very angry patron sent an e-mail that ended with the following sentences: "I am sick and tired of you feeding these stray cats. Send them back where they belong. Perhaps you people could move to El Salvador or Mexico."

Kaleda, who has expanded the programs to reach even more Hispanics, says that she often engages in conversations with patrons who don't like the library's Spanish-language services. She tries to appease them by explaining that the community is changing and that recognizing that change can be painful. Dina Chrils, the director of the library, sends everyone the same response: "Thank you for your input. We will keep it in mind when planning Library Services."[35]

The Reverend Dwight Wolter, who had wanted to reach out to the Latino community ever since he arrived in Patchogue, finally found an ingenious way to do so. He gives away new and used bicycles to anyone who needs transportation and can't afford wheels. But he drew the ire of an important segment of the Latino community when he announced in July 2010 that he would begin collecting money to contribute to Jeffrey Conroy's commissary account in prison. Eddington too provoked much criticism when he and his wife, Patricia, an elected official, each sent a letter to Judge Doyle asking him for clemency in sentencing Jeff. Eddington wrote that the killing was "deplorable" and needed to be punished, but he added, "I have to believe that, for a young man raised in such a family, redemption is possible."[36]

The day Jeff was sentenced to twenty-five years in prison, his father lost his composure in a heartbreaking scene that left no doubt what the true outcome of the case was. Eight families were shattered. "He was fucking seventeen!" Bob Conroy yelled the moment Judge Doyle issued his sentence. From his seat, next to his lawyer, Jeff paled and looked pained. His sister in the audience began sobbing. "You think this is mercy, for crying out loud? Jesus fucking Christ!" Conroy started walking toward the door as he yelled at the judge. The courtroom was quiet, as people sat in the benches, twisting their bodies to get a better view but not daring to say a word. Conroy banged on the door on his way out, already surrounded by police officers. His children followed him quietly as Jeff was escorted out of the courtroom and the judge, impassively, returned to his reading of the sentence. The family vowed to appeal.

Broke after his son's trial, Conroy turned to the Legal Aid Society in Suffolk County for help. A lawyer there, John Dowden, argued the appeal on December 7, 2012, more than two years after the trial. He presented a brief with eleven points that, he said, would merit a retrial. Dowden argued that Jeff was denied his right to a fair trial when the court failed to respond meaningfully to a juror note requesting a read-back of the cross-examination of Detective McLeer, and that the judge had erred when he instructed the jury to regard Jeff's statement regarding the culpability of Chris not as a fact but as a comment that reflected Jeff's state of mind. Dowden also argued that the sentence imposed on Jeff was harsh and excessive and that it should be modified in the interest of justice.[37] But Dowden lost his argument and the court confirmed the conviction. Though the Conroys still have the option of going before the New York Court of Appeals and beyond, Jeff is likely to remain imprisoned at least until he's eligible for parole in 2030, the year he will turn thirty-nine.

To this day, Conroy remains aggrieved by the sentence. Jeff is held at the Clinton Correctional Facility, a maximum-security prison built in 1844 that houses about twenty-seven hundred men in Dannemora, a village 365 miles from Medford.[38] Conroy visits him as often as he can, which is not very often, because it's a long trip and gasoline is expensive, but father and son talk on the phone often and Jeff writes from prison. A *Wikipedia* entry for the prison lists Jeff among the many "notable inmates" who have done their time at Clinton. It breaks Conroy's already pained and fragile heart to know that his son lives with some of the most hardened criminals in the state, including Joel Rifkin, a serial killer serving a 203-year sentence. "He's surrounded by bad men," he told me once and complained about how Jeff had begun cursing a great deal.

Conroy has had several recent health scares but tries to remain strong, the head of a household that has changed dramatically since Jeff was arrested. Now separated from his wife, he lives with three of his children in the same house where Jeff grew up. The last time I visited, the house was in much better shape than when we first met right after the trial. The grass was green and lush; there were potted flowers, and the place had a sense of order and normalcy.

In a brief exchange of text messages in early 2013, Conroy wrote me: "It is just totally wrong how they made him the county's scapegoat. I don't know if that's how you feel. But 25 years is bullshit." Then he asked me how I felt, if I thought that justice was served by sentencing a seventeen-year-old to such a long prison term. I told him the truth: I don't know. Because even after three years of reporting and writing this book, there is a lot I will never know.

What I think I do know is that Jeffrey Conroy didn't set out to kill anybody that night. I also know that the atmosphere that existed in Suffolk County in the first decade of the century would have made an unequivocal impression on any youngster: Jeff and his friends must have felt that their entertainment of hunting "beaners" had the tacit and implicit approval of the adults in their world.

A recent national study shows that a large number of Americans, influenced by negative images in the media, hold unfavorable and even hostile views of Hispanics. According to the study, conducted by the National Hispanic Media Coalition, many Americans hold the media stereotype of Latinos largely as maids, gardeners, dropouts, and criminals. At least a third of non-Hispanic Americans believe that half or more of the nation's almost fifty-six million Hispanics are undocumented immigrants with large families and little education.[39]

On the fourth anniversary of Lucero's death, a vigil was held in a Methodist church in Patchogue. About seventy-five people attended the November 25, 2012, event, including Mayor Pontieri. A large photo of Lucero in rust-colored overalls was placed at the altar, and it seemed to loom over the audience. The friendship quilts the women of Medford and Patchogue had painstakingly made hung in the back.

Before the event started, Bob Conroy drove by the church and called Joselo Lucero to his car. Neither one of them wanted to describe to me what transpired, but someone who is close to both men and was standing by heard Conroy apologize. His gesture is not surprising. Conroy had apologized at least twice before, including once during a pretrial hearing when he shook Joselo's hand.[40] The day of the fourth-anniversary vigil, Conroy took his apology a step further and asked Joselo if he could come into the church. Joselo told him that the event was open to all. But Conroy drove away. He said he didn't want to attract attention to himself on such a solemn occasion. Joselo was left a little shaken by the unexpected encounter but quickly recovered.

Inside the church, near the altar, there were yellow, red, and orange flowers. A man, accompanied by his own guitar playing, sang a song about the difficulties in attaining the American dream. "Here I am, after ten years, living in the United States, without papers. I'm still illegal," he sang. A local woman read a long poem she had written about the trial of Jeffrey Conroy, which she called "In the Courtroom," and then Joselo, wearing a camel-colored suit and a white shirt, took the microphone.

"I don't know what to say," he began, and then, of course, he had plenty to say, because in the years since his brother's death, Joselo has blossomed into a public figure, a young man who wears dark shades to hide his sad eyes and who makes forceful statements in his still tentative but improving English. Joselo has moved from Patchogue and now works as outreach coordinator at the Hagedorn Foundation—a nonprofit organization based on Long Island that supports and promotes social equality. Frequently he speaks to college and high school students, and he participates in symposiums, conferences, and television programs about hate crimes and immigration. His attire has improved—he no longer wears baseball caps to public events—but he retains his shy smile and his inbred politeness.

That day, in front of the altar, he talked about Sandy, the superstorm that had just swept over the Northeast killing 149 people, 42 of them in New York alone. Lucero linked that tragedy to the plight of immigrants.

"Immigrants are the ones who will be rebuilding after Sandy," he said. "The day laborers are the ones who will rebuild the homes that keep you warm."

He was right. Five weeks after Sandy, the *New York Times* reported that day laborers were working seven days a week rebuilding homes destroyed by Sandy. One of the workers interviewed for the article said the sudden infusion of money had allowed him to buy a computer, bicycles, and new shoes for his two sons in Ecuador.[41]

In Patchogue, there was little damage from the storm. Water rose approximately four feet deep in many homes along the shore, trees were down, and people lost power, but most neighborhoods had their electricity back on in seventy-two hours. Some houses need major reconstruction work, but no one was left homeless, Pontieri said.

"Like most things in Patchogue, its past is what saved it from the ravages of today," Pontieri told me, explaining that in the early 1950s, the mayor at the time, George Lechtrecker, had created a thirty-acre park on the waterfront. It was that park that protected and buffered most homes from the serious damage that other Long Island communities suffered during the 2012 storm.[42]

The past also helped Patchogue survive the killing of Lucero, Pontieri insisted, because the village is and always has been an immigrant enclave. The faces and the languages have changed but the ethos is the same: newcomers trying to find in pretty and orderly suburbia their own little piece of heaven.

Pontieri may be right. How do immigrants find their way to suburbia if not following those who came before they did? How do parents ever recuperate from the grave mistakes of their children? How does anyone account for the capriciousness of wind and rising water? Superstorm Sandy, like all major weather systems, had a mind of its own. In 1992, Hurricane Andrew ravaged portions of South Florida, leaving others untouched. I remember walking around a doomed neighborhood called Country Walk in Dade County and finding one solitary pale green wall standing amid total devastation. There were pictures of smiling children with braces on the wall, and reclining against it, an elegant table with a set of glasses and a bottle of liquor. Intact.

Perhaps Sandy spared Patchogue because the park barrier built fifty years earlier did what it was supposed to do. Or perhaps Sandy, with a mind of its own, spared Patchogue because the village had had enough.

ACKNOWLEDGMENTS

I could not have written this book without the goodwill and cooperation of the men and women in Patchogue and in Gualaceo who
sat with me for extensive rounds of interviews and conversations
or answered my phone calls and e-mails on numerous occasions
during three years. Most of them are cited throughout the book,
as this is their story, not mine, but I want to thank them here,
because without their help I would have had nothing more than
a good idea. In no particular order, they are Jean Kaleda, Gilda
Ramos, Mayor Paul Pontieri, the Reverend Dwight Wolter,
Angel Loja, Jack Eddington, Ambassador Jorge López Amaya,
Julio Espinoza and his family, Pamela Suárez, Rabbi Joel Levinson, Hans Henke, Diana M. Berthold, Megan O'Donnell, Detective Lola Quesada, Michael Mostow, Martha Vázquez, Joselo
Lucero and his family, Macedonio Ayala, Denise Overton, Mayor
Marco Tapia, Father Julio Castillo, and Bob Conroy.

    I relied a great deal on the good journalism of reporters who
got to the story before I did, chiefly Angel Canales, Tamara Bock,
Jennifer Jo Janisch, Ted Hesson, Sumathi Reddy, Margaret

(Molly) Altizer, and Bart Jones. Angel and Tamara generously shared the transcripts of their documentary, *Running Wild: Hate and Immigration on Long Island*. Ted and Sumathi not only shared their notes, expertise, and friendship, but they also drove me to and from the courthouse in Riverhead too many times to count. Ted, Bart, and Molly also read the manuscript; Molly especially made numerous and terrific comments that improved the book immensely.

Gretchen Van Dyck and Ray Katz assisted me during the early stages of research. Their help tracking down trial documents and researching the history of hate in America was an essential building block to my own reporting and writing. Michael Sorrentino, Sarah Hartmann, and Mark Nolan helped me understand Patchogue better. Fernando León, Marlene Matute, William Murillo, and Andrea Ledesma did the same in Gualaceo. I'm eternally grateful for their generosity of spirit and camaraderie.

Court reporter Dana Marconi worked diligently to get me the trial transcripts I needed, often on deadline. Michael Lieberman of the Anti-Defamation League patiently helped me understand the intricacies of hate crime laws. Laura Itzkowitz took charge of the monumental task of organizing the book's references, and she did so with grace and calm despite a punishing deadline. Ambassador Gonzalo Andrade graciously agreed to read the sections of the manuscript that deal with the recent history of Ecuador and made available important research regarding Ecuadorian emigration. And S. Mitra Kalita, over lunch one day, said the words that unlocked the writing of this book.

Sarah, Diane, Peter, Kay, and María helped me tremendously with my children. With friends like these, a working mom can actually finish writing a book. Sam Freedman, as ever, provided advice and encouragement, as did Lindy Hess, dear friend and early champion of this project.

My agent, Anna Ghosh, understood the book before she had even read the proposal and was immediately enthusiastic. She led me to my editor at Beacon Press, Gayatri Patnaik, an immigrant herself, who has made it a personal and professional mission to publish books that advance the national conversation on immigration. She, along with all the other good people at Beacon Press, has lovingly tended to this book. In particular, I want to thank Beacon's director, Helene Atwan; Tom Hallock, director of sales and marketing; Bob Kosturko, creative director, who designed the beautiful cover; Beth Collins, who put it all together skillfully; Rachael Marks, editorial assistant, who was always available, always helpful, always professional and friendly; and freelancer Chris Dodge, the best copy editor I've had since I left the *Times*.

I'm indebted to Columbia University for providing the resources to research and write the book, with three grants: the Diversity Research Fellowship Award and (twice) the Research and Travel Grant of the Institute of Latin American Studies. Esteban Andrade, program manager of the institute, was a great source of contacts and information. Nick Lemann, Bill Grueskin, and Laura Muha—my colleagues at the Graduate School of Journalism—allowed me to take the time to complete this project and were very creative with my schedule when I couldn't take any more time off.

My children, Juan Arturo, Lucas, and Marcelo, were the inspiration and motivation to tell this story. More than once I left the dinner table to take notes inspired by our talks. Yet they sacrificed much to the book's completion, and they got way too used to my peering at them over my reading glasses with a glazed look. "Thinking of your book?" they often asked. Yes, of course, but I also was, and I always am, thinking of them first. It is my hope that they will remember this tumultuous period of our lives as a time of growth and learning.

NOTES

Prologue

1. "Most Expensive ZIP Codes, 2006," *Forbes*, http://www.forbes.com/lists/2006/7/NY_Rank_1.html.

2. Bruce Lambert, "Study Calls L.I. Most Segregated Suburb," *New York Times*, June 5, 2002.

3. Telephone interview with Joselo Lucero, January 5, 2010.

4. Mirta Ojito, "Away from the Big City, Seeking a New Life but Facing New Tensions," *New York Times*, September 30, 1996.

5. Paul Pontieri's quote from interview on April 13, 2010.

6. Mark Potok, "Anti-Latino Hate Crimes Rise for Fourth Year in a Row," Southern Poverty Law Center, October 29, 2008, http://www.splcenter.org/blog/2008/10/29/anti-latino-hate-crimes-rise-for-fourth-year.

7. "Hating Marcelo," *Bob Edwards Show*, aired December 22, 2009, http://www.bobedwardsradio.com/hating-marcelo.

8. Ted Hesson, "Suffolk County Appoints New Head of Hate Crimes Unit," *Long Island Wins*, January 8, 2011, http://www.longislandwins.com.

9. "Many in U.S. Illegally Overstayed Their Visas," *Wall Street Journal*, April 7, 2013.

10. Steven A. Camarota, "Immigrants in the United States, 2010: A Profile of America's Foreign-Born Population," Center for Immigration Studies, August 2012, http://www.cis.org/2012-profile-of-americas -foreign-born-population.

11. Steven A. Camarota, "100 Million More: Projecting the Impact of Immigration on the U.S. Population, 2007 to 2060," Center for Immigration Studies, August 2007, http://cis.org/impact_on_population.html.

12. Laura Meckler, "Hispanic Future in the Cards; Whites to Represent 43% of U.S. by 2060, Down from 63% Today, Census Projects," *Wall Street Journal*, December 13, 2012.

13. Sabrina Tavernise, "Numbers of Children of Whites Falling Fast," *New York Times*, April 6, 2011.

14. Jack Eddington's quote from interview on May 26, 2010.

15. Sabrina Tavernise and Robert Gebeloff, "Immigrants Make Paths to Suburbia, Not Cities," *New York Times*, December 14, 2010.

16. Conor Dougherty and Miriam Jordan, "Stirring Up the Melting Pot," *Wall Street Journal*, September 7, 2012.

17. "Suffolk County QuickFacts from the US Census Bureau," US Census Bureau, http://quickfacts.census.gov/qfd/states/36/36103.html.

18. Kirk Semple, "A Killing in a Town Where Latinos Sense Hate," *New York Times*, November 14, 2008.

19. Tamara Boch and Angel Canales, unpublished transcript of documentary *Running Wild: Hate and Immigration on Long Island*, aired on WLIW-TV, November 11, 2009.

20. *Climate of Fear: Latino Immigrants in Suffolk County, N.Y.*, Southern Poverty Law Center, 2009, http://www.splcenter.org/get-informed/ publications/climate-of-fear-latino-immigrants-in-suffolk-county-ny.

21. Ibid.

22. Interviews with Eddington, May 26, 2010–November 12, 2012.

23. *Climate of Fear*.

24. Interview with Paul Pontieri, February 27, 2012.

Chapter 1: A Bloody Knife

Unless otherwise specified, the information in this chapter comes from interviews with Angel Loja, May 30, 2011–December 3, 2012.

1. People of the State of New York v. Jeffrey Conroy, Supreme Court of the State of New York, County of Suffolk No. 3032A-2008, 236A-2009, excerpt of trial (March 24, 2010).

2. Señor de Andacocha tourist information pamphlet.

3. Ibid.

4. Centro de Estudios Internacionales (Barcelona, Spain) and FLACSO (organization), *Emigración y Política Exterior En Ecuador*, Agora (Quito: Centro de Estudios Internacionales: FLACSO, Sede Académica de Ecuador: Abya Yala, 2005), 101.

CHAPTER 2: PAINTED BIRDS IN THE AIR
Unless otherwise specified, information in this chapter comes from several interviews with Julio Espinoza, January 2010–September 2012.

1. "History [of Ecuador]," http://www.frommers.com/destinations/ecuador/0811020044.html.

2. *Report of the Visa Office 1981* (US Department of State, Bureau of Consular Affairs, 1981).

3. Kyle and Goldstein, *Migration Industries*, 5.

4. Ibid., 4.

5. Ibid., 4–5.

6. Ibid., 5.

7. Portes and Rumbaut, *Immigrant America*.

8. Ibid., 40, 41, 59.

9. Kyle and Goldstein, *Migration Industries*, 5.

10. Ibid., 6.

11. Frank S. Costanza, "Planting Roots on Long Island: Surging Hispanic Population Hopes to Break Barriers in America," *Long Island Advance*, October 10, 2002.

CHAPTER 3: WELCOME TO PATCHOGUE
Unless otherwise specified, information in this chapter comes from interviews with Jean Kaleda and Gilda Ramos, 2010–2012.

1. John N. Berry, "Gilda Ramos," *Library Journal* 136, no. 4 (March 1, 2011): 30.

2. Draft of an unpublished article by Jean Kaleda, "Public Libraries and Spanish Language Outreach: The Importance of Community Partnerships."

3. Ibid.

4. Ibid.

5. Frank S. Costanza, "Planting Roots on Long Island: Surging Hispanic Population Hopes to Break Barriers in America," *Long Island Advance*, October 10, 2002.

6. Draft of unpublished article by Jean Kaleda.

7. Julia Preston, "Immigration Cools as Campaign Issue: Largely Absent from Debate, but Candidates Refine Positions," *New York Times*, October 29, 2008.

8. Elisabeth Bumiller and Marc Lacey, "McCain Winds Up Latin Trip in Mexico: Candidate Endorses Immigration Reform," *New York Times*, July 4, 2008.

9. Robert Pear and Carl Hulse, "Immigration Bill Fails to Survive Senate Vote," *New York Times*, June 28, 2007.

10. Ted Hesson, "Five Ways the Immigration System Changed after 9/11," Univision News, September 11, 2012.

11. "The Great Immigration Panic," editorial, *New York Times*, June 3, 2008.

12. "Pushing Back on Immigration," editorial, *New York Times*, July 21, 2008.

13. Michael Powell and Michele Garcia, "Pa. City Puts Illegal Immigrants on Notice," *Washington Post*, August 22, 2006.

14. Adam Nossiter, "Nearly 600 Were Arrested in Factory Raid, Officials Say," *New York Times*, August 27, 2008.

15. Susan Saulny, "Hundreds Are Arrested in U.S. Sweep of Meat Plant," *New York Times*, May 13, 2008.

16. Thayer Evans, "160 Arrested in Immigration Raid at a Houston Plant," *New York Times*, June 26, 2008.

17. Janie Lorber, "King, Others Call for More Secure Border Fence," *Newsday*, June 11, 2008.

18. Dave Marcus, "Suffolk County: Speaking Up for Hispanics," *Newsday*, September 17, 2008.

Chapter 4: Not in My Backyard

1. Details about Paul Pontieri's life come from interviews, 2010–2012.

2. LaGumina, *From Steerage to Suburb*, 1.

3. Thomas and Znaniecki, *The Polish Peasant in Europe and America*.

4. LaGumina, *From Steerage to Suburb*, 32–33.

5. "Patchogue: Breve Historia," Patchogue-Medford Library, n.d., http://www.pmlib.org/espatchbreve.

6. Ibid.

7. Garland, *Gangs in Garden City*, 34.

8. Jackson, *Crabgrass Frontier*, 13.

9. Garland, *Gangs in Garden City*, 33–39.

10. "Patchogue: Breve Historia."

11. Information about Farmingville comes from James E. Claffey, "Anti-Immigrant Violence in Suburbia," *Social Text* 24, no. 3 (2006): 74–75.

12. Ibid.

13. Paul J. Smith, "Anti-Immigrant Xenophobia around the World," *International Herald Tribune*, February 14, 1996.

14. Claffey, "Anti-Immigrant Violence in Suburbia."

15. *Climate of Fear: Latino Immigrants in Suffolk County, N.Y.*, Southern Poverty Law Center, 2009, 11–13, http://www.splcenter.org/get-informed/publications/climate-of-fear-latino-immigrants-in-suffolk-county-ny.

16. Claffey, "Anti-Immigrant Violence in Suburbia," 77, 78.

17. Charlie LeDuff, "Immigrant Workers Tell of Being Lured and Beaten," *New York Times*, September 20, 2000; Slavin: "Queens Man Is Convicted in L.I. Attack on Mexicans," *New York Times*, December 13, 2001; Wagner, "Sentence Reduced in Beating Case," *New York Times*, March 29, 2006.

18. LeDuff, "Immigrant Workers Tell of Being Lured and Beaten."

19. Claffey, "Anti-Immigrant Violence in Suburbia."

20. "Fact-checking Lou Dobbs," from *60 Minutes*, May 6, 2007, uploaded March 11, 2008, by TruthInImmigration, http://www.youtube.com.

21. Bill O'Reilly and Geraldo Rivera, "Angry Fight Immigration," from *The O'Reilly Factor*, Fox News, April 5, 2007, http://www.youtube.com.

22. "Criminals Shot by Joe Horn Are Illegal Aliens," from *The O'Reilly Factor*, Fox News, December 5, 2007, uploaded December 5, 2007, by Dan Amato, http://www.youtube.com.

23. Buchanan, *State of Emergency*, 5.

24. Huntington, *Who Are We?*, 181.

25. Ibid., 185.

26. Kalita, *Suburban Sahibs*, 3.

27. Charlie LeDuff, "Tensions Persist after Suffolk Vote on Immigrant Workers," *New York Times*, September 2, 2000.

28. *Climate of Fear*, 8.

29. Ibid., 11.

30. Ibid., 8.

31. Ibid., 11.

32. Ibid., 19.

33. Ibid.

34. Ibid.

CHAPTER 5: BEANER JUMPING

1. Information about Christopher Overton comes from interviews with Denise Overton, April 4, 2012– December 10, 2012.

2. Interview with Denise Overton.

3. The narrative of the events that transpired in the evening of November 8, 2008, comes from the confessions of Jeffrey Conroy (*Long Island Wins*, January 19, 2010, http://www.longislandwins.com/), José Pacheco (*Long Island Wins*, April 9, 2010), Christopher Overton (*Long Island Wins*, April 7, 2010), Jordan Dasch (*Long Island Wins*, February 23, 2010), Nicholas Hausch (*Long Island Wins*, March 31, 2010), Kevin Shea (*Long Island Wins*, February 5, 2010), and Anthony Hartford (*Long Island Wins*, April 7, 2010), as well as the court testimony of Conroy and Hausch. Where possible, their version of events has been corroborated by interviews with Bob Conroy and Denise Overton.

4. Tamara Boch and Angel Canales, unpublished transcript of documentary *Running Wild: Hate and Immigration on Long Island*, aired on WLIW-TV, November 11, 2009.

5. Levin, *Hate Crimes Revisited*, 17–23.

6. Ibid., 23.

7. Ibid., 25.

8. People of the State of New York v. Jeffrey Conroy, Supreme Court of the State of New York, County of Suffolk Nos. 236A-2009, 252A-2009, 3032A-2009, sentencing hearing (May 26, 2010).

9. Unless otherwise noted, all the information about Jeffrey Conroy's childhood and adolescence comes from interviews with Bob Conroy conducted December 6, 2010–January 4, 2013.

10. Information about Pamela Suárez comes from interviews conducted with her on June 29, 2011, and July 1, 2011.

11. Anne Barnard, "Admired by Many, but to Police a Killer," *New York Times*, November 24, 2008.

12. Manny Fernandez, "A Hate Crime Killer Denies Being So Hateful," *New York Times*, April 30, 2010.

13. From a May 29, 2012, interview with someone close to the Conroys who didn't want to be identified for fear of offending the family.

14. Ibid.

15. Levin, *Hate Crimes Revisited*, 27.

16. Ibid., 47.

17. *Deputized*, directed by Susan Hagedorn and Amanda Zinoman (Seedworks Films, 2012).

18. Robin Finn, "A Principal Struggles with the Killing's Aftermath," *New York Times*, November 23, 2008.

19. From a 2012 phone interview with Clarissa Espinosa.

20. Patrick Whittle, "Patchogue ESL Classes to Remain," *Newsday*, December 17, 2008.

21. From an interview with Michael Mostow, May 29, 2012.

22. "Long Island Nassau Suffolk County New York Political Forum," *The Schwartz Report*, July 25, 2005, http://www.theschwartzreport.com/.

23. Jennifer Sinco Kelleher, "School Wrestles with Issues of Race," *Newsday*, November 18, 2008.

24. Michael M. Grynbaum, "Cheer Fades as Stocks Plunge 9%," *New York Times*, December 2, 2008.

25. Ray Allen Billington, "The Burning of the Charlestown Convent," *New England Quarterly: A Historical Review of New England Life and Letters* 10, no. 1 (March 1937): 4–24.

26. Bennett, *The Party of Fear*.

27. Scott Zesch, "Chinese Los Angeles in 1870–1871: The Makings of a Massacre," *Southern California Quarterly* 90 (Summer 2008): 109–58.

28. George E. Cunningham, "The Italian, a Hindrance to White Solidarity in Louisiana, 1890–1898," *Journal of Negro History* 50 (January 1965): 25–26.

29. John G. Bitzes, "The Anti-Greek Riots of 1909—South Omaha," *Nebraska History* 51 (1970): 16–17.

30. Richard Griswold del Castillo, "The Los Angeles 'Zoot Suit Riots' Revisited: Mexican and Latin American Perspectives," *Mexican Studies* 16, no. 2 (Summer 2000): 367–91.

31. Gerstenfeld, *Hate Crimes*, 89–90.

32. Roger Daniels, *Coming to America: A History of Immigration and Ethnicity in American Life*, 2nd ed. (New York: Perennial, 2002), xii.

33. Sucheng Chan, "A People of Exceptional Character: Ethnic Diversity, Nativism, and Racism in the California Gold Rush," *California History* 79, no. 2 (Summer 2000): 44–85.

34. Richard H. Peterson, "The Mexican Gold Rush: Illegal Aliens of the 1850s," *Californians* 3 (June 1985): 19.

35. William R. Kenny, "Mexican-American Conflict on the Mining Frontier, 1848–52," *Journal of the West* 6 (October 1967): 587.

36. Francisco A. Rosales, *Pobre Raza! Violence, Justice, and Mobilization among México Lindo Immigrants, 1900–1936* (Austin: University of Texas Press, 1999), 78–81.

37. Brentin Mock, "Immigration Backlash: Hate Crimes against Latinos Flourish," *Southern Poverty Law Center Intelligence Report*, no. 128 (Winter 2007), http://www.splcenter.org/.

38. Rosales, *Pobre Raza!*, 78.

39. Ibid., 77–78.

40. Ibid., 107.

41. Ibid., 102.

42. Ibid., 105.

43. Nancy Cervantes, Sasha Khokha, and Sasha Murray, "Hate Unleashed: Los Angeles in the Aftermath of Proposition 187," *Chicano-Latino Law Review* 8 (1995): 2.

44. Carrasco, "Latinos in the United States," 197.

45. Cervantes, Khokha, and Murray, "Hate Unleashed," 8.

46. Ibid., 14.

47. Mock, "Immigration Backlash."

48. Ibid.

49. Ibid.

50. Ibid.

51. Ibid.

52. Peter E. Bortner, "Donchak and Piekarsky Face Nine Years in Prison for Mexican's Beating Death," *Times-Tribune* (Wilkes-Barre, PA), February 24, 2011, www.thetimes-tribune.com.

53. Tamara Boch and Angel Canales, unpublished transcript of documentary *Running Wild: Hate and Immigration on Long Island*, aired on WLIW-TV, November 11, 2009.

54. All the details of the attack on Sierra comes from his testimony, New York v. Conroy, Supreme Court of the State of New York, County of Suffolk No. 3032A-2008, 236A-2009, excerpt of trial (March 23, 2010).

55. Boch and Canales, *Running Wild*.

56. Ibid.

57. Ted Hesson, "Marcelo Lucero Trial: Jeffrey Conroy's Written Confession," *Long Island Wins*, January 19, 2010, http://www.longislandwins.com/.

CHAPTER 6: UNWANTED

1. Details about Angel Loja's life and about how he spent the day with Marcelo Lucero on November 8, 2008, come from interviews with Loja, May 30, 2011–December 3, 2012.

2. Tamara Boch and Angel Canales, unpublished transcript of documentary *Running Wild: Hate and Immigration on Long Island*, aired on WLIW-TV, November 11, 2009.

3. Jennifer Jo Janish, "Where Two Rivers Separate: Hate Crimes against Hispanics and the Immigration Debate on Long Island," master's thesis, Graduate School of Journalism, Columbia University, 2009.

4. Details about Marcelo Lucero's life in Gualaceo come from interviews with his mother in Ecuador on July 17, 2010.

5. Janish, "Where Two Rivers Separate."

6. Boch and Canales, *Running Wild*.

7. Ibid.

8. Interview with Macedonio Ayala, December 6, 2010.

9. Marcelo Lucero's letters were provided by his mother and translated by the author.

10. Janish, "Where Two Rivers Separate."

CHAPTER 7: A MURDER IN THE SUBURBS

1. The narrative of the events that transpired in Patchogue on the evening of November 8, 2008, comes from the confessions of Jeffrey Conroy (*Long Island Wins*, January 19, 2010), José Pacheco (*Long Island Wins*, April 9, 2010), Christopher Overton (*Long Island Wins*, April 7, 2010), Jordan Dasch (*Long Island Wins*, February 23, 2010), Nicholas Hausch (*Long Island Wins*, March 31, 2010), Kevin Shea (*Long Island Wins*, February 5, 2010), and Anthony Hartford (*Long Island Wins*, April 7, 2010), as well as the trial testimony of Conroy, Hausch, and Angel Loja.

2. Details about the train's schedule on the night of November 8, 2008, come from Salvatore Arena, spokesman, Metropolitan Transportation Authority, New York City.

3. Manny Fernandez, "Aid for L.I. Attack Victim Took Time, Court Is Told," *New York Times*, March 19, 2010.

4. Sumathi Reddy and Carl MacGowan, " 'Not a Good Idea': Witness Says Teens Looked to Beat 'a Mexican' but His Warning Went Unheeded, He Testifies," *Newsday*, March 20, 2010.

5. Manny Fernandez, "Aid for L.I. Attack Victim Took Time, Court Is Told."

6. Ibid.

7. All of the information about Christopher Schiera comes from his

trial testimony: People of the State of New York v. Jeffrey Conroy, Supreme Court of the State of New York, County of Suffolk No. 3032A-2008, 236A-2009, excerpt of trial (March 18, 2010).

8. "A Brief History of Patchogue Ambulance Co.," Patchogue Ambulance Company, http://www.patchogueambulance.com/pachistory.htm.

9. Quotes come from Michael Richardsen's testimony: New York v. Conroy, Supreme Court of the State of New York, County of Suffolk No. 3032A-2008, 236A-2009, excerpt of trial (March 18, 2010).

10. Details about the emergency crew's attempt to save Marcelo Lucero's life come from Christopher Schiera's trial testimony: New York v. Conroy, Supreme Court of the State of New York, County of Suffolk No. 3032A-2008, 236A-2009, excerpt of trial (March 18, 2010).

11. Manny Fernandez, "Ambulance's Delay May Be Issue in L.I. Hate-Crime Trial," *New York Times*, March 18, 2010.

12. New York v. Conroy, Supreme Court of the State of New York, County of Suffolk No. 3032A-2008, 236A-2009, excerpt of trial (April 5, 2010).

13. Information about Detective McLeer's interrogation of Jeffrey Conroy comes from the detective's testimony: New York v. Conroy, Supreme Court of the State of New York, County of Suffolk No. 3032A-2008, 236A-2009, excerpt of trial (April 5, 2010).

14. This detail comes from interviews conducted with Bob Conroy, December 6, 2010–January 4, 2013.

15. Quotes and information in this section come from Angel Loja's testimony: New York v. Conroy, Supreme Court of the State of New York, County of Suffolk No. 3032A-2008, 236A-2009, excerpt of trial (March 24, 2010), 33.

16. Information about Octavio Cordovo comes from his testimony: New York v. Conroy, Supreme Court of the State of New York, County of Suffolk No. 3032A-2008, 236A-2009, excerpt of trial (March 30, 2010).

17. Interview with Bob Conroy, July 24, 2012.

18. This short conversation comes from Ted Hesson, "Marcelo Lucero Case: Jeffrey Conroy's Mother Testifies in His Defense," *Long Island Wins*, April 9, 2010, http://www.longislandwins.com/.

19. Information about the manslaughter charge comes from Detective McLeer's testimony: New York v. Conroy, Supreme Court of the State of New York, County of Suffolk No. 3032A-2008, 236A-2009, excerpt of trial (April 5, 2010).

20. Interview with Bob Conroy, July 24, 2012.

CHAPTER 8: A TORN COMMUNITY

1. Details about Paul Pontieri's reaction to the murder come from an interview with him on February 27, 2012.

2. According to Kathleen Bleck, senior research analyst of Command 2000 of the Suffolk County Police Department, there were six murders in Patchogue in the period between January 1, 2002, and July 31, 2012. There were no murders in the years 2005, 2006, 2007, 2009, and 2012.

3. Kirk Semple, "A Killing in a Town Where Latinos Sense Hate," *New York Times*, November 14, 2008.

4. Interviews with Denise Overton, April 4, 2012–December 10, 2012.

5. Details about the Reverend Dwight Wolter's activities after learning of Marcelo Lucero's death come from interviews with Wolter, November 7, 2010–February 19, 2013.

6. Sandra Dunn and Silvia Heredia, eds., "For Marcelo," in *Latinas Write/ Escriben* (Sag Harbor, NY: Herstory Writers Workshop, 2011), 65.

7. Information on Lola Quesada's life and career comes from an interview in January 2012.

8. Details about Julio Espinoza's reaction to the murder comes from interview with him, February 1, 2012.

9. Details about what Kaleda was doing when she heard about the murder and how she reacted comes from interview with her, February 1, 2012.

10. Interview with Gilda Ramos, February 1, 2012.

11. Dan Janison, "Spin Cycle: Levy's Response Walks a Fine Line," *Newsday*, November 13, 2008.

12. Steve Levy et al., "Letters," *Newsday*, November 14, 2008.

13. Details about Paul Pontieri's hopes comes from an interview with him, February 27, 2012.

14. "Jack Eddington, Suffolk County Legislator," uploaded by *Long Island Wins*, November 12, 2008, and "Luis Valenzuela, Long Island Immigrant Alliance," uploaded by *Long Island Wins*, November 13, 2008, http://www.youtube.com/.

15. "Dwight Wolter, the Congregational Church of Patchogue," uploaded by *Long Island Wins*, November 13, 2008, http://www.youtube.com/.

16. "Joselo Lucero, Marcelo Lucero's Brother," uploaded by *Long Island Wins*, November 13, 2008, http://www.youtube.com/.

17. Details about Joselo Lucero's life and his reaction to his brother's death from Tamara Boch and Angel Canales, unpublished transcript of documentary *Running Wild: Hate and Immigration on Long Island*, aired on WLIW-TV, November 11, 2009.

18. Herz and Nogueira, *Ecuador vs. Peru*, 47.

19. Jack Eddington's life story comes from interviews with him, May 26, 2010–November 12, 2012, and from his unpublished memoir, "Jack in the Box: One Man's Journey of Self-Discovery."

20. Details about Jack Eddington's performance at the meeting comes from "Community Forum at Temple Beth El in Patchogue—Legislator Jack Eddington Speaks," uploaded by *Long Island Wins*, December 8, 2008, http://www.youtube.com/.

21. Angela Macropoulos, "In Mourning an Immigrant, a Call for Unity on Long Island," *New York Times*, November 16, 2008.

22. Information about the service for Marcelo Lucero comes from interviews with Reverend Wolter, November 7, 2010–November 15, 2012.

23. Details about Joselo Lucero during the service for his brother come from Jennifer Jo Janish, "Where Two Rivers Separate: Hate Crimes against Hispanics and the Immigration Debate on Long Island," master's thesis, Graduate School of Journalism, Columbia University, 2009.

24. Dwight Lee Wolter, "The Beginning of Justice for Marcelo Lucero," *God's Politics* (blog), *Sojourners*, http://sojo.net/blogs/2010/07/08/beginning-justice-marcelo-lucero.

25. Keith Herbert et al., "Service Brings Out Strong Emotions," *Newsday*, November 16, 2008.

26. Macropoulos, "In Mourning an Immigrant."

27. Ibid.

28. Jennifer Jo Janish, "Hate," *Guernica*, April 1, 2010, http://www.guernicamag.com/features/1654/hate.

29. Ibid.

CHAPTER 9: A LITTLE PIECE OF HEAVEN

1. All details of the arrival of the body in Gualaceo and funeral come from Bart Jones, "Reports from Ecuador: A Homecoming Marked by Tears," *Newsday*, November 20, 2008.

2. Details about the house Marcelo Lucero built come from an interview with his mother, Doña Rosario, in Gualaceo, Ecuador, July 17, 2010.

3. Details regarding the impact of emigration from Gualaceo come from comments made by Father Julio Castillo and Mayor Marco Tapia during separate interviews in Gualaceo, Ecuador, July 18, 2010.

4. Orellana, *Patrimonio Cultural de Gualaceo*, 15.

5. Bart Jones, "Reports from Ecuador: The Lost Dads of Ecuador," *Newsday*, November 18, 2008.

6. Hurtado, *Portrait of a Nation*, 157.

7. Information about the landslide comes from an interview with Fernando León, publisher of *Semanario El Pueblo*, December 7, 2012, and "Ecuador Landslide Buries Mining Site, Killing at Least 60," *New York Times*, May 11, 1993.

8. Legrain, *Immigrants*, 69.

9. Mirta Ojito, "People They Left Behind Want Emigrants Back," *Miami Herald*, August 1, 2010.

10. Bart Jones, "Reports from Ecuador: A Friend's Life Cut Short," *Newsday*, November 19, 2008.

11. Ibid.

12. Ibid.

13. Bart Jones, "LI Hate Killing: Sorrow for a Son Lost to Violence," *Newsday*, November 21, 2008.

14. Ibid.

15. "Kristallnacht," PBS, n.d., http://www.pbs.org/; interview with Rabbi Joel Levinson, September 13, 2012.

16. All details of the November 19, 2008, meeting come from Molly Altizer-Evans, "Calming Residents' Safety Fears," *Long Island Advance*, November 25, 2008, http://www.longislandadvance.net/.

17. Ibid.

18. Details about the teenagers' arraignment come from Cara Buckley, "Teenagers' Violent 'Sport' Led to Killing, Officials Say," *New York Times*, November 21, 2008.

19. Quotes come from interviews with Bob Conroy, December 6, 2010–January 4, 2013.

20. Sumathi Reddy, "Timeline of Events in the Federal Hate Crime Probe," *Newsday*, November 8, 2008, and Andrew Strickler, "Ready to Take the Reins," *Newsday*, November 26, 2008.

21. Strickler, "Ready to Take the Reins," and Gen X Revert, "The Murder of Marcelo Lucero Continues to Shake Things up Here in Suffolk County," *A Long Island Catholic*, November 26, 2008, http://revert edxer.blogspot.com/.

22. Strickler, "Ready to Take the Reins."

23. Lawrence Downes, "A Hate-Crime Circus Comes to Patchogue," *New York Times*, December 5, 2008.

24. Interviews conducted with Reverend Wolter, November 7, 2010–November 15, 2012.

25. Buckley, "Teenagers' Violent 'Sport' Led to Killing, Officials Say."

26. Robin Finn, "A Principal Struggles with the Killing's Aftermath," *New York Times*, November 23, 2008.

27. Girl booed off the stage: *Deputized*, directed by Susan Hagedorn and Amanda Zinoman (Seedworks Films, 2012).

28. Patrick Whittle, "Patchogue ESL Classes to Remain," *Newsday*, December 17, 2008.

29. Michael Sorrentino, "Patchogue Patch," *Patchogue Patch*, May 27, 2010, http://patchogue.patch.com/.

30. Elise Pearlman, "Film Based on Lucero Murder to Play LI Film Festival," *Patchogue Patch*, July 15, 2010, http://patchogue.patch.com/articles/film-based-on-lucero-murder-to-play-li-film-festival.

31. Michael Sorrentino, "Medford SBU Student Wins Scholarship for Lucero Essay," *Patchogue Patch*, September 9, 2010, http://patchogue.patch.com/.

32. Ted Hesson, "Remembering the Marcelo Lucero Killing, Residents Seek to Mend Hearts with Quilting Project," *Long Island Wins*, October 7, 2010, http://www.longislandwins.com/.

33. *Climate of Fear: Latino Immigrants in Suffolk County, N.Y.* (Montgomery, AL: Southern Poverty Law Center), 2009, http://www.splcenter.org/get-informed/publications/climate-of-fear-latino-immigrants-in-suffolk-county-ny.

34. Ibid.

35. Ibid.

36. Information comes from a class lecture by Pablo Calle, US representative of the National Secretariat for Migrant Affairs, in the Immigration Reporting Seminar of the Graduate School of Journalism, Columbia University, March 8, 2011, and from an interview with Jorge W. López, general consul of Ecuador in New York, January 11, 2013.

37. Bart Jones, "There Is a Lot of Pain Here," *Newsday*, November 17, 2008.

38. Sumathi Reddy, "Central Islip: Group Plays Tribute to Lucero," *Newsday*, October 23, 2009.

39. Laura Rivera and Dave Marcus, "Lucero's Mother Comes to Face Teens," *Newsday*, February 17, 2009.

40. Details about Joselo Lucero's reaction to his encounter with Levy come from Michael Amon, "Levy Meets Luceros," *Newsday*, November 9, 2009.

CHAPTER 10: TRIAL AND PUNISHMENT

1. Information about Megan O'Donnell's life and her preparation for the trial comes from an interview with her, June 23, 2011.

2. People of the State of New York v. Jeffrey Conroy, Supreme Court of the State of New York, County of Suffolk No. 3032A-2008, 236A-2009, opening statements (March 18, 2010).

3. "Film Extras: Interview with Suffolk County Assistant District Attorney Megan O'Donnell," *Not in Our Town*, http://www.niot.org/.

4. Manny Fernandez, "Teenager Charged in L.I. Hate Crime Plans to Testify," *New York Times*, April 8, 2010, and Sheriff GI Compartment, Incident File Report, GIU-Inmate Security Risk Group Assessment, November 10, 2008, author: Steven Lundquist, Suffolk County Sheriff's Office.

5. "Film Extras."

6. The charges come from Megan O'Donnell's opening statement: New York v. Conroy, Supreme Court of the State of New York, County of Suffolk No. 3032A-2008, 236A-2009, opening statements (March 18, 2010).

7. Information about Keahon comes from Manny Fernandez, "Veracity of the Defendant Is Key in Hate-Killing Trial," *New York Times*, April 10, 2010.

8. Ann Givens, "Showman in the Courtroom: Attorney Bill Keahon Is Both a Believer in Every Person's Right to a Vigorous Defense and Unafraid of Bold Tactics," *Newsday*, September 16, 2007.

9. "Film Extras"; Sumathi Reddy, "Fourth Teen Pleads Guilty in Lucero Beating Trial," *Newsday*, February 25, 2010.

10. "Hate Crimes Act—Ch. 107, 2000—NY DCJS," New York State Division of Criminal Justice Services, http://www.criminaljustice.ny.gov/.

11. Phone interview with Michael Lieberman, director, Civil Rights Policy Planning Center, Anti-Defamation League, February 22, 2013.

12. "Facts for Features: Hispanic Heritage Month 2012: Sept. 1–Oct. 15," US Census Bureau, August 6, 2012, http://www.census.gov/.

13. "What Motivates Hate Offenders?," National Institute of Justice, January 9, 2008, http://www.nij.gov/.

14. James Barron, "2 Men Sentenced in Beating Death of Ecuadorean Immigrant in Brooklyn," *New York Times*, August 6, 2010.

15. Information about the jurors comes from the author's e-mail correspondence with *Newsday* reporter Sumathi Reddy.

16. Sumathi Reddy, "Jurors Picked for Lucero Slay Trial," *Newsday*, March 13, 2010.

17. Sumathi Reddy, "Riverhead: Slay-case Jurors Tough to Find," *Newsday*, March 5, 2010.

18. Manny Fernandez, "In Jury Selection for Hate Crime, a Struggle to Find Tolerance," *New York Times*, March 9, 2010.

19. Information about the jurors comes from the author's correspondence with *Newsday* reporter Sumathi Reddy.

20. Fernandez, "In Jury Selection for Hate Crime, a Struggle to Find Tolerance."

21. Reddy, "Jurors Picked for Lucero Slay Trial."

22. Manny Fernandez, "Aid for L.I. Attack Victim Took Time, Court Is Told," *New York Times*, March 20, 2010.

23. Manny Fernandez, "Ambulance's Delay May Be Issue in L.I. Hate-Crime Trial," *New York Times*, March 18, 2010.

24. Sumathi Reddy and Carl MacGowan, "Cop: Teen Had Knife on Him," *Newsday*, March 23, 2010.

25. Manny Fernandez, "Jurors in Suffolk Hate-Crime Trial Are Shown Photo of Defendant's Swastika Tattoo," *New York Times*, March 24, 2010.

26. Quote comes from Angel Loja's testimony, New York v. Conroy, Supreme Court of the State of New York, County of Suffolk No. 3032A-2008, 236A-2009, excerpt of trial (March 24, 2010).

27. Kathleen Kerr and Carl MacGowan, "Riverhead: Expert: Lucero's DNA on Knife," *Newsday*, April 1, 2010. And from Stuart Dawson's testimony, New York v. Conroy, Supreme Court of the State of New York, County of Suffolk No. 3032A-2008, 236A-2009, excerpt of trial (March 31, 2010).

28. Manny Fernandez, "Blood on Defendant's Knife Was Victim's, Scientist Says," *New York Times*, April 1, 2010.

29. Manny Fernandez, "Teenager Testifies about Attacking Latinos for Sport," *New York Times*, March 29, 2010.

30. Ibid.

31. Ann Givens and Carl MacGowan, "Conroy 'Upset' after Conviction," *Newsday*, April 21, 2010.

32. Kathleen Kerr, Carl MacGowan, and Bart Jones, "Conroy Testifies He Didn't Stab Lucero," *Newsday*, April 9, 2010.

33. Joye Brown, "A Stunning Twist as Conroy Testifies at Trial," *Newsday*, April 8, 2010.

34. Ibid.

35. Manny Fernandez, "Veracity of the Defendant Is Key in Hate-Killing Trial," *New York Times*, April 10, 2010.

36. Brown, "A Stunning Twist as Conroy Testifies at Trial."

37. Kerr, MacGowan, and Jones, "Conroy Testifies He Didn't Stab Lucero."

38. Manny Fernandez, "In Testimony, Teenager Charged with Hate Killing Recants His Confession," *New York Times*, April 9, 2010.

39. Alfonso A. Castillo, "Suffolk County: Neighbor's Shocking Find," *Newsday*, July 29, 2008.

40. Erik German and Alfonso A. Castillo, "East Patchogue: Slay Suspect Denies Gun," *Newsday*, August 5, 2008.

41. Castillo, "Suffolk County: Neighbor's Shocking Find."

42. Andrew Smith, "Guilty in Fatal E. Patchogue Shooting," *Newsday*, May 18, 2011.

43. Andrew Smith, "25 Years for Manslaughter," *Newsday*, September 7, 2011.

44. Manny Fernandez, "Verdict Is Manslaughter in L.I. Hate Crime Trial," *New York Times*, April 20, 2010.

45. Kathleen Kerr, Carl MacGowan, and Andrew Strickler, "Historic Words in a Packed Courtroom," *Newsday*, April 20, 2010.

46. Givens and MacGowan, "Conroy 'Upset' after Conviction."

47. Carl MacGowan, "Community Reacts to Conroy Verdict," *Newsday*, April 19, 2010.

48. Kerr, MacGowan, and Strickler, "Historic Words in a Packed Courtroom."

49. Sumathi Reddy, "Guilty Verdict in Hate Crime," *Wall Street Journal*, April 19, 2010.

50. Fernandez, "Verdict Is Manslaughter in L.I. Hate Crime Trial."

51. Joye Brown, "In Reaching Verdict, Hate Stood Out," *Newsday*, April 20, 2010.

52. Fernandez, "Verdict Is Manslaughter in L.I. Hate Crime Trial."

EPILOGUE

1. Ian Urbina, "Federal Hate Crime Cases at Highest Level Since '01," *New York Times*, December 18, 2009.

2. Langton and Planty, *Hate Crime*.

3. Associated Press, "Teen in Bias Killing Hid Knife in Boxer Shorts," *New York Daily News*, November 24, 2008.

4. Touré, "Inside the Racist Mind," *Time*, May 7, 2012; http://ideas.time.com/2012/04/19/inside-the-racist-mind.

5. Manny Fernandez, "A Hate Crime Killer Denies Being So Hateful," *New York Times*, April 30, 2010.

6. Sumathi Reddy, "Patchogue Hate Crime Defendant: 'I'm Not a Monster,'" *Newsday*, November 1, 2009.

7. Andrew Strickler and James Carbone, "Teen in Lucero Case Talks Briefly," *Newsday*, June 12, 2010.

8. Quotes come from a letter from Thomas Shea Sr., March 21, 2012.

9. Luis Almonte as the Administrator of the Estate of Oswaldo Lucero a/k/a Marcelo Lucero v. Jeffrey Conroy, et al., Supreme Court of the State of New York County of Suffolk No. 09–43986, verified complaint, June 25, 2010.

10. Jose Antonio Vargas, "Not Legal Not Leaving," *Time*, June 25, 2012; http://www.time.com/time/magazine/article/0,9171,2117243,00.html.

11. Marc Hugo Lopez and Ana Gonzalez-Barrera, "Inside the 2012 Latino Electorate," Pew Research Hispanic Center, June 3, 2013, www.pewhispanic.org/2013/06/03/inside-the-2012-latino-electorate/.

12. Cindy Y. Rodriguez, "Latino Vote Key to Obama's Re-Election," CNN .com, November 9, 2012, http://www.cnn.com/2012/11/09/politics/latino-vote-key-election.

13. "¡Estimados Republicanos! The GOP's Immigration and Hispanic Debacles," editorial, *Wall Street Journal*, November 9, 2012.

14. Julia Preston, "Latino Leaders Warn Congress on Immigration," *New York Times*, December 13, 2012.

15. Julia Preston, "Beside a Path to Citizenship, a New Path on Immigration," *New York Times*, April 16, 2013; David Nakamura, "Immigration Bill Filed in Senate; Opponents Hope to Use Delays to Kill It," *Washington Post*, April 17, 2013.

16. Suzy Khimm, "Obama Is Deporting Immigrants Faster than Bush, Republicans Don't Think That's Enough," *Washington Post*, August 27, 2012.

17. Suzy Khimm, "Want Tighter Border Security? You're Already Getting It," *Washington Post*, January 29, 2013.

18. Jeffrey Passel, D'Vera Cohn, and Ana Gonzalez-Barrera, "Net Migration from Mexico Falls to Zero—and Perhaps Less," Pew Research Hispanic Center, April 23, 2012; http://www.pewhispanic.org/2012/04/23/net-migration-from-mexico-falls-to-zero-and-perhaps-less.

19. John Valenti, "Suspects Sought in Robberies of Hispanic Men," *Newsday*, May 15, 2013.

20. E-mail to author from Mayor Paul Pontieri, June 22, 2013.

21. US Department of Justice, Civil Rights Division, letter addressed to Mr. Steve Levy, Suffolk County Executive, September 13, 2011, Re: Suffolk County Police Department Technical Assistance Letter.

22. Ibid.

23. Will Van Sant et al., "Feds to Suffolk on Hate Crime Probes: Need to Do Better," *Newsday*, September 15, 2011.

24. Paul Pontieri, "Pontieri's Speech from Ecuador Trip," *Patchogue Patch*, July 1, 2010, http://patchogue.patch.com/articles/pontieris-speech -from-ecuador-trip.

25. Jo Napolitano, "LI Library Takes Home a National Prize," *Newsday*, December 18, 2010.

26. Jennifer Medina, "California Eases Tone as Latinos Make Gains," *New York Times*, February 17, 2013.

27. Griselda Nevarez, "Tucson School District Poised to Restore Mexican American Studies," Arizona Ethnic Studies Network, http://azethnic studies.com/archives/531.

28. Meredith Hoffman, "Study Finds That Immigrants Are Central to Long Island Economy," *New York Times*, October 27, 2011.

29. Ibid.

30. Adam Davidson, "Coming to America: Are Illegal Immigrants Actually Detrimental to the U.S. Economy?" *New York Times Magazine*, February 17, 2003.

31. Ted Hesson, "Steve Levy Unwittingly Gives $17,500 to Immigrant Rights Groups," *Long Island Wins*, February 15, 2012, http://www.long islandwins.com/.

32. "A New Day in Suffolk? Here's Hoping," editorial, *New York Times*, January 17, 2012.

33. James Will, "Suffolk County Aids Non-English Speakers," *Wall Street Journal*, November 15, 2012.

34. Rick Brand, "Clearly, Bellone Is No Levy on Immigration," *Newsday*, July 14, 2012.

35. E-mail to author from Jean Kaleda.

36. Rick Brand, "Suffolk Pols Write Judge Supporting Lucero Killer," *Newsday*, May 29, 2010.

37. Supreme Court: State of New York Appellate Division, Second Department, The People of the State of New York, Plaintiff–Respondent, against Jeffrey Conroy, Defendant-Appellant, appellant's brief, filed June 12, 2012.

38. Carl MacGowan, "Conroy Settles in at Prison, as Dad, Pastor Raise Funds," *Newsday*, July 5, 2010.
39. Luisita López Torregrosa, "Media Feed Bias against Latinos," *New York Times*, September 18, 2012.
40. Sumathi Reddy, "A Cordial Exchange," *Newsday*, March 20, 2010.
41. Joseph Berger, "For Day Laborers, Used to Scraping By, Hurricane Creates a Wealth of Work," *New York Times*, December 31, 2012.
42. Interview with Paul Pontieri, December 20, 2012.

BIBLIOGRAPHY

Allport, Gordon W. *The Nature of Prejudice*. Cambridge, MA: Addison-Wesley, 1954.

Bennett, David Harry. *The Party of Fear: From Nativist Movements to the New Right in American History*. Chapel Hill: University of North Carolina Press, 1988.

Buchanan, Patrick J. *State of Emergency: The Third World Invasion and Conquest of America*. New York: Thomas Dunne Books/St. Martin's Press, 2006.

Carrasco, Gilbert. "Latinos in the United States: Invitation and Exile." In *Immigrants Out! The New Nativism and the Anti-Immigrant Impulse in the United States*, edited by Juan F. Perea. Critical America. New York: New York University Press, 1997.

Daniels, Roger. *Coming to America: A History of Immigration and Ethnicity in American Life*. 2nd ed. New York: Perennial, 2002.

Eddington, John, and Beth Rosato. *First Survive, Then Thrive: A Journey from Crisis to Transformation*. Tempe, AZ: American Federation of Astrologers, 1998.

Garland, Sarah. *Gangs in Garden City: How Immigration, Segregation, and Youth Violence Are Changing America's Suburbs*. New York: Nation Books, 2009.

Gaylin, Willard. *Hatred: The Psychological Descent into Violence*. New York: PublicAffairs, 2003.

Gerstenfeld, Phyllis B. *Hate Crimes: Causes, Controls, and Controversies*, 2nd ed. Los Angeles: Sage, 2011.

Hall, Nathan. *Hate Crime*. Crime and Society Series. Cullompton, UK: Willan, 2005.

Henke, Hans. *Patchogue: Queen City of Long Island's South Shore: In the Twentieth Century*. Blue Point, NY: AGC Printing & Design, n.d.

———. *Patchogue: Queen City of Long Island's South Shore: The Early Years*. Blue Point, NY: AGC Printing & Design, 2003.

Herz, Mónica, and João Pontes Nogueira. *Ecuador vs. Peru: Peacemaking amid Rivalry*. International Peace Academy Occasional Paper Series. Boulder, CO: Lynne Rienner, 2002.

Huntington, Samuel P. *Who Are We? The Challenges to America's Identity*. New York: Simon & Schuster, 2004.

Hurtado, Osvaldo. *Portrait of a Nation: Culture and Progress in Ecuador*. Lanham, MD: Madison Books, 2010.

Jackson, Kenneth T. *Crabgrass Frontier: The Suburbanization of the United States*. New York: Oxford University Press, 1985.

Kalita, S. Mitra. *Suburban Sahibs: Three Immigrant Families and Their Passage from India to America*. New Brunswick, NJ: Rutgers University Press, 2003.

Kyle, David J., and Rachel Goldstein. *Migration Industries: A Comparison of the Ecuador-US and Ecuador-Spain Cases*. Florence, Italy: European University Institute, 2011.

LaGumina, Salvatore L. *From Steerage to Suburb: Long Island Italians*. New York: Center for Migration Studies, 1988.

Langton, Lynn, and Michael Planty. *Hate Crime, 2003–2009*. Washington, DC: US Department of Justice, Bureau of Justice Statistics, 2011. http://www.bjs.ojp.usdoj.gov.

Lefkowitz, Bernard. *Our Guys: The Glen Ridge Rape and the Secret Life of the Perfect Suburb*. Men and Masculinity 4. Berkeley: University of California Press, 1997.

Legrain, Philippe. *Immigrants: Your Country Needs Them*. Princeton, NJ: Princeton University Press, 2007.

Levin, Jack. *Hate Crimes Revisited: America's War against Those Who Are Different*. Boulder, CO: Westview Press, 2002.

———. *Why We Hate*. Amherst, NY: Prometheus Books, 2004.

O'Neill, Patrice. *Not in Our Town: Light in the Darkness*. Aired on PBS, 2011.

Orellana, Diego Demetrio. *Patrimonio Cultural de Gualaceo*. Extensión de Gualaceo: Universidad Alfredo Pérez Guerrero, 2011.

BIBLIOGRAPHY

Perry, Barbara. *In the Name of Hate: Understanding Hate Crimes*. New York: Routledge, 2001.

Portes, Alejandro, and Rubén G. Rumbaut. *Immigrant America: A Portrait*, 3rd ed. Berkeley: University of California Press, 2006.

Rosales, Francisco A. *Pobre Raza! Violence, Justice, and Mobilization among México Lindo Immigrants, 1900–1936*. Austin: University of Texas Press, 1999.

Thomas, William Isaac, and Florian Znaniecki. *The Polish Peasant in Europe and America*. New York: Alfred A. Knopf, 1927.

Wolter, Dwight Lee. *Forgiving Our Grownup Children*. Cleveland, OH: Pilgrim Press, 1998.

———. *Forgiving Our Parents: For Adult Children from Dysfunctional Families*. Center City, MN: Hazelden Foundation, 1989.

———. *A Life Worth Waiting For! Messages from a Survivor*. Minneapolis: CompCare, 1989.

———. *My Child, My Teacher, My Friend: One Man's View of Parenting in Recovery*. Minneapolis: CompCare, 1991.